Reconstructing Womanhood

Reconstructing Womanhood

The Emergence of the
Afro-American Woman Novelist

HAZEL V. CARBY

OXFORD UNIVERSITY PRESS
New York   Oxford

Oxford University Press

Oxford   New York   Toronto
Delhi   Bombay   Calcutta   Madras   Karachi
Petaling Jaya   Singapore   Hong Kong   Tokyo
Nairobi   Dar es Salaam   Cape Town
Melbourne   Auckland

and associated companies in
Berlin   Ibadan

First published in 1987 by Oxford University Press, Inc.,
200 Madison Avenue, New York, New York 10016

First issued as an Oxford University Press paperback, 1989

Oxford is a registered trademark of Oxford University Press

Library of Congress Cataloging-in-Publication Data
Carby, Hazel V.
Reconstructing womanhood.
"Bibliography of texts by Black women authors" : p.
Bibliography: p.
1. American fiction—Afro-American authors—History and criticism.
2. American fiction—Women authors—History and criticism.
3. American fiction—19th century—History and criticism.
4. Afro-American women in literature.
5. Women and literature—United States.
6. Feminism and literature—United States.
I. Title.
PS153.N5C37   1987   813'.4'099287   87-11055
ISBN 0-19-504164-X
ISBN 0-19-506071-7 (pbk.)

9 8 7

Printed in the United States of America

For my parents

Acknowledgments

No intellectual endeavor is ever the work of one individual; I have received a great deal of support, both financial and intellectual. I would like to thank the Social Science Research Council of Great Britain and the Afro-American Studies Program at Yale University, for providing me with money for research, and Wesleyan University for a sabbatical to complete the book. The library staff at Sterling Memorial Library and Beinecke Library at Yale, at Olin Library at Wesleyan, at the New York Public Library, at the Schomberg Center for Research in Black Culture, and at the Moorland-Spingarn Research Center provided me with invaluable assistance. For intellectual support and encouragement I am grateful to John Blassingame, Nancy Cott, the late Charles T. Davis, and Michael Green. For their extensive critical comments and insights I owe particular thanks to Joanne Braxton, Henry Louis Gates, Jr., Valarie Hartmann, Ketu Katrak, Richard Slotkin, Mary Helen Washington, Susan Willis, and Jean Yellin. To all my colleagues at Birmingham, Yale, and Wesleyan universities I owe thanks for their stimulating and supportive friendship. Paul Gilroy, Vron Ware, Errol Lawrence, Val Amos, and Pratibha Parma have long been sisters and brothers in the political struggle for black liberation. For his rigorous intellect, political acumen, and theoretical insights, and for being the best teacher I ever had, I am indebted to Stuart Hall. For his extensive editorial assistance, his constant emotional support and encouragement, and for being my best friend, I thank Michael Denning.

A different version of Chapter Five appeared as "'On the Threshold of Woman's Era': Lynching, Empire and Sexuality in Black Feminist Theory," in *Critical Inquiry* 12 (Autumn 1985): 262–77, copyright © 1985 by the University of Chicago.

Contents

1   "Woman's Era"
     Rethinking Black Feminist Theory   3

2   Slave and Mistress
     Ideologies of Womanhood under Slavery   20

3   "Hear My Voice, Ye Careless Daughters"
     Narratives of Slave and Free Women before Emancipation   40

4   "Of Lasting Service for the Race"
     The Work of Frances Ellen Watkins Harper   62

5   "In the Quiet, Undisputed Dignity of
     My Womanhood"
     Black Feminist Thought after Emancipation   95

6   "Of What Use Is Fiction?"
     Pauline Elizabeth Hopkins   121

7   "All the Fire and Romance"
     The Magazine Fiction of Pauline Hopkins   145

8   The Quicksands of Representation
     Rethinking Black Cultural Politics   163

     Notes   177

     Bibliography of Texts by Black Women Authors   199

     General Bibliography   205

     Index   217

Reconstructing Womanhood

1

"Woman's Era"

Rethinking Black Feminist Theory

On May 20, 1893, Frances Harper addressed the World's Congress of Representative Women assembled as part of the Columbian Exposition in Chicago. She encouraged her audience to see themselves standing "on the threshold of woman's era" and urged that they be prepared to receive the "responsibility of political power."[1] Harper was the last of six black women to address the delegates; on the previous two days Fannie Barrier Williams, Anna Julia Cooper, Fannie Jackson Coppin, Sarah J. Early, and Hallie Quinn Brown had been the black spokeswomen at this international but overwhelmingly white women's forum. Williams spoke of the women "for whom real ability, virtue, and special talents count for nothing when they become applicants for respectable employment" and asserted that black women were increasingly "a part of the social forces that must help to determine the questions that so concern women generally."[2] Anna Julia Cooper described the black woman's struggle for sexual autonomy as "a struggle against fearful and overwhelming odds, that often ended in a horrible death. . . . The painful, patient, and silent toil of mothers to gain a fee simple title to the bodies of their daughters, the despairing fight . . . to keep hallow their own persons." She contrasted the white woman who "could at least plead for her own emancipation" to the black women of the South who have to "suffer and struggle and be silent" and made her concluding appeal to "the solidarity of humanity, the oneness of life, and the unnaturalness and injustice of all special favoritisms, whether of sex, race, country, or condition."[3] Fannie

3

Jackson Coppin declared that the conference should not be "indifferent to the history of the colored women of America," for their fight could only aid all women in their struggle against oppression," and Sarah J. Early and Hallie Quinn Brown gave detailed accounts of the organizations that black women had established.[4]

It appeared that the Columbian Exposition had provided the occasion for women in general and black women in particular to gain a space for themselves in which they could exert a political presence. However, for black women the preparations for the World's Congress had been a disheartening experience, and the World's Congress itself proved to be a significant moment in the history of the uneasy relations between organized black and white women. Since emancipation black women had been active within the black community in the formation of mutual-aid societies, benevolent associations, local literary societies, and the many organizations of the various black churches, but they had also looked toward the nationally organized suffrage and temperance movements, dominated by white women, to provide an avenue for the expression of their particular concerns as women and as feminists. The struggle of black women to achieve adequate representation within the women's suffrage and temperance movements had been continually undermined by a pernicious and persistent racism, and the World's Congress was no exception. While Harper, Williams, Cooper, Coppin, Early, and Brown were on the women's platform, Ida B. Wells was in the Haitian pavilion protesting the virtual exclusion of Afro-Americans from the exposition, circulating the pamphlet she had edited, *The Reason Why: The Colored American is not in the World's Columbian Exposition.*[5]

The fight for black representation had begun at the presidential level with an attempt to persuade Benjamin Harrison to appoint a black member to the National Board of Commissioners for the exposition. The president's intransigent refusal to act led the black community to focus their hopes on the Board of Lady Managers appointed to be "the channel of communication through which all women may be brought into relation with the exposition, and through which all applications for space for the use of women or their exhibits in the buildings shall be made."[6] Two organizations of black women were formed, the Woman's Columbian Association and the Women's Columbian Auxiliary Association, and both unsuccessfully petitioned the Board of Lady Managers to establish mechanisms of representation for black Americans. Sympathetic sentiments were expressed by a few members of the board, but no appointment was made, and some members of the board threatened to resign rather than work with a black representative. Indeed, the general belief of the board members was that black women were incapable of any organized critique of their committee and that a white woman must be behind such "articulate and sustained protests."[7] The fact that six black women eventually addressed the World's Congress was not the result of a practice of sisterhood or evidence of a concern to provide a black political presence but part of a discourse of exoticism that pervaded the fair. Black Americans were included in a highly selective manner as part of exhibits with other ethnic groups which reinforced conventional racist attitudes of the American imagination. The accommodation of racial diversity in ethnic villages at the fair was an attempt to scientifically legitimate racist assumptions, and, as one historian notes, "the results were devastating not only for American blacks, Native Americans, and the Chinese, but also for other non-white peoples of the world."[8]

The Columbian Exposition was widely regarded as "the greatest fair in history."[9] The "White City," symbol of American progress, was built to house the exposition in Jackson Park on the shores of Lake Michigan in Chicago. It has been characterized by a contemporary cultural critic as simultaneously "a fitting conclusion of an age" and the inauguration of another. "It lays bare a plan for a future. Like the Gilded Age, White City straddles a divide: a consummation and a new beginning."[10] For black Americans it was "literally and figuratively a White City" which symbolized "not the material progress of America, but a moral regression—the reconciliation of the North and South at the expense of Negroes."[11] At the time, black visitors expressed their resentment at their virutal exclusion by renaming the fair "the great American white elephant" and "the white American's World's Fair,"; Frederick Douglass, attending the fair as commissioner from Haiti, called the exposition "a whited sepulcher."[12] The Columbian Exposition embodied the definitive failure of the hopes of emancipation and reconstruction and inaugurated an age that was to be dominated by "the problem of the color-line."[13]

To appear as a black woman on the platform of the Congress of Representative Women was to be placed in a highly contradictory position, at once part of and excluded from the dominant discourse of white women's politics. The contradictions which were experienced by these women and other black women who tried to establish a public presence in the nineteenth century will form the focus of this book. The arguments are theoretical and political, responding to contemporary black and white feminist cultural politics. The historical and literary analyses are materialist, interpreting individual texts in relation to the dominant ideological and social formations in which they were produced. The book has four major concerns.

First, in order to gain a public voice as orators or published writers, black women had to confront the dominant domestic ideologies and literary conventions of womanhood which excluded them from the definition "woman." This book traces these ideologies of womanhood as they were adopted, adapted, and transformed to effectively represent the material conditions of black women, and it explores how black women intellectuals reconstructed the sexual ideologies of the nineteenth century to produce an alternative discourse of black womanhood.

Second, this historical account questions those strands of contemporary feminist historiography and literary criticism which seek to establish the existence of an American sisterhood between black and white women. Considering the history of the failure of any significant political alliances between black and white women in the nineteenth century, I challenge the impulse in the contemporary women's movement to discover a lost sisterhood and to reestablish feminist solidarity. Individual white women helped publish and promote individual black women, but the texts of black women from ex-slave Harriet Jacobs to educator Anna Julia Cooper are testaments to the racist practices of the suffrage and temperance movements and indictments of the ways in which white women allied themselves not with black women but with a racist patriarchal order against all black people. Only by confronting this history of difference can we hope to understand the boundaries that separate white feminists from all women of color.[14]

Third, though Afro-American cultural and literary history commonly regards the late nineteenth and early twentieth centuries in terms of great men, as the Age of Washington and Du Bois, marginalizing the political contributions of black women, these were the years of the first flowering of black women's autonomous organizations and a period of intense intellectual activity and pro-ductivity. An examination of the literary contributions of Frances Harper and Pauline Hopkins and the political writings of Anna Julia Cooper and Ida B. Wells will reconstruct our view of this period. Writing in the midst of a new "black women's renaissance," the contemporary discovery and recognition of black women by the corporate world of academia, publishing, and Hollywood—marked by the celebrity of Alice Walker and Toni Morrison—I try to establish the existence of an earlier and perhaps more politically resonant rennaissance so we may rethink the cultural politics of black women.

Fourth, this book is also a literary history of the emergence of black women as novelists. To understand the first novels which were written at the end of the nineteenth century, one has to understand not only the discourse and context in which they were produced but also the intellectual forms and practices of black women that preceded them. I examine narratives of slave and free women, the relation of political lecturing to the politics of fiction, and a variety of essay, journalistic, and magazine writing. Conse-quently, this book is not a conventional literary history, nor is it limited to drawing on feminist or black feminist literary theories, but it is a cultural history and critique of the forms in which black women intellectuals made political as well as literary interventions in the social formations in which they lived.

During the period in which this book was conceived, researched, and written, two fields of academic inquiry emerged: black feminist literary criticism and black women's history. As a first step toward assessing what has come to be called black feminist theory, I want to consider its history and to analyse its major tendencies.

It is now a decade since Barbara Smith published "Toward a Black Feminist Criticism" (1977), addressing the conditions of both politics and literature that she felt could provide the necessary basis for an adequate consideration of black women's literature.[15] Smith argued that since the "feminist movement was an essential precon-dition to the growth of feminist literature, criticism, and women's studies," the lack of an autonomous black feminist movement contributed to the neglect of black women writers and artists, there being no "political movement to give power or support to those

who want to examine Black women's experience." Hence, without a
political movement there was no black feminist political theory to
form a basis for a critical approach to the art of black women.
Smith argued for the development of both the political movement
and the political theory so that a black feminist literary criticism
would embody "the realization that the politics of sex as well as the
politics of race and class are crucially interlocking factors in the
works of Black women writers" (170). To support her argument,
Smith indicted a variety of male critics and white feminist critics for
their sexist and racist assumptions which prevented the critical
recognition of the importance of the work of black women writers.

In many ways, "Toward a Black Feminist Criticism" acted as a
manifesto for black feminist critics, stating both the principles and
the conditions of their work. Smith argued that a black feminist
approach should have a primary commitment to the exploration of
the interrelation of sexual and racial politics and that black and
female identities were "inextricable elements in Black women's writings." Smith also asserted that a black feminist critic should "work
from the assumption that Black women writers constitute an identi-
fiable literary tradition" (174). Smith was convinced that it was
possible to reveal a verifiable literary tradition because of the
common experience of the writers and the shared use of a black
female language.

> The use of Black women's language and cultural experience in books *by*
> Black women *about* Black women results in a miraculously rich coalesc-
> ing of form and content and also takes their writing far beyond the
> confines of white/male literary structures. The Black feminist critic
> would find innumerable commonalities in works by Black women. (174)

A second principle that Smith proposed to govern black feminist
critical practice was the establishment of precedents and insights in
interpretation within the works of other black women. The critic
should write and think "out of her own identity," asserted Smith,
the implication being that the identity of the critic would be synony-
mous with that of the author under scrutiny. The identities that
most concerned Smith were those of a black feminist and a black
lesbian. The principles of interpretation that she employed, she
hoped, would combine to produce a new methodology, a criticism
that was innovative and constantly self-conscious of the relation-

ship between its own perspective and the political situation of all black women. Black feminist criticism, in Smith's terms was defined as being both dependent on and contributing to a black feminist political movement (175). Convinced of the possibilities for radical change, Smith concluded that it was possible to undertake a "total reassessment of Black literature and literary history needed to reveal the Black woman-identified woman" (182–83).

Smith's essay was an important statement that made visible the intense repression of the black female and lesbian voice. As a critical manifesto it represented a radical departure from the earlier work of Mary Helen Washington, who had edited the first contemporary anthology of black women's fiction, *Black-Eyed Susans*, two years earlier.[16] Washington did not attempt to define, explicitly, a black feminist critical perspective but concentrated on recovering and situating the neglected fiction of black women writers and establishing the major themes and images for use in a teaching situation.[17] However, there are major problems with Smith's essay as a critical manifesto, particularly in its assertion of the existence of an essential black female experience and an exclusive black female language in which this experience is embodied. Smith's essay assumes a very simple one-to-one correspondence between fiction and reality, and her model of a black feminist critical perspective is undermined as a political practice by being dependent on those who are, biologically, black and female. For Smith, her reliance on common experiences confines black feminist criticism to black women critics of black women artists depicting black women. This position can lead to the political cul de sac identified by Alice Walker as a problem of white feminist criticism in her essay "One Child of One's Own."[18] Walker criticized the position taken by Patricia Meyer Spacks, in the introduction to her book *The Female Imagination*, where she justified her concentration on the lives of white middle-class women by reiterating Phyllis Chesler's comment: "I have no theory to offer of Third World female psychology in America. . . . As a white woman, I'm reluctant and unable to construct theories about experiences I haven't had." To which Spacks added. "So am I." Walker challenged Spacks's exclusive concentration on white middle-class writers by asking:

> Why only these? Because they are white, and middle class, and because, to Spacks, female imagination is only that. Perhaps, however, this *is* the

white female imagination, one that is "reluctant *and unable* to construct theories about experiences I haven't had." (Yet Spacks never lived in nineteeenth-century Yorkshire, so why theorize about the Brontës?)[19]

Walker's point should be seriously considered, for a black feminist criticism cannot afford to be essentialist and ahistorical, reducing the experience of all black women to a common denominator and limiting black feminist critics to an exposition of an equivalent black "female imagination."

In 1982, Smith's manifesto was reprinted in a text which attempted to realize its project.[20] *All the Women Are White, All the Blacks Are Men, But Some of Us Are Brave*, edited by Gloria T. Hull, Patricia Bell Scott, and Barbara Smith, was a text dedicated to the establishment of black women's studies in the academy.

> Merely to use the term "Black women's studies" is an act charged with political significance. At the very least, the combining of these words to name a discipline means taking the stance that Black women exist—and exist positively—a stance that is in direct opposition to most of what passes for culture and thought on the North American continent. To use the term and to act on it in a white-male world is an act of political courage.[21]

To state unequivocally, as the editors do, that black women's studies is a discipline is a culminating act of the strand of black feminist theory committed to autonomy. The four issues that the editors see as being most important in relation to black women's studies acknowledge no allies or alliances:

> (1) the general political situation of Afro-American women and the bearing this has had upon the implementation of Black women's studies; (2) the relationship of Black women's studies to Black feminist politics and the Black feminist movement; (3) the necessity for Black women's studies to be feminist, radical, and analytical; and (4) the need for teachers of Black women's studies to be aware of our problematic political positions in the academy and of the potentially antagonistic conditions under which we must work.[22]

However, in the foreword to the book, Mary Berry, while criticizing women's studies for not focusing on black women, recognized that women's studies exists on the "periphery of academic life, like Black

Studies."[23] Where, then, we can ask, lie black women's studies? On the periphery of the already marginalized, we could assume, a very precarious and dangerous position from which to assert total independence. For, as Berry acknowledged, pioneering work on black women was undertaken by white as well as black women historians, and black women's studies has a crucial contribution to make to the understanding of the oppression of the whole of the black community. Berry, then, implicity understood that work on black women should be engaged with women's studies and Afro-American studies. The editors acknowledged the contributions to the volume made by white female scholars but were unclear about the relation of their work to a black feminism. They constantly engaged, as teachers and writers, with women's studies and Afro-American studies, yet it is unclear how or whether black women's studies should transform either or both of the former.[24] The editors acknowledged with dismay that "much of the current teaching and writing about Black women is not feminist, is not radical, and unfortunately is not always even analytical" and were aggressively aware of the pitfalls of mimicking a male-centered canonical structure of "great black women." In opposition to teaching about exceptional black women, the editors were committed to teaching as an act that furthered liberation in its exploration of "the experience of supposedly 'ordinary' Black women whose 'unexceptional' actions enabled us and the race to survive."[25] *But Some of Us Are Brave* was a collective attempt to produce a book that could be a pedagogical tool in this process.

An alternative approach to black feminist politics is embodied in Deborah McDowell's 1980 essay, "New Directions for Black Feminist Criticism," and in Barbara Christian's *Black Feminist Criticism: Perspectives on Black Women Writers.*[26] McDowell, like Smith, showed that white female critics continued to perpetrate against black women the exclusive practices they condemned in white male scholarship by establishing the experience of white middle-class women as normative within the feminist arena. She also attacked male critics for the way in which their masculine-centered values dominated their criticism of the work of black women writers (186–87). However, the main concern of McDowell's essay was to look back at "Toward a Black Feminist Criticism" in order to assess the development of black feminist scholarship.

While acknowledging the lack of a concrete definition for or substantial body of black feminist criticism, McDowell argued that "the theories developed thus far have often lacked sophistication and have been marred by slogans, rhetoric, and idealism" (188). Two very important critiques of Smith's position were made by McDowell. She questioned the existence of a monolithic black female language (189) and problematized what she saw to be Smith's oversimplification and obscuring of the issue of lesbianism. McDowell called for a firmer definition of what constituted lesbianism and lesbian literature and questioned "whether a lesbian aesthetic is not finally a reductive approach to the study of Black women's literature" (190).

Moreover, unlike Smith's asserting the close and necessary links between a black feminist political framework and a black feminist criticism, McDowell was concerned to warn feminist critics of "the dangers of political ideology yoked with aesthetic judgment" and worried that Smith's "innovative analysis is pressed to the service of an individual political persuasion" (190). McDowell made more complex the relationship between fiction and criticism on the one hand and the possibilities of social change in the lives of the masses of black women on the other and also doubted the feasibility of a productive relationship between the academy and political activism.

McDowell's project was to establish the parameters for a clearer definition of black feminist criticism. Like Smith, McDowell applied the term to "Black female critics who analyze the works of Black female writers from a feminist or political perspective" but also departed from Smith's definitions when she extended her argument to state that

> the term can also apply to any criticism written by a Black woman regardless of her subject or perspective—a book written by a male from a feminist or political perspective, a book written by a Black woman or about Black women authors in general, or any writings by women. (191)

Thus, McDowell identified the need for a specific methodology while at the same time producing a very mystifying definition of her own. The semantic confusion of the statement gives cause to wonder at the possibiltiy that an antifeminist celebration of a racist tract could be called black feminist as long as it was written by a black woman! Surely black feminist theory is emptied of its feminist content if the perspective of the critic doesn't matter.

Nevertheless, McDowell posed very pertinent questions that have yet to be adequately answered regarding the extent to which black and white feminist critics have intersecting interests and the necessity for being able to discern culturally specific analytic strategies that may distinguish black from white feminist criticism. McDowell also argued for a contextual awareness of the conditions under which black women's literature was produced, published, and reviewed, accompanied by a rigorous textual analysis which revealed any stylistic and linguistic commonalities across the texts of black women. She regarded the parameters of a tradition as an issue to be argued and established, not assumed, and warned against an easy reliance on generalities, especially in relation to the existence of a black female "consciousness" or "vision" (196). Like Washington, McDowell stressed that the "immediate concern of Black feminist critics must be to develop a fuller understanding of Black women writers" but did not support a "separatist position" as a long-term strategy and argued for an exploration of parallels between the texts of black women and those of black men. However, McDowell did not include the possibility of a black feminist reading of literature written by either white male or female authors, and while she called for black feminist criticism to ultimately "expand to embrace other modes of critical inquiry," these modes remain unspecified. In an attack against "critical absolutism," McDowell concluded by making an analogy between Marxism as dogma and black feminist criticism as a separatist enterprise, an anaolgy which did not clarify her political or theoretical position and confused her appeal for a "sound, thorough articulation of the Black feminist aesthetic" (196–97).

As opposed to the collective act of *But Some of Us Are Brave*, Christian has collected together her own essays written between 1975 and 1984. The introduction, "Black Feminist Process: In the Midst of . . . ," reflects the structure of the collection as a whole as the essays cover the period of the development of contemporary black feminist criticism. However, the book does not exemplify the history of the development of contemporary black feminist criticism but rather concentrates on situating the contributions of an individual critic over the period of a decade. Christian's work has been concerned with establishing a literary history of black women's writing and has depended very heavily on the conceptual apparatus of stereotypes and images.[27] However, it is necessary to confront Christian's assertions that the prime motivation for nineteenth- and early twentieth-century black writers was to confront the negative images of blacks held by whites and to dispute the simplistic model of the literary development of black women writers indicated by such titles as "From Stereotype to Character."[28] Christian's work represents a significant strand of black feminist criticism that has concentrated on the explication of stereotypes at the expense of engaging in the theoretical and historical questions raised by the construction of a tradition of black women writing. Indeed, in the introduction to *Black Feminist Criticism*, Christian herself raises some of the questions that are left unanswered in the body of her work so far but which are crucial to understanding or defining a black feminist critical practice:

> What is a literary critic, a black woman critic, a black feminist literary critic, a black feminist social literary critic? The adjectives mount up, defining, qualifying, the activity. How does one distinguish them? The need to articulate a theory, to categorize the activities is a good part of the activity itself to the point where I wonder how we ever get around to doing anything else. What do these categories tell anyone about my method? Do I do formalist criticism, operative or expressive criticism, mimetic or structuralist criticism? . . . Can one theorize effectively about an evolving process? Are the labels informative or primarily a way of nipping questions in the bud? What are the philosophical questions behind my praxis? (x–xi)

Christian, unlike many feminist critics, divorces what she considers to be sound critical practice from political practice when she states that what irks her about "much literary criticism today" is that "so often the text is but an occasion for espousing [the critic's] philosophical point of view—revolutionary black, feminist, or socialist program."[29] Thus, ten years after the term *black feminist criticism* was coined, it is used as the title of a book as if a readership would recognize and identify its parameters; yet, in the very attempt to define itself, even in the work of one individual critic, the contradic-

tory impulses of black feminist criticism are clear. In a review of
Christian's book, Hortense Spillers points to the ideological nature
of the apparent separation between the critical project and its
political dimensions:

> The critical projects that relate to the African-American community
> point to a crucial aspect of the entire theme of liberation. The same
> might be said for the career of feminist inquiry and its impact on the
> community: in other words, the various critical projects that intersect
> with African-American life and thought in the United States comple-
> ment the actualities of an objective and historic situation, even if, in the
> name of the dominant ruling discourses, and in the interests of the
> ruling cultural and political apparatus, the convergence between intel-
> lectual and political life remains masked.[30]

What I want to advocate is that black feminist criticism be
regarded critically as a problem, not a solution, as a sign that
should be interrogated, a locus of contradictions. Black feminist
criticism has its source and its primary motivation in academic
legitimation, placement within a framework of bourgeois humanis-
tic discourse. But, as Cornel West has argued in a wider context, the
dilemma of black intellectuals seeking legitimation through the
academy is that

> it is existentially and intellectually stultifying for black intellectuals. It is
> existentially debilitating because it not only generates anxieties of de-
> fensiveness on the part of black intellectuals; it also thrives on them. The
> need for hierarchical ranking and the deep-seated racism shot through
> bourgeois humanistic scholarship cannot provide black intellectuals
> with either the proper ethos or conceptual framework to overcome a
> defensive posture. And charges of intellectual inferiority can never be
> met upon the opponent's terrain—to try to do so only intensifies one's
> anxieties. Rather the terrain itself must be viewed as part and parcel of
> an antiquated form of life unworthy of setting the terms of contempo-
> rary discourse.[31]

This critique is applicable for a number of reasons. Black feminist
criticism for the main part accepts the prevailing paradigms predominant in the academy, as has women's studies and Afro-Ameri-

can studies, and seeks to organize itself as a discipline in the same way. Also, it is overwhelmingly defensive in its posture, attempting to discover, prove, and legitimate the intellectual worthiness of black women so that they may claim their rightful placement as both subjects and creators of the curriculum.

Black feminist theory continues to be shaped by the tensions apparent in feminist theory in general that have been characterized by Elaine Showalter as three phases of development. To paraphrase and adapt her model, these would be (1) the concentration on the mysogyny (and racism) of literary practice; (2) the discovery that (black) women writers had a literature of their own (previously hidden by patriarchal [and racist] values) and the development of a (black) female aesthetic; and (3) a challenge to and rethinking of the conceptual grounds of literary study and an increased concern with theory.[32] Though it is not possible to argue that these different approaches appear chronologically over the last ten years in black feminist work, it is important to recognize that in addition to the specific concerns of black feminist theory it shares a structural and conceptual pattern of questions and issues with other modes of feminist inquiry.

Black feminist criticism has too frequently been reduced to an experiential relationship that exists between black women as critics and black women as writers who represent black women's reality. Theoretically this reliance on a common, or shared, experience is essentialist and ahistorical. Following the methodologies of mainstream literary criticism and feminist literary criticism, black feminist criticism presupposes the existence of a tradition and has concentrated on establishing a narrative of that tradition. This narrative constitutes a canon from these essentialist views of experience which is then placed alongside, though unrelated to, traditional and feminist canons. This book does not assume the existence of a tradition or traditions of black women writing and, indeed, is critical of traditions of Afro-American intellectual thought that have been constructed as paradigmatic of Afro-American history.

One other essentialist aspect of black feminist criticism should be considered: the search for or assumption of the existence of a black female language. The theoretical perspective of the book is that no language or experience is divorced from the shared context in which different groups that share a language express their differing group interests. Language is accented differently by competing groups, and therefore the terrain of language is a terrain of power relations.[33] This struggle within and over language reveals the nature of the structure of social relations and the hierarchy of power, not the nature of one particular group. The sign, then, is an arena of struggle and a construct between socially organized persons in the process of their interaction; the forms that signs take are conditioned by the social organization of the participants involved and also by the immediate conditions of their interactions. Hence, this book will argue that we must be historically specific and aware of the differently oriented social interests within one and the same sign community. In these terms, black and feminist cannot be absolute, transhistorical forms (or form) of identity.

Reconstructing Womanhood embodies a feminist critical practice that pays particular attention to the articulation of gender, race, and class.[34] Social, political, and economic analyses that use class as a fundamental category often assert the necessity for white and black to sink their differences and unite in a common and general class struggle. The call for class solidarity is paralleled within contemporary feminist practice by the concept of sisterhood. This appeal to sisterhood has two political consequences that should be questioned. First, in order to establish the common grounds for a unified women's movement, material differences in the lives of working-class and middle-class women or white and black women have been dismissed. The search to establish that these bonds of siterhood have always existed has led to a feminist historiography and criticism which denies the hierarchical structuring of the relations between black and white women and often takes the concerns of middle-class, articulate white women as a norm.

This book works within the theoretical premises of societies "structured in dominance" by class, by race, and by gender and is a materialist account of the cultural production of black women intellectuals within the social relations that inscribed them.[35] It delineates the sexual ideologies that defined the ways in which white and black women "lived" their relation to their material conditions of existence. Ideologies of white womanhood were the sites of racial and class struggle which enabled white women to negotiate their subordinate role in relation to patriarchy and at the same time to ally their class interests with men and against establishing an alliance with black women. We need more feminist work that interrogates sexual ideologies for their racial specificity and acknowledges whiteness, not just blackness, as a racial categorization. Work that uses race as a central category does not necessarily need to be about black women.

An emphasis on the importance of establishing historically specific forms of racism should also apply to gender oppression. It is not enough to use the feminist theoretical back door to assert that because racism and sexism predate capitalism there is no further need to specify their particular articulation with economic systems of oppression. On the contrary, racisms and sexisms need to be regarded as particular historical practices articulated with each other and with other practices in a social formation. For example, the institutionalized rape of black women as slaves needs to be distinguished from the institutionalized rape of black women as an instrument of political terror, alongside lynching, in the South. Rape itself should not be regarded as a transhistorical mechanism of women's oppression but as one that acquires specific political or economic meanings at different moments in history.

For feminist historiography and critical practice the inclusion of the analytic categories of race and class means having to acknowledge that women were not only the subjects but also the perpetrators of oppression. The hegemonic control of dominant classes has been secured at the expense of sisterhood. Hegemony is never finally and utterly won but needs to be continually worked on and reconstructed, and sexual and racial ideologies are crucial mechanisms in the maintenance of power. For women this has meant that many of their representative organizations have been disabled by strategies and struggles which have been race-specific, leading to racially divided movements like the temperance and suffrage campaigns. No history should blandly label these organizations "women's movements," for we have to understand the importance of the different issues around which white and black women organized and how this related to their differing material circumstances. A revision of contemporary feminist historiography should investigate the different ways in which racist ideologies have been constructed and made operative under different historical conditions. But, like sexual ideologies, racism, in its appeal to the natural order of things, appears as a transhistorical, essentialist category, and critiques of racism can imitate this appearance.

This book is a contribution to such a revision, a revision that examines the boundaries of sisterhood, for the contradictions faced by the black women intellectuals at the Columbian Exposition continue to haunt the contemporary women's movement.

2

Slave and Mistress

Ideologies of Womanhood under Slavery

The institution of slavery is now widely regarded as the source of stereotypes about the black woman, and it is therefore important to concentrate, initially, on the antebellum period in the United States in order to explore the implications of this assertion.[1] Catherine Clinton, a feminist historian, has argued in *The Plantation Mistress* that "woman is, in part, a cultural creation," and it is this cultural creation, the mythical aspect of the requisites of womanhood, that I will examine in the context of the cultural and political power of sexual ideologies under slavery.[2] In order to perceive the cultural effectivity of ideologies of black female sexuality, it is necessary to consider the determining force of ideologies of white female sexuality: stereotypes only appear to exist in isolation while actually depending on a nexus of figurations which can be explained only in relation to each other. Therefore, I will discuss and analyze ideologies of white Southern womanhood, as far as they influence or shape ideologies of black womanhood, and will argue that two very different but interdependent codes of sexuality operated in the antebellum South, producing opposing definitions of motherhood and womanhood for white and black women which coalesce in the figures of the slave and the mistress.

It is also necessary to situate narratives by black women within the dominant discourse of white female sexuality in order to be able to comprehend and analyze the ways in which black women, as writers, addressed, used, transformed, and, on occasion, subverted the dominant ideological codes. I will define the dynamics of the most popular social convention of female sexuality, the "cult of true womanhood," and assess its influence on the literary conventions that produced the heroine of the sentimental novel. Finally, the cultural and political influence of the cult of true womanhood will be shown to permeate the representations of black women in abolitionist literature, in general, and male slave narratives, in particular.

In his book *The Slave Community*, historian John Blassingame has argued that

> In many instances, historians have been misled by analyzing only one literary stereotype. The accuracy of the literary treatment of the plantation can be determined, however, only when several of the stereotypes of the slave are examined. This is all the more necessary because the legitimacy of each stereotype is tied irrevocably to the legitimacy of all the others.[3]

Blassingame recognized that "the portrait of the slave which emerges from antebellum Southern literature is complex and contradictory." He charted a dialectical relationship between the simultaneous existence of two male slave stereotypes, a rebellious and potentially murderous "Nat" and a passive, contented "Sambo," but Blassingame did not place these two stereotypes within the whole network of figurations forming a complex metaphorical system that functioned as an ideological explanation of the social relations of the South. While acknowledging that an analysis of one male slave stereotype will not allow access to an understanding of the mythology of the "Old South," Blassingame accepted that a dissection of the complex of male stereotypes could provide this understanding. The relationship between male and female representations and the complex and contradictory nature of figurations of the black woman as slave was ignored. This neglect of an account of ideologies of womanhood led to a very limited and indeed stereotypical response in Blassingame's discussion of slave women. A slave woman, he argued, could be "neither pure nor virtuous"; existing in circumstances of sexual subordination, "women were literally forced to offer themselves willingly" to their masters.[4] The interpretive ambivalence evident in the juxtaposition of "forced" and "willingly" indicates the spectrum of representation of the female slave from victim to active collaborator and a historical reluctance to condemn as an act of rape what is conceived in patriarchal terms to be sexual compliance. It is not an exaggeration to state that the formation of stereotypes of black female sexuality has been reproduced unquestioningly in contemporary historiography even where other aspects of the institution of slavery have been under radical revision.[5]

However, it is important to emphasize that my objective is not to prove that stereotypes contradict plantation realities. Any analysis that measures literary stereotypes against an empirically proven "reality" is motivated by the desire to find correspondences or noncorrespondences between literary figurations and actual social behavior and assumes that literary forms are mere reflections of reality. Such an analysis regards literary stereotypes as a directly related expression of social processes in terms of resemblance, homology, or analogy. In contrast, in my examination of dominant ideologies and literary conventions I will argue that the objective of stereotypes is not to reflect or represent a reality but to function as a disguise, or mystification, of objective social relations. The texts I will refer to, therefore, will not be presented as reflections of "real life" as it "was," but as representing and reconstructing history for us from particular viewpoints under specific historical conditions.

It is necessary to historicize literary practices to be able to adequately consider the particular constraints in operation, for example, in the writing of a slave narrative by a man as opposed to a woman, constraints that were influenced by factors of race and gender and were inflected very differently in a diary by a Southern white woman.[6] While acknowledging that forms of racism and patriarchy are older than the economic system of slavery in the United States and the Caribbean, it is also possible to recognize the particular ways in which racism and black sexuality are articulated in the patriarchal system of the antebellum South. As a literary product of these specific sets of social relations, narratives by black women embody the tension between the author's desire to privilege her experience and being able to speak only within a discourse of conventionally held beliefs about the nature of black womanhood. I am going to establish what these conventions were before assessing how black women who wrote used, transformed, or rejected them.

The dominating ideology to define the boundaries of acceptable female behavior from the 1820s until the Civil War was the "cult of true womanhood."[7] Barbara Welter, a feminist historian, has characterized its basic tenets: "the attributes of True Womanhood, by which a woman judged herself and was judged by her husband, her neighbors and society, could be divided into four cardinal virtues— piety, purity, submissiveness and domesticity. . . . With them she was promised happiness and power."[8] In the particular instance of white Southern womanhood, Julia Cherry Spruill, author of *Women's Life and Work in the Southern Colonies* (1938), also attests to the power of these conventions. In her excellent survey of the texts that were formative in the production of images of noble womanhood, Spruill concludes that these books "had an incalculable influence in fixing the conception of the proper nature of woman throughout the following century."[9]

In any assessment of the power of this image of "true womanhood" it is important to consider two aspects of its cultural effect: it was dominant, in the sense of being the most subscribed to convention governing female behavior, but it was also clearly recognizable as a dominating image, describing the parameters within which women were measured and declared to be, or not to be, women. Scholarship that has concentrated on the history of women in the United States during the nineteenth century has tended to focus on the issue of true womanhood, as a popularly held but misconceived set of beliefs that need to be tested against well-researched "realities" of women's lives. Historian Ann Scott, in her contemporary book on Southern women, *The Southern Lady*, follows the earlier course charted by Spruill and summarizes the purpose of her work in the following way:

> . . . to describe the culturally defined image of the lady; to trace the effect this definition had on women's behavior; to describe the realities of women's lives which were often at odds with the image; to describe and characterize the struggle of women to free themselves from the confines of cultural expectation and find a way to self-determination.[10]

Like Scott, most contemporary women's historians assert that the majority of white women in the antebellum period were not living embodiments of true womanhood, but they have paid little attention to an analysis of the function of the ideology. Concern with historical accuracy and authenticity has not revealed the generative power of the cult of true womanhood as ideology, and the narrow concentration of its effects on the lives of white women only has needlessly limited the perspective of feminist historiography.

I have chosen an alternative avenue of investigation, one which considers and assesses the importance of the image as a definer of what constituted a woman and womanhood. What needs to be discerned through these ideological complexities is that the cult of true womanhood resolves contradictions in the sets of social relations in which women were located. The ideology of true womanhood attempted to bring coherence and order to the contradictory material circumstances of the lives of women. Within the economic, political, and social system of slavery, women were at the nexus of its reproduction. Clinton has argued that

> Without the oppression of *all* women, the planter class could not be assured of absolute authority. In a biracial slave society where "racial purity" was a defining characteristic of the master class, total control of the reproductive females was of paramount concern for elite males. Patriarchy was the bedrock upon which the slave society was founded, and slavery exaggerated the pattern of subjugation that patriarchy had established.[11]

While agreeing with Clinton that the planter class needed to oppress all women, what I would add to this general observation is that the planters' control over reproduction had entirely different consequences for white women and for black women. Clinton suggests that antebellum sexual ideology "sought to bind up a woman's self-concept completely with her 'biological destiny,' " her duty to her husband being "to provide him with heirs" and her duty to her country "to produce citizens."[12] For white women of the elite planter class, Clinton's argument is perfectly sound; they were viewed as the means of the consolidation of property through the marriages of alliance between plantation families, and they gave birth to the inheritors of that property. But female heirs could also inherit; as Clinton herself recognizes, "sons received land and daughters, slaves."[13] As a slave, the black woman was in an entirely different relation to the plantation patriarch. Her reproductive destiny was bound to capital accumulation; black women gave birth to property and, directly, to capital itself in the form of slaves, and all slaves inherited their status from their mothers.

The sexual ideology of the period thus confirmed the differing material circumstances of these two groups of women and resolved the contradiction between the two reproductive positions by balancing opposing definitions of womanhood and motherhood, each dependent on the other for its existence. In Clinton's historical analysis of the plantation mistress, she argues that white slave-owners used "similar methods of keeping blacks and women excluded from spheres of power . . . and employed near-identical ideological warfare against them."[14] But if women, as an undifferentiated group, are compared to blacks, or slaves, as an undifferentiated group, then it becomes impossible to see the articulations of racism within ideologies of gender and of gender within the ideologies of racism.

The parameters of the ideological discourse of true womanhood were bound by a shared social understanding that external physical appearance reflected internal qualities of character and therefore provided an easily discernible indicator of the function of a female of the human species: men associated "the idea of female softness and delicacy with a correspondent delicacy of constitution" and recoiled if a woman spoke of "her great strength, her extraordinary appetite," or "her ability to bear excessive fatigue."[15] While fragility was valorized as the ideal state of woman, heavy labor required other physical attributes. Strength and ability to bear fatigue, argued to be so distasteful a presence in a white woman, were positive features to be emphasized in the promotion and selling of a black female field hand at a slave auction. It is worth considering that a delicate constitution was an indicator of class as well as racial position; woman as ornament was a social sign of achieved wealth, while physical strength was necessary for the survival of women in the cotton fields, in the factories, or on the frontier.

To qualify as a "true woman," the possession of virtue was an imperative. Barbara Welter argues in her essay that "Purity was as essential as piety to a young woman, its absence as unnatural and unfeminine. Without it she was, in fact, no woman at all, but a member of some lower order."[16] Chastity, or a chaste reputation, as Clinton has shown, was a commodity.[17] In terms of social and literary conventions, the qualities of piety and purity were displayed through action and behavior. In literature these qualities could be represented in a physical aura that surrounded the heroine. In a popular novel of 1852, *Eoline, or Magnolia Vale*, Caroline Lee Hentz writes that "Eoline, with her fair hair, and celestial blue eyes bending over the harp . . . really seemed 'little lower than the angels,' and an aureola of purity and piety appeared to beam around her brow."[18] The dark physical presence of the black woman who lacked these two essential qualities was constructed in opposition to the heroine. In another popular novel, Metta Victoria Victor's *Maum Guinea and Her Plantation Children* (1861), the case for the black woman was argued in a tone of an appeal to irrefutable evidence: "The idea of modesty and virtue in a Louisiana colored-girl might well be ridiculed; as a general thing, she has neither."[19] Black women were not represented as the same order of being as their mistresses; they lacked the physical, external evidence of the presence of a pure soul.

Within the discourse of the cult of true womanhood, wifehood and motherhood were glorified as the "purpose of a woman's being"; the home was the sphere of all a woman's actions.[20] The prime objective of a woman's life was to obtain a husband and then to keep him pleased; duties focused entirely on the bearing and rearing of heirs and caring for the household. In order to qualify as a paragon of virtue it was necessary to repress all overt sexuality. Feminine sexuality was limited to a display of heightened sensibilities and refinements and a titillating charm. As historian Barbara Berg has illustrated in her history of American feminism, *The Remembered Gate*, "The cult of purity denied that [white] women had natural sex drives," for the dominant view was that "the best mothers, wives and managers of households know little or nothing of sexual indulgence. Love of home, children and domestic duties are the only passions they feel."[21]

Popular sentimental novels of the period featured heroines who aptly demonstrated the appropriate aspirations for a young woman. A subgenre of this form, the plantation novels, contained the first of a series of literary "Southern belles."[22] An archetype of this figure was the character of Bel Tracy in John Pendleton Kennedy's *Swallow Barn* (1832). Bel combined charm with an aristocratic heritage, skills in music with skills in horse riding, but all her accomplishments are motivated by the vein of romance that desired, above all, a cavalier.[23] Marriage itself, however, meant the belle had to be transformed into a chaste matron residing on a domestic pedestal. In 1835, Thomas R. Drew published an exposition, "On the Characteristic Differences between the Sexes, and on the Position and Influence of Woman in Society," in the *Southern Literary Messenger*. Drew maintained that the belle could be rewarded male "protection" for the use of female "qualities that delight and fascinate" men. He defined these qualities of "[g]race, modesty and loveliness" as being "the charms which constitute [a woman's] power."[24] Clinton also observes that "throwing charm was the paramount duty of the female sex."[25] The concept of charm, in this particular construction of female sexuality, works as a mediator between the contradictory aspects of a chaste versus a titillating sexuality. Sexuality can be used to tempt but must be placed within a shell of modesty, meekness, and chastity; in other words, it must be repressed.

Overt sexuality, on the other hand, emerged in images of the black woman, where "charm" revealed its relation to the dark forces of evil and magic. The effect of black female sexuality on the white male was represented in an entirely different form from that of the figurative power of white female sexuality. Confronted by the black woman, the white man behaved in a manner that was considered to be entirely untempered by any virtuous qualities; the white male, in fact, was represented as being merely prey to the rampant sexuality of his female slaves. A basic assumption of the principles underlying the cult of true womanhood was the necessity for the white female to "civilize" the baser instincts of man. But in the face of what was constructed as the overt sexuality of the black female, excluded as she was from the parameters of virtuous possibilities, these baser male instincts were entirely uncontrolled. Thus, the white slave master was not regarded as being responsible for his actions toward his black female slaves. On the contrary, it was the female slave who was held responsible for being a potential, and direct, threat to the conjugal sanctity of the white mistress.

The constitution of the white female was conventionally portrayed as appropriately delicate, an outward manifestation of an inner sensitivity and refinement. In his *Narrative of the Life of Frederick Douglass an American Slave* (1845), Frederick Douglass described one of his mistresses in the following terms: "a woman of the kindest heart and finest feelings. . . . Her face was made of heavenly smiles, and her voice of tranquil music."[26] These "finest feelings" and heightened sensibilities were a recurring motif in the literature of the period. Their cultivation was advocated in handbooks on female behavior, and the display of fine sensibilities became a conventional mechanism in diaries, letters, novels, and slave narratives. In Douglass's *Narrative*, "slavery prove[d] as injurious" to his mistress as it did to Douglass himself. A "pious, warm, and tender-hearted woman" was completely corrupted by the effects of living within the institution of slavery.[27]

Conventions of sensitivity and refinement were also mobilized in rejections of the brutality of the slave system. Mary Boykin Chesnut, an aristocratic plantation mistress, recorded in her diary that she had seen "a Negro woman sold upon the block at auction" and that this sight, above the crowd, made her "faint, seasick," for "the creature looked so like" her own maid.[28] Such sensitivity and compassion were often ascribed to mistresses, by slaves in their own narratives, in ways that revealed a paternalism which reduced the slave to the status of a hapless child.[29]

However, the terrain of sensibilities was highly contradictory. A sensitivity that was heightened into an awareness of slavery as a brutal social system often existed simultaneously with a rejection of the humanity of slaves as brute creatures. A display of finer feelings worked to affirm the superiority of white sensibilities, and of white people as a group, over and above the slaves who were constructed as being incapable of harboring feelings or of generating grief. Fine sensibilities could, at the same time, be present as the "natural" attributes of the white mistress and as delicate and fragile as the constitution that housed them. When Douglass described in detail the effect of slavery on the natural grace of his mistress, both a physical and a spiritual decay occurred simultaneously:

> But alas, this kind heart had but a short time to remain such. The fatal poison of irresponsible power was already in her hands, and soon commenced its infernal work. That cheerful eye, under the influence of slavery, soon became red with rage; that voice, made of all sweet accord, changed to one of harsh and horrid discourse; and that angelic face gave place to that of a demon.[30]

This particular use of the convention by Douglass was not without irony, for the mistress contained the poison in her own hands; she was not forced to drink it.

The framing of moral virtue in the constitution of womanhood was a double-edged convention, ranging from compassion and sympathy to moral superiority and coercion. Mary Chesnut's diary contains evidence of such ambivalence and a consciousness of contradiction. Chesnut declared that "[t]he best way to take Negroes to your heart [was] to get as far away from them as possible."[31] Having just read Harriet Beecher Stowe's *Uncle Tom's Cabin*, Chesnut responded: "Topsys I have known, but none that were beaten or ill-used. Evas are mostly in the heaven of Mrs. Stowe's imagination. People can't love things dirty, ugly, and repulsive, simply because they ought to do so, but they can be good to them at a distance; that's easy."[32]

If we consider carefully the contradictory aspects of the ideology of true womanhood as a literary and social convention, it is possible to discern the limits of those analyses that seek to compare a stereotype with reality. Ann Scott has argued that the image of Southern white womanhood was inadequate to describe the day-to-day life of the white woman in the antebellum South because the stereotype applied only to a small percentage of women and because it did not accurately portray the experience of even this elite group. Scott has maintained that "Few aspects of woman's work accorded so poorly with the image of the delicate, frivolous, submissive woman, than the responsibility for managing slaves." "Supervising slaves," Scott concludes, "was difficult, demanding, frustrating, and above all never-ending."[33] This statement identifies the source of the contradictory nature of the image of womanhood in its relation to the system of slavery, but Scott's analysis does not consider the reason for the maintenance of the ideology if the image of woman it contained did not coincide with experience. In Scott's work the image of the Southern lady remains just that, an image, a stereotype unrelated to any others. What needs to be questioned is the necessity for the constant reiteration, in books, journals, and newspapers, that wives had to be submissive to patriarchal practices. Scott attempts to argue that the power of the patriarch had to be constantly reaffirmed because the control that white women exercised in running the home, raising children, and setting standards of behavior, though practiced within a restricted domain, was nevertheless a power. Scott's work established that any change in the role of women, or the institution of slavery, meant a downfall of the family structure. Clinton has agreed that "either a change in the status of women or the downfall of slavery" would have brought about "the end of southern civilization."[34] However, neither connects social relations at a material level with the ideologies that worked to perpetuate those social relations. Scott considers the image of the Southern lady in isolation; she undertakes no analysis of the power relation between a slave and her mistress, and her focus on the everyday concerns of the Southern lady is not situated within the wider sets of social relations in which the "everyday" is embedded. Any historical investigation of the ideological boundaries of the cult of true womanhood is a sterile field without a recognition of the dialectical relationship with the alternative sexual code associated with the black woman. Existing outside the definition of true womanhood, black female sexuality was nevertheless used to define what those boundaries were. The contradictions at a material and ideological level can clearly be seen in the dichotomy between repressed and overt representations of sexuality and in the simultaneous existence of two definitions of motherhood: the glorified and the breeder.

Josiah Quincy noted in his journal in 1773 that

> The enjoyment of a negro or mulatto woman is spoken of as quite a common thing: no reluctance, delicacy or shame is made about the matter. It is far from being uncommon to see a gentleman at dinner, and his reputed offspring a slave to the master of the table. . . . The fathers neither of them blushed or seemed disconcerted. They were called men of worth, politeness and humanity.[35]

Delicacy, shame, blushing, and being disconcerted were not the conventions governing patriarchal behavior but qualities attributed to white women. It was accusations of improper behavior of white women with black men that were publicly thought to be shocking, condemned, and swiftly punished. Ideologies of white womanhood coalesced and became more rigid at the same historical moment that the miscegenation laws were extended, laws which, in practice, were primarily directed toward relationships between black men and white women. At this same historical juncture it became illegal to import more slaves, so that internal breeding through slave women became a more crucial addition to plantation capital. That the slave followed the condition of his or her mother necessitated the raising of protective barriers, ideological and institutional, around the form of the white mother, whose progeny were heirs to the economic, social, and political interests in the maintenance of the slave system.

However, the idea of the essential purity of the white woman contained the seeds of its own destruction, an internal contradiction. Virtue had to be preserved until marriage, but marriage itself brought an end to innocence.[36] The core of the apple was rotten with the patriarchal manipulation of black and white female sexuality: the slave had been raped, and the mistress had to survive by clinging to the delusion that the apple was still whole:

> Under slavery we live surrounded by prostitutes, yet an abandoned woman is sent out of any decent house. . . . Like the patriarchs of old our men live all in one house with their wives and their concubines; and the mulattoes one sees in every family partly resemble the white children. Any lady is ready to tell you who is the father of all the mulatto children in everybody's household, but her own. Those, she seems to think, drop from the clouds.[37]

Consciousness of the contradiction, here so clearly expressed by Mary Chesnut, did not mean that it was to the advantage of the white mistress that the ideology be dismantled and exposed. The social relations of slavery, which the ideology mystified, determined that the interests of the mistress lay with the slave master, not with the slave. The ideology of true womanhood allowed the white mistress to live her contradictory position. It offered a way of making sense of the role that the white woman had to play, of resolving the contradictions that could otherwise shatter the pedestal on which she stood, a stool supported by the institution of slavery. One wonders if Chesnut detected the irony and clarity of the vision of her female slave recorded in her diary:

> Martha Adamson is a beautiful mulatress, as good looking as they ever are to me. I have never seen a mule as handsome as a horse, and I know I never will; no matter how I lament and sympathize with its undeserved mule condition. . . . She is so nearly white. How could she marry that

horrid Negro? It is positively shocking! She answered that she inherits the taste of her white father, that her mother was black.[38]

Martha Adamson spoke here across the ideological and material boundary that separated mistress and slave. The figure of the "beautiful mulatress" and the slave's response to her white mistress embody the contradictory position of black and white women in the sexual dynamics of the slave system.

Black women, in gaining their public presence as writers, would directly confront the political and economic dimensions of their subjugation. They had to define a discourse of black womanhood which would not only address their exclusion from the ideology of true womanhood but, as a consequence of this exclusion, would also rescue their bodies from a persistent association with illicit sexuality. It is to the representations of black female sexuality that I will now turn in order to illustrate the depth of the polarity between ideologies of black and white womanhood.

As I have already suggested, the figurations of black women existed in an antithetical relationship with the values embodied in the cult of true womanhood, an absence of the qualities of piety and purity being a crucial signifier. Black womanhood was polarized against white womanhood in the structure of the metaphoric system of female sexuality, particularly through the association of black women with overt sexuality and taboo sexual practices. Frances Smith Foster has argued, in *Witnessing Slavery: The Development of Ante-bellum Slave Narratives* (1979), that

the black woman became closely identified with illicit sex. If the "negress" were not a hot-blooded, exotic whore, she was a cringing terrified victim. Either way she was not pure and thus not a model of womanhood. Moreover, her ability to survive degradation was her downfall. As victim she became the assailant, since her submission to repeated violations was not in line with the values of sentimental heroines who died rather than be abused. Her survival of these ordeals and continued participation in other aspects of slave life seemed to connote, if not outright licentiousness, at least a less sensitive and abused spirit than that of white heroines.[39]

In fiction, it is not only the proslavery novel that should be indicted for a racist portrayal of black women; antislavery and abolitionist writers also drew on a racist and stereotypical characterizations.

David Levy, a literary critic who has surveyed the field of anti-slavery novels, concluded, "Those who attacked slavery in fiction portrayed the races in precisely the same terms as those who defended it."[40] Among the women writers of popular novels of the period, cited by Levy for their racist portrayal of slave characters, are E. D. E. N. Southworth, Sara Joseph Hale, Mary Hayden Pike, and Metta Victoria Victor.[41] Identifying and cataloguing the perpetrators of racist stereotyping as Levy has done, however, does not reveal how ideologies actually worked to construct both racial and sexual referents.

Popular white women novelists often used their texts to explore the boundaries of the cult of true womanhood and to challenge some of the most confining strictures in definitions of female sexuality. A close reading of these books reveals that this process of questioning the ideology applied only to the white female characters; black women in these texts exist only to confirm their own lack of womanly attributes in contrast to the abundance of virtues in their mistresses. Caroline Lee Hentz, in *Eoline, or Magnolia Vale*, created an exalted heroine, active, articulate, and white, who defied patriarchal authority. Eoline, the heroine, had a black maid, Gatty, who was rendered literally dumb. In opposition to Eoline's powerful use of language to define, challenge, and transform the limitations of her existence, Hentz imposed upon Gatty the language of self-abnegation. Gatty spoke only to say that she was "nothing but a negro, and no business to ask questions." Eoline silenced Gatty with the command, "you must not suspect, you must not think, you must not speak."[42] Thinking, articulate, reasoning black women were represented only as those who looked white: mulattoes, quadroons, or octoroons. The character of Maum Guinea, in Victor's *Maum Guinea*, was portrayed as an exception to this general rule. Victor created Maum to speak of herself as different from most black people: "I was allers deeper in my feelings dan most colored folks; and missus' teaching made me so."[43] This capacity for sensitivity had been cultivated by a white mistress and led directly to a correct appreciation of the "true" values of womanhood. Maum was seen to grant her love to her beautiful daughter Judy, who inherited the blue eyes and golden curls of her father, Maum's master, while she withheld such adoration from her other children, whose father was Maum's husband and blacker than herself. She vented her anger at the institutionalized condition of Judy, arguing that "she *wasn't* a nigger" and that therefore "she *shouldn't* be a slave."[44] The consequence of such narrative devices was that the black woman was made to speak her own absence from the definition "woman." White women writers debated the parameters of the dominant sexual ideology and questioned its inherent value structure, but they did not question its underlying concept, that woman meant white. Maum wanted her daughter Judy to approximate the attributes of true womanhood, but Victor resolved the potential contradiction that was raised by Judy's white appearance by placing her, as octoroon, in relation to illicit sexuality. Maum's desires for Judy to fulfill herself as a "true woman" could not be achieved, and she was left to vent her bitterness against God. As a black female character, Maum has a comprehension of social relations that was limited by the author: she could not understand why God allowed her "to bring up my girl pious and modest, jes' to let a white man take her and defile her when he'd a mind to?"[45]

In the most popular antislavery novel ever produced, *Uncle Tom's Cabin* (1852), Harriet Beecher Stowe was unable to embody the values of true womanhood in a black female character and, instead, bestowed them upon her protagonist, Uncle Tom, a black male.[46] Emmeline and Cassie were the two pale black female characters that existed only to become prey to the sexual appetite of the slave master, Simon Legree. This association with illicit sex was repeated in the history of the third octoroon character, Cassie. Upon the sudden death of her father, Cassie became a concubine who was eventually sold to repay gambling debts. The selling of Cassie left her white male lover free to legitimately marry an authentic embodiment of true womanhood who, unlike Cassie, was more than superficially "white."

Measured against the sentimental heroines of domestic novels, the black woman repeatedly failed the test of true womanhood because she survived her institutionalized rape, whereas the true heroine would rather die than be sexually abused. Comparison between these figurations of black versus white womanhood also encouraged readers to conclude that the slave woman must be less sensitive and spiritually inferior.

It was not, however, only within the confines of popular fiction that the sexuality of the black female slave was associated with the illicit. William Lloyd Garrison, a leading abolitionist, could use the absence of the qualities of virtue and chastity in the lives of slave women as part of his campaign for the abolition of the slave system in the pages of the major abolitionist newspaper *The Liberator* (1853):

> There are in this country a million females who have no protection for their chastity, and who may be ravished by their masters or drivers with impunity!! There are born every year more than SIXTY THOUSAND infant slaves who are *illegitimate!* a large proportion of whom have *white fathers*—some of these are the most distinguished men at the south—who sell them as they would pigs or sheep!! *Is not this perdition upon earth*—A BURNING HELL IN THE VERY BOSOM OF OUR COUNTRY—A VOLCANO OF LUST AND IMPURITY, *threatening to blast every plant of virtue, and to roll its lava tide over all that is beautiful to the eye, or precious in the sight of God?*[47]

Garrison's sexual metaphors for black women extended from passionate whore to hapless, cringing victim.

An analysis of slave narratives by men reveals a conventional portrayal of mothers, sisters, and daughters as victims, of either brutal beatings or sexual abuse. The victim appeared not just in her own right as a figure of oppression but was linked to a threat to, or denial of, the manhood of the male slave. Black manhood, in other words, could not be achieved or maintained because of the inability of the slave to protect the black woman in the same manner that convention dictated the inviolability of the body of the white woman. The slave woman, as victim, became defined in terms of a physical exploitation resulting from the lack of the assets of white womanhood: no masculine protector or home and family, the locus of the flowering of white womanhood.

The issue of miscegenation, in male slave narratives, provided a narrative occasion for the juxtaposition of the figure of the mistress with that of her female slave. A double victimization was often constructed usually in the form of a mother, sister, or daughter who became subject to the sexual abuse of the master and subsequent physical and mental abuse by the mistress. A classic instance of this type of juxtaposition occurred in the history of Ellen Craft, as told by her husband, William Craft, in *Running a Thousand Miles for Freedom* (1860).[48] Ellen's father was her first master, her mother his slave. Ellen was almost white in color, so nearly so that the tyrannical old lady to whom she first belonged became so annoyed at finding her frequently mistaken for a child of the family, that she gave her when eleven years of age to a daughter, as a wedding present. This separated my wife from her mother, and also from several other dear friends. But the incessant cruelty of her old mistress made the change of owners, or treatment so desirable, that she did not grumble much at this cruel separation.[49]

The slave man's desire for action to prevent abuse to mother, daughter, sister, or wife, or to take revenge against their brutal treatment, had in William Craft's words, "to be buried beneath the iron heel of despotism."

In contrast, in the slave narratives written by black women the authors placed in the foreground their active roles as historical agents as opposed to passive subjects; represented as acting their own visions, they are seen to take decisions over their own lives. They document their sufferings and brutal treatment but in a context that is also the story of resistance to that brutality. Lucy Delany, in *From the Darkness Cometh the Light, or Struggles for Freedom*, related her mother's fight for her own and her children's freedom after their father was sold down South.[50] Lucy's mother had been born in a free state and kidnapped into slavery. Having successfully planned and encouraged the escape of her eldest daughter, Nancy, to Canada, Lucy's mother subsequently rebelled against the authority of her mistress and was taken to the auction block and sold to the highest bidder. Three weeks later she escaped to Chicago but was tracked down under the fugitive slave law. Fearing the revenge that could be taken against Lucy, her mother decided to return with her captors. Undaunted, however, she eventually sued successfully for her own freedom on the grounds that she was originally kidnapped. In her mother's absence Lucy's trial began. Her spirit of independence, engendered by her mother, led her to argue with her mistress, who threatened her with a whipping. Lucy rebelled against such a beating, and arrangements were made for her to be sold. Lucy's mother fought a long court case to sue for the freedom of her daughter, pleading that as a free woman she could not have given birth to a slave, and won her case.

The narrative of Lucy Delany used conventions of heroism and greatness, normally associated only with the adventurous group of male slave narratives. Her mother's virtues, declared Lucy, were as "bright rays as ever emanated from the lives of the great ones of the earth," though to others, Lucy added, she would appear to have only "the common place virtues of an honest woman."[51] Such comments worked on two levels to disrupt conventional patterns of expected female behavior. In the absence of a male to protect and preserve the family, Lucy elevated her mother's actions to the realm of heroism, transferring codes of conventional male sexuality. But Lucy's second statement carried an understated irony, for the "common place virtues" were those denied to the black woman within the dominant ideology of womanhood. Gaining recognition as an "honest woman" was the struggle of Lucy's mother throughout the text.

Lucy and her mother were represented as a mutually supportive unit; they worked together and survived. Kate Drumgoold's narrative, *A Slave Girl's Story* (1895), also included an account of a female family unit working to support each other when the mother had finally gathered them all together after separation. These female households were portrayed as complete families, even if not conventional in structure. The authors did not describe such family structures as aberrant because they lacked a male head of household. Mothers were constructed as figures to be emulated by their daughters writing the narratives. Drumgoold described her mother's defiance of the term *slave* in phrases similar to the praise Delany reserved for her mother. "My mother was one that the master could not do anything to make her feel like a slave and she would battle with them to the last that she would not recognize them as her lord and master and she was right."[52]

In the narrative by Mary Prince, *A West Indian Slave* (1831), such a female household was entirely absent. Mary Prince was sold away from her mother, and each of her sisters was sold to a different master. Mary did receive teaching in rudimentary spelling from Fanny Williams, the daughter of Captain and Mrs. Williams, to whom she was sold and, later in her life, stressed that both she and the daughter of a later master were beaten. In this way Prince established in her narrative that certain sympathies and similarities could exist between a white woman and her black female slave. However, *A West Indian Slave* also revealed a conscious perception of the consequences of Prince's black womanhood in its essential difference from white womanhood. Prince demonstrated her awareness of the attempt to reduce her to nonwoman, to nonhuman, in the description of her sale. She was valued as a breeder. She was handled and examined like cattle, Prince stated, while prospective buyers "talked about my shape and size in like words . . . as if I could no more understand their meaning than the dumb beasts."[53] Through her narrative, Prince was able to affirm her ability to judge those who would deny her humanity and to morally condemn those masters who threatened her sexual autonomy.

While the portrayal of black women as defiant, refusing to be brutalized by slavery, countered their representation as victims, it also militated against the requirements of the convention of true womanhood. As Caroline Gilman, a white, Southern, antebellum "lady" wrote in her *Recollections of a Southern Matron*: "the three golden threads with which domestic happiness is woven . . . [are] to repress a harsh answer, to confess a fault, and to stop (right or wrong) in the midst of self-defense, in gentle submission."[54] The attempt to establish an independent and public narrative voice meant that black women had to counter simultaneously the implications of their exclusion from being women, as defined by the cult of true womanhood, and their representation as victim, whether of rape or of barter.

Frances Foster, in *Witnessing Slavery*, has documented the conventional pressures that shaped the slave narrative to conform to the demands of the reading public. Foster argues that in order to sell and to function as part of the movement for the abolition of slavery, "the viability of the slave family had to be denied, to increase the pathos of the homeless victim."[55] As a consequence of this, Foster continued, the rare instances of nuclear family relationships in slave narratives were highly romanticized. Marion Starling, in her work on slave narratives, has emphasized the importance of conventional uses of adventure, especially in relation to escape. However, both Foster and Starling concentrate mainly on male slave narratives. Neither critic feels that an alternative mode of analysis is necessary for examining female slave narratives. From the few examples of slave narratives by women given so far, it can be seen clearly that the viability of the slave family was not necessarily denied in those narratives published after abolition but could even be asserted as effective without the presence of male heads of households. Slave narratives by women, about women, could also mobilize the narrative forms of adventure and heroism normally constituted within ideologies of male sexuality. However, these portraits of black women did not eliminate association with illicit sexuality, nor did they contradict conventional interpretations of black female sexuality. Rather, the cult of true womanhood drew its ideological boundaries to exclude another definition of black women from "woman." The image of the strong, nonsubmissive black female head of a household did not become a positive image, but, on the contrary, because it transgressed what Gilman referred to as the three "golden threads," it became a figure of oppressive proportions with unnatural attributes of masculine power. Independent black women were destined to become labeled black matriarchs.

Angela Davis, considering slavery as a source of stereotypes of black women, has pointed to the links between the image of the matriarch and accusations of complicity between black women and white men in the subordination of the black man.[56] Sexual relations between black women and white men are often used as evidence of the existence of such complicity during the existence of the slave system. Thus, the institutionalized rape of black women has never been as powerful a symbol of black oppression as the spectacle of lynching. Rape has always involved patriarchal notions of women being, at best, not entirely unwilling accomplices, if not outwardly inviting a sexual attack. The links between black women and illicit sexuality consolidated during the antebellum years had powerful ideological consequences for the next hundred and fifty years.

In the narratives discussed in the next chapter, the issue involved in the establishment of a public voice will be related to the necessity for black women, as writers, to develop their own discourse of black womanhood. Though the cult of true womanhood did not remain the dominant ideological code, it should be remembered that the exclusion of black women from dominant codes of morality continued throughout the century. In 1895, the catalyst for the formation of the National Association of Colored Women was a public attack on the immorality of all black women. In Harriet Jacobs's slave narrative, which provides the main focus of analysis in the next chapter, a coherent framework for a discourse of black womanhood emerged for the first time. However, the rape of black women in the South continued to be an institutionalized weapon of oppression after emancipation, and the representation of the struggle for sexual autonomy was to remain a crucial organizing device of the narrative structures of black women writers.

3

"Hear My Voice,
Ye Careless Daughters"

Narratives of Slave and Free Women
before Emancipation

A survey of the general terrain of images and stereotypes produced by antebellum sexual ideologies is a necessary but only preliminary contribution to understanding how the ideology of true womanhood influenced and, to a large extent, determined the shape of the public voice of black women writers. What remains to be considered is how an ideology that excluded black women from the category "women" affected the ways in which they wrote and addressed an audience. The relevance of this question extends beyond the writing of slave narratives, and I will first examine texts written by free black women living in the North before turning to a slave narrative, Harriet Jacobs's *Incidents in the Life of a Slave Girl*.

In 1850, Nancy Prince published in Boston her *Life and Travels*. A free woman, Nancy Prince declared that her object in writing was not "a vain desire to appear before the public"; on the contrary, her book was the product of her labor by which she hoped to sustain herself. In other words, Prince regarded her writing as her work. The publication of her *Life and Travels* was the occasion for an assertion of Prince's intention to retain and maintain her independence:

The Almighty God our heavenly father has designed that we eat our bread by the sweat of our brow; that all-wise and holy Being has designed and requires of us that we be diligent, using the means, that with his blessing we may not be burdensome, believing we shall be directed and go through.[1]

But this statement was double-edged: it was at once an assertion of her present condition and a comment on her history which was retold in the main body of the text. Prince's assertion appealed to the values of the "Protestant ethic," while the opening pages of her text were an apt demonstration of economic racial discrimination; however hard the young Nancy and her family labored in the North, the fruits of that society were not granted to them. At fourteen years old, Nancy replaced a sick friend in service and "thought herself fortunate" to be with a religious family, as she herself had received religious instruction and had been taught "right from wrong" by her grandfather. Prince recounted the details of her arduous duties and cruel treatment and then interrogated the hypocritical religion of her employers:

Hard labor and unkindness were too much for me; in three months, my health and strength were gone. I often looked at my employers, and thought to myself, is this your religion? I did not wonder that the girl who had lived there previous to myself, went home to die. They had family prayers, morning and evening. Oh! yes, they were sanctimonious! I was a poor stranger, but fourteen years of age, imposed upon by these good people. (11–12)

After seven years of "anxiety and toil," Prince married and went to live in Russia, where her husband was employed and where there was "no prejudice against color" (20–23). Prince established her international perspective in a section which detailed life in Russia and then condemned the racism which permeated the United States, North and South. In a direct address to her audience, which Prince considered to be primarily a Northern readership, she described how, upon her return to her own country, "the weight of prejudice . . . again oppressed [her]," even while she retained her belief in ultimate justice:

God has in all ages of the world punished every nation and people for their sins. The sins of my beloved country are not hid from his notice;

his all-seeing eye sees and knows the secrets of all hearts; the angels that kept not their first estate but left their own habitations, he hath reserved in everlasting chains unto the great day. (43)

By extending the logic of religious conviction, Prince revealed the hypocrisy at the heart of American society. Her thinly veiled threat of revenge gained additional power from her earlier, obviously sympathetic response to those she had witnessed rebelling against the injustices of Russian society.

The dignity and power of Prince's narrative was gained from her position at once inside and outside the society she wished to condemn. Her narrative voice was given strength through her presentation of herself as a true practitioner of Christian principles who was able to comment on the hypocritical attitudes and forms of behavior that she saw practiced throughout the country. Prince used her knowledge of other societies to compare and contrast with her own. Somewhat ironically, she commented that she "may not see as clearly as some" because of the weight of oppression, but, of course, this rhetorical device revealed exactly how appropriate a witness and how effective a narrator of racist practices she was (42). Prince made clear her double position inside U.S. society as a citizen and outside it as an outcast because of her color; her final narrative position, however, was above "this world's tumultuous noise," at the side of the ultimate judge (89).

In her narrative, one action in particular used, but also questioned, a fundamental attribute of true womanhood: the possession of sexual purity. Having discovered that her eldest sister had been "deluded away" into a brothel and become a prostitute, Prince responded: "[t]o have heard of her death, would not have been so painful to me, as we loved each other very much" (12). This statement was in accord with conventional expectations of the importance of sexual purity; death was easier to accept than loss of virtue. However, Prince did not continue to follow the conventional pattern of regarding her sister as "lost" forever but searched for, found, and rescued her. Far from seizing the narrative opportunity to condemn her sister, Prince claimed her "soul as precious" and revealed the contradiction of a sexual ideology that led her sister to feel she was neither "fit to live, nor fit to die." Returning her sister to the bosom of a family Prince declared not shame but a sense of "victory" (13–16). As author, Prince used the structure of spiritual autobiography not to conform to a conventional representation of experience but to begin to question the limits of those conventions as they contradicted aspects of her own experience. *A Narrative of the Life and Travels of Mrs. Nancy Prince. Written by Herself* is an early example of a black woman who attempted to use a conventional narrative form, spiritual autobiography, in unconventional ways.[2] Princes's adoption of a public voice assumed and asserted the authority of her experience.

The conviction that writing was work was attested to by another free black woman, Harriet Wilson, in her narrative *Our Nig; or, Sketches from the Life of a Free Black* (1859).[3] A comparison of Wilson's motives for writing with those of Prince is fruitful. Wilson stated in her preface:

> In offering to the public the following pages, the writer confesses her inability to minister to the refined and cultivated, the pleasure supplied by abler pens. It is not for such these crude narrations appear. Deserted by kindred, disabled by failing health, I am forced to some experiment which shall aid me in maintaining myself and my child without extinguishing this feeble life.

Prince established that her book was the product of her labor, and Wilson appealed to her audience to buy her narrative as a product of her labor so that she and her son could survive. But, unlike Prince, Wilson sought her patronage not from a white Northern audience but from her "colored brethren." Wilson attempted to gain authority for her public voice through a narrative that shared its experience with a black community which she addressed as if it were autonomous from the white community in which it was situated.

In his introduction to Wilson's text, Henry Louis Gates, Jr., calls it the first novel by a black writer because of its use of the plot conventions of sentimental novels (xiii). But the use of these particular conventions can be found not only in the novel but also in many slave narratives. I would argue that *Our Nig* can be most usefully regarded as an allegory of a slave narrative, a "slave" narrative set in the "free" North. The first indication of the possibility of an allegorical reading occurs in the subtitle, "Sketches from the Life of a Free Black, in a Two-Story White House, North. Showing That Slavery's Shadows Fall Even There." Wilson used her voice as a black woman addressing a black audience to condemn racism in the North and criticize abolitionists. This placed Wilson in a position similar to that of Prince, both inside and outside the society subject to critique. Whereas Prince gained narrative dignity and power from her experience of other countries, her outcast status, and her "true" religious principles, Wilson's narrative authority derived from an assertion of independence from the patronage of the white community. Her narrative was written apart from any links to the abolitionist movement, and her direct appeal to the black community marginalized a white readership.

The "two-story white house" can be interpreted initially as the equivalent of the Southern plantation, in which the protagonist, Frado, was held in virtual slavery. Scenes of punishment and brutality, whippings, and beatings were evoked, as in a conventional slave narrative, to document the relentless suffering and persecution to which the slave was subject. The Northern house, like its Southern counterpart, was the sovereign territory of a tyrant, ruled by a mistress whom Wilson described as being "imbued with *southern principles*" (preface). Mrs. Bellmont, the white mistress, was described as having power over the whole family—husband, sons, daughters, and Frado—and was symbolic of the power of the South. The domestic realm, within which Wilson represented Mrs. Bellmont as the ultimate power, was the terrain of struggle over the treatment of Frado in which debates about the position and future of blacks in the United States are re-created. Sensitivity and compassion were to be found in some members of the family, including Mr. Bellmont and one of his sons, but their protests were ignored; the power of the mistress, like the power of the South, was never effectively challenged. The actions of Mrs. Bellmont determine and structure the overall pattern of her slave's life in the house; a house which increasingly resembles the nation, as the resolve of Mrs. Bellmont's opponents to improve Frado's conditions disintegrated at the slightest possibility of conflict. Mr. Bellmont was portrayed as preferring to leave the house to the tyrannical rages of his wife, hiding until the recurring ruptures receded and Frado had again been punished. In a close resemblance to the position of many abolitionists, Mr. Bellmont and his son offered sympathy and loud protestations but were unwilling to assert the moral superiority of their position by fighting the mistress, the South, and imposing an alternative social order. Both men merely dressed Frado's wounds and turned their backs when battles were renewed. The two-story house was an allegory for the divided nation in which the object of controversy and subject of oppression was *Our Nig*. Like Prince, Wilson gained her narrative authority from adapting literary conventions to more adequately conform to a narrative representation and re-creation of black experience. It is important to identify the source of many of these conventions in the sentimental novel and also to recognize that Wilson's particular use of sentimental conventions derives from the sentimental novel via slave narratives to produce a unique allegorical form. That *Our Nig* did not conform to the parameters of contemporary domestic fiction can be attributed to this cultural blend.

The issue of conformity to conventions has been linked to questions concerning the authenticity of slave narratives by historians, particularly in the case of Harriet Jacobs's narrative, *Incidents in the Life of a Slave Girl* (1861).[4] Arguing, convincingly, that historians need to recognize both the "uniqueness" and the "representativeness" of the slave narrative, John Blassingame, in *The Slave Community*, concluded that Jacobs's narrative is inauthentic because it does not conform to the guidelines of representativeness.[5] Blassingame questioned the narrative's orderly framework and the use of providential encounters and continued:

> the story is too melodramatic: miscegenation and cruelty, outraged virtue, unrequited love, and planter licentiousness appear on practically every page. The virtuous Harriet sympathizes with her wretched mistress who has to look on all of the mulattoes fathered by her husband, she refuses to bow to the lascivious demands of her master, bears two children for another white man, and then runs away and hides in a garret in her grandmother's cabin for seven years until she is able to escape to New York. . . . In the end, all live happily ever after.[6]

With regard to internal evidence and the question of the authority of the public voice, the critique that Blassingame offers focuses heavily, though perhaps unconsciously, on the protagonist, Linda Brent, as conventional heroine.

In comparing slave narratives to each other, historians and literary critics have relied on a set of unquestioned assumptions that interrelate the quest for freedom and literacy with the establishment of manhood in the gaining of the published, and therefore public, voice. The great strength of these autobiographies, Blassingame states, is that, unlike other important sources, they embody the slaves' own perception of their experiences. Yet it is taken for granted that this experience, which is both unique and representative, is also male:

> If historians seek to provide some understanding of the past experiences of slaves, then the autobiography must be their point of departure; in the autobiography, more clearly than in any other source, we learn what went on in the minds of *black men*. It gives us a window to the "inside half" of the slave's life which never appears in the commentaries of "outsiders." Autobiographers are generally so preoccupied with conflict, those things blocking their hopes and dreams, that their works give a freshness and vitality to history which is often missing in other sources.[7]

The criteria for judgment that Blassingame advances here leave no room for a consideration of the specificity and uniqueness of the black female experience. An analogy can be made between Blassingame's criticism of *Incidents* as melodrama and the frequency with which issues of miscegenation, unrequited love, outraged virtue, and planter licentiousness are found foregrounded in diaries by Southern white women, while absent or in the background of the records of their planter husbands. Identifying such a difference should lead us to question and consider the significance of these issues in the lives of women as opposed to men, not to the conclusion that the diaries by women are not credible because they deviate from the conventions of male-authored texts. Any assumption of the representativeness of patriarchal experience does not allow for, or even regard as necessary, a gender-specific form of analysis. Indeed, the criteria chosen by Blassingame as the basis for his dismissal of the narrative credibility of Jacobs's narrative are, ideologically, the indicators of a uniquely female perspective.

Jean Fagan Yellin, a literary historian, critic, and biographer of Jacobs, has (from external evidence) established the authenticity of Jacobs's narrative.[8] Jacobs wrote under the pseudonym Linda

Brent. *Incidents in the Life of a Slave Girl* was first published in Boston in 1861, under the editorship of Lydia Maria Child, and a year later it appeared in a British edition.[9] In the discussion that follows, the author will be referred to as Jacobs, but, to preserve narrative continuity, the pseudonym Linda Brent will be used in the analysis of the text and protagonist.

Incidents in the Life of a Slave Girl is the most sophisticated, sustained narrative dissection of the conventions of true womanhood by a black author before emancipation. It will be the object of the following analysis to demonstrate that Jacobs used the material circumstances of her life to critique conventional standards of female behavior and to question their relevance and applicability to the experience of black women. Prior to a close examination of the text itself, it is necessary to document briefly the conditions under which Jacobs wrote her autobiography and gained her public voice.

At the time of writing, Jacobs worked as a domestic servant for and lived with Nathaniel P. Willis and his second wife, the Mr. and Mrs. Bruce of the text. Unlike either his first or second wife, Nathaniel Willis was proslavery. Against Jacobs's wishes but to protect her from the fugitive slave law, the second Mrs. Willis persuaded her husband that Jacobs should be purchased from her owners and manumitted by the family. Because of her suspicions of Nathaniel Willis, Jacobs did not want him to be aware that she was writing of her life in slavery; the need for secrecy and the demands of her domestic duties as nurse to the Willis children forced Jacobs to write at night.[10] Jacobs recognized that the conditions under which she lived and wrote were very different from those under which other female authors were able to write and under which her audience, "the women of the North," lived. In her preface, Linda Brent stated:

> Since I have been at the North, it has been necessary for me to work diligently for my own support, and the education of my children. This has not left me much leisure to make up for the loss of early opportunities to improve myself; and it has compelled me to write these pages at irregular intervals, whenever I could snatch an hour from Household duties. (xiii)

Unlike her white female audience or contemporary authors, Jacobs had neither the advantages of formal education nor contemplative leisure. She contrasted both her past life as a slave and her present condition, in which the selling of her labor was a prime necessity, with the social circumstances of her readership. Jacobs thus established the context within which we should understand her choice of epigram, from Isaiah (32:2): "Rise up, ye women that are at ease! Hear my voice, Ye careless daughters! Give ear unto my speech" (iv). Jacobs had achieved her freedom from slavery, but she was still bound to labor for the existence of herself and her children.

The closing pages of *Incidents* contrasted the "happy endings" of the conventional domestic novel with the present condition of the narrator, Linda Brent:

> Reader, my story ends with freedom; not in the usual way with marriage. . . . We are as free from the power of slaveholders as are the white people of the north; and though that, according to my ideas, is not saying a great deal, it is a vast improvement in *my* condition. (207)

Contrary to Blassingame's interpretation, *Incidents* does not conform to the conventional happy ending of the sentimental novel. Linda Brent, in the closing pages of her narrative, was still bound to a white mistress.

Jacobs's position as a domestic servant contrasted with the lives of the white women who surrounded and befriended her. Mrs. Willis, though she was instrumental in gaining her manumission, had the power to buy her and remained her employer, her mistress. Jacobs's letters to Amy Post, although to a friend, revealed her consciousness of their different positions in relation to conventional moral codes. Desiring a female friend who would write some prefatory remarks to her narrative, Jacobs consulted Post, but the occasion led her to indicate that the inclusion of her sexual history in her narrative made her "shrink from asking the sacrifice from one so good and pure as yourself."[11] It was as if Jacobs feared that her own history would contaminate the reputation of her white friend. Lydia Maria Child, who became Jacobs's editor, and Harriet Beecher Stowe, with whom Jacobs had an unfortunate brush, were both described by her as "satellite[s] of so great magnitude."[12] This hierarchy in Jacobs's relations with white women was magnified through the lens of conventional ideas of true womanhood when they appeared in print together, for Jacobs's sexuality was compromised in the very decision to print her story and gain her public voice. As she wrote to Post, after Post had agreed to endorse her story, "Woman can whisper her cruel wrongs into the ear of a very dear friend much easier than she can record them for the world to read."[13] Jacobs had children but no husband and no home of her own. In order to be able to represent herself in conventional terms as a "true" woman, Jacobs should have had a husband to give meaning to her existence as a woman. As I described in the previous chapter, any power or influence a woman could exercise was limited to the boundaries of the home. Linda Brent, in the concluding chapter of her narrative, recognized that this particular definition of a woman's sphere did not exist for her, and this factor ensured her dependence on a mistress. She stated, "I do not sit with my children in a home of my own. I still long for a hearthstone of my own, however humble. I wish it for my children's sake far more than my own" (207).

The ideological definition of the womanhood and motherhood of Linda Brent (and Jacobs) remained ambivalent as Linda Brent (and Jacobs) were excluded from the domain of the home, the sphere within which womanhood and motherhood were defined. Without a "woman's sphere," both were rendered meaningless. Nevertheless, the narrative of Linda Brent's life stands as an exposition of her womanhood and motherhood contradicting and transforming an ideology that could not take account of her experience. The structure of Jacobs's narrative embodied the process through which the meaning of Linda Brent's and Jacobs's motherhood and womanhood were revealed. Jacobs, as author, confronted an ideology that denied her very existence as a black woman and as a mother, and, therefore, she had to formulate a set of meanings that implicitly and fundamentally questioned the basis of true womanhood. *Incidents* demystified a convention that appeared as the obvious, common-sense rules of behavior and revealed the concept of true womanhood to be an ideology, not a lived set of social relations as she exposed its inherent contradictions and inapplicability to her life.[14]

Jacobs rejected a patronizing offer by Harriet Beecher Stowe to incorporate her life story into the writing of *The Key to Uncle Tom's Cabin*. This incorporation would have meant that her history would have been circumscribed by the bounds of convention, and Jacobs responded that "it needed no romance." The suggestion that

Stowe might write, and control, the story of Jacobs's life raised
issues far greater than those which concerned the artistic and aesthetic merit of her narrative; Jacobs "felt denigrated as a mother,
betrayed as a woman, and threatened as a writer by Stowe's action."[15] Jacobs knew that to gain her own public voice, as a writer,
implicated her very existence as a mother and a woman; the three
could not be separated. She also knew from experience, as did
Prince and Wilson, that the white people of the North were not
completely free from the power of the slaveholders, or from their
racism. To be bound to the conventions of true womanhood was to
be bound to a racist, ideological system.

Many slave authors changed the names of people and places in
their narratives to protect those still subject to slavery. However,
Jacobs's need for secrecy in the act of writing and her fear of scorn
if discovered meant that her pseudonym, Linda Brent, functioned
as a mechanism of self-protection. The creation of Linda Brent as a
fictional narrator allowed Jacobs to manipulate a series of conventions that were not only literary in their effects but which also
threatened the meaning of Jacobs's social existence. The construction of the history of Linda Brent was the terrain through which
Jacobs had to journey in order to reconstruct the meaning of her
own life as woman and mother. The journey provided an alternative path to the cult of true womanhood and challenged the readers
of *Incidents* to interrogate the social and ideological structures in
which they were implicated and to examine their own racism.
Jacobs denied that she wrote to "excite sympathy" for her own
"sufferings" but claimed that she wanted to "arouse the women of
the North to a realizing sense of the condition of two millions of
women at the South, still in bondage, suffering what I suffered, and
most of them far worse" (xiv). Jacobs established that hers was the
voice of a representative black female slave, and in a contemporary
interpretation this appeal is defined as being an appeal to the
sisterhood of all women:

> Seen from this angle of vision, Jacobs' book—reaching across the gulf
> separating black women from white, slave from free, poor from rich,
> reaching across the chasm separating "bad" women from "good"—
> represents an attempt to establish an American sisterhood and to acti-
> vate that sisterhood in the public arena.[16]

However, these bonds of sisterhood are not easily or superficially evoked. "Sisterhood" between white and black women was realized rarely in the text of *Incidents*. Jacobs's appeal was to a potential rather than an actual bonding between white and black women. The use of the word *incidents* in the title of her narrative directs the reader to be aware of a consciously chosen selection of events in Jacobs's life.[17] Many of the relationships portrayed between Linda Brent and white women involve cruelty and betrayal and place white female readers in the position of having to realize their implication in the oppression of black women, prior to any actual realization of the bonds of "sisterhood."

The narrative was framed by Linda Brent's relationships to white mistresses. The relationship to Mrs. Willis with which the narrative concluded has already been discussed. The opening chapter, "Childhood," described Linda's early disillusion with a mistress whom she loved and trusted. Linda's early childhood was happy, and only on the death of her mother did Linda learn that she was a slave. *Sister* and *sisterhood* were made ambiguous terms for relationships which had dubious consequences for black women. Early in the text Linda referred to her mother and her mother's mistress as "foster sisters" because they were both fed at the breast of Linda's grandmother. This intimate "sisterhood" as babes was interrupted by the intervention of the starkly contrasting hierarchy of their social relationship. Linda's grandmother, the readers were told, had to wean her own daughter at three months old in order to provide sufficient food for her mistress's daughter. Although they played together as children, Linda's mother's slave status was reasserted when she had to become "a most faithful servant" to her "foster sister." At the side of the deathbed of Linda's mother, her mistress promised her that "her children [would] never suffer for anything" in the future. Linda described her subsequent childhood with this mistress as "happy," without "toilsome or disagreeable duties." A diligent slave, Linda felt "proud to labor for her as much as my young years would permit," and she maintained a heart "as free from care as that of any free born white child" (4–5).

Unlike Kate Drumgoold in *A Slave Girl's Story*, Linda Brent did not attempt to replace this mistress as surrogate mother. The phrase carefully chosen by Jacobs was "almost like a mother." The juxtaposition of the concepts of a carefree childhood with laboring registered an experience alien to that of the readership. This gentle disturbance to middle-class ideas of childhood moved toward a climactic shock at the death of the mistress, when Linda was bequeathed to the daughter of her mistress's sister. Linda and her community of friends had been convinced that she would be freed, but, with bitterness, Linda recalled the years of faithful servitude of her mother and her mistress's promise to her mother. In a passage that used a narrative strategy similar to that used by Prince in her *Life and Travels*, Jacobs's narrator indicted the behavior of her mistress according to conventional moral codes. Linda Brent reasserted the religious doctrine espoused by her mistress to condemn her action and reveal the hypocrisy of her beliefs:

> My mistress had taught me the precepts of God's word: "Thou shalt love thy neighbor as thyself." "Whatsoever ye would that men should do unto you, do ye even so unto them." But I was her slave, and I suppose she did not recognize me as her neighbor. (6)

The disparity between "almost a mother" and the lack of recognition as "neighbor" highlighted the intensity of Jacobs's sense of betrayal. Having taught her slave to read and spell, this mistress had contributed to the ability of Jacobs to tell her tale, but the story Jacobs told condemned the mistress, for it was her "act of injustice" that initiated the suffering in Linda Brent's life.

Because of the hierarchical nature of their social, as opposed to emotional, relationships, white mistresses in the text were placed in positions of power and influence over the course of the lives of slave women, an influence that was still being exerted at the close of the narrative after Linda's emancipation. Linda did not recount the actions of her mistress as if they were only an individual instance of betrayal but placed them within a history of acts of betrayal toward three generations of women in her family: herself, her mother, and her grandmother. Each served as faithful servant, each trusted to the honor of her mistress, and each was betrayed. The reconstruction of these acts through time and over generations was an attempt to assert their representative status within a historical perspective of dishonesty and hypocrisy.

The polarization between the lives of white sisters and black sisters was a recurring motif. The material differences in their lives that determined their futures and overwhelmed either biological relation or emotional attachment were continually stressed in the text. Linda Brent told the reader:

> I once saw two beautiful children playing together. One was a fair white child; the other was her slave, and also her sister. When I saw them embracing each other, and heard their joyous laughter, I turned sadly away from the lovely sight. I foresaw the inevitable blight that would fall on the little slave's heart. I knew how soon her laughter would be changed to sighs. The fair child grew up to be a still fairer woman. From childhood to womanhood her pathway was blooming with flowers. . . . How had those years dealt with her slave sister, the little playmate of her childhood? She was also very beautiful; but the flowers and sunshine of love were not for her. She drank the cup of sin, and shame, and misery, whereof her persecuted race are compelled to drink. (28–29)

Any feminist history that seeks to establish the sisterhood of white and black women as allies in the struggle against the oppression of all women must also reveal the complexity of the social and economic differences between women. Feminist historiography and literary criticism also need to define the ways in which racist practices are gender-specific and sexual exploitation racialized. The dialectical nature of this process is reconstructed in the "incidents" that Jacobs reconstructed between the slave woman and her mistress.

Linda Brent described her second mistress, Mrs. Flint, in ways that utilized the conventions of an antebellum ideal of womanhood while exposing them as contradictory:

> Mrs. Flint, like many southern women, was totally deficient in energy. She had not strength to superintend her household affairs; but her nerves were so strong, that she could sit in her easy chair and see a woman whipped, till the blood trickled from every stroke of the lash. (10)

Mrs. Flint forced Linda Brent to walk barefoot through the snow because the "creaking" of her new shoes "grated harshly on her refined nerves" (17). In these and other passages the conventional figure of the plantation mistress is ironically undermined. The qualities of delicacy of constitution and heightened sensitivity, attributes of the Southern lady, appear as a corrupt and superficial veneer that covers an underlying strength and power in cruelty and brutality.

Linda Brent realized that because of Dr. Flint's overt sexual advances and intentions she represented an actual as well as potential threat to the dignity and pride of Mrs. Flint. Jacobs demonstrated the slave's capacity to analyze the grief and pain of her mistress; the slave, however, waited in vain for a reciprocal display of kindness or sympathy. The sisterhood of the two abused women could not be established, for Mrs. Flint, who "pitied herself as a martyr . . . was incapable of feeling for the condition of shame and misery in which her unfortunate, helpless slave was placed" (32).

In an attempt to appeal directly to the compassion of her white Northern readers, Jacobs contrasted the material conditions of black female slaves with their own lives:

> O, you happy free women, contrast *your* New Year's day with that of the poor bond-woman! With you it is a pleasant season, and the light of the day is blessed. . . . Children bring their little offerings, and raise their rosy lips for a caress. They are your own, and no hand but that of death can take them from you. But to the slave mother New Year's day comes laden with peculiar sorrows. She sits on a cold cabin floor, watching the children who may all be torn from her the next morning; and often does she wish that she and they might die before the day dawns. (14)

Linda Brent was a demonstration of the consequences for motherhood of the social and economic relations of the institution of slavery. Jacobs recognized that plantation mistresses were subject to forms of patriarchal abuse and exploitation, but because they gave birth to the heirs of property they were also awarded a degree of patriarchal protection. Slave women gave birth to the capital of the South and were therefore, in Linda Brent's words, "considered of no value, unless they continually increase their owner's stock" (49). Upon this hierarchical differential in power relations an ideology was built which ensured that two opposing concepts of motherhood and womanhood were maintained. As Linda Brent argued, "that which commands admiration in the white woman only hastens the degradation of the female slave" (27). If a slave woman attempted to preserve her sexual autonomy, the economic system of slavery was threatened: "[I]t [was] deemed a crime in her to wish to be virtuous" (29).

The barriers to the establishment of the bonding of sisterhood were built in the space between the different economic, political, and social positions that black women and white women occupied in the social formation of slavery. Their hierarchical relationship was determined through a racial, not gendered, categorization. The ideology of true womanhood was as racialized a concept in relation to white women as it was in its exclusion of black womanhood. Ultimately, it was this racial factor that defined the source of power of white women over their slaves, for, in a position of dependence on the patriarchal system herself, the white mistress identified her interests with the maintenance of the status quo. Linda Brent concluded:

> No matter whether the slave girl be as black as ebony or as fair as her mistress. In either case, there is no shadow of law to protect her from insult, from violence, or even from death; all these are inflicted by friends who bear the shape of men. The mistress, who ought to protect the helpless victim, has no other feelings towards her but those of jealousy and rage. (26–27)

Jacobs thus identified that mistresses confirmed their own social position at the expense of denying the humanity of their slaves particularly when they were insecure in their own relation to patriarchal power: "I knew that the young wives of slaveholders often thought their authority and importance would be best established and maintained by cruelty" (94).

The Northern women who formed Jacobs's audience were implicated in the preservation of this oppression in two ways. In a passage that directly addressed the reader, Linda Brent accused Northerners of allowing themselves to be used as "bloodhounds" to hunt fugitives and return them to slavery (34–35). More subtly, Linda Brent also illustrated how Northerners were not immune to the effects of the slave system or to the influence of being able to wield a racist power when she described how, "when northerners go to the south to reside, they prove very apt scholars. They soon imbibe the sentiments and disposition of their neighbors, and generally go beyond their teachers. Of the two, they are proverbially the

hardest masters" (44). *Incidents* also documented the numerous
acts of racist oppression that Linda Brent had to suffer while in the
Northern states. A major motive for her escape from the South was
her determination to protect her daughter, Ellen, from the sexual
exploitation she herself had experienced. However, Ellen was subject to sexual harassment in the household in which she lived and
worked as a servant in New York, which made Linda Brent question
the nature and extent of her freedom in the "free" states of the
North. Described as being in a position of "servitude to the Anglo-
Saxon race," Linda Brent urged the whole black community to defy
the racism of Northerners, so that "eventually we shall cease to be
trampled underfoot by our oppressors" (180–82).

This spirit of defiance characterized Jacobs's representations of
all Linda Brent's encounters with her master. Conventional feminine qualities of submission and passivity were replaced by an
active resistance. Although Flint had "power and law on his side,"
she "had a determined will," and "there was might in each." Her
strength and resourcefulness to resist were not adopted from a
reservoir of masculine attributes but were shown to have their
source in her "woman's pride, and a mother's love for [her] children" (87). Thus, Jacobs developed an alternative set of definitions
of womanhood and motherhood in the text which remained in
tension with the cult of true womanhood.

The slave became the object of the jealousy and spite of her
mistress; Jacobs wrote that Mrs. Flint even vented her anger on
Linda Brent's grandmother for offering Linda and her children
protective shelter: "She would not even speak to her in the street.
This wounded my grandmother's feelings, for she could not retain
ill will against the woman who she had nourished with her milk
when a babe" (91). In an effective adaptation of convention it was
Linda Brent's grandmother who was portrayed as a woman of
genuine sensitivity. The two women were polarized: the grandmother exuded a "natural" warmth, but Mrs. Flint, as Jacobs's
choice of name emphasized, displayed an unnatural, cold, and hard
heart. For the grandmother, the act of nurturing gave rise to
sustained feelings of intimacy; Mrs. Flint's rejection of this mother-
ing relationship implied that she was an unnatural woman. Linda
Brent stated that she was "indebted" to her grandmother for all her
comforts, "spiritual or temporal" (9). It was the grandmother's
labor that fed and clothed her when Mrs. Flint neglected her slave's

material needs, and it was the grandmother who stood as the source
of a strong moral code in the midst of an immoral system. In a
considerable number of ways, Jacobs's figure of the grandmother
embodied aspects of a *true* womanhood; she was represented as
being pure and pious, a fountainhead of physical and spiritual
sustenance for Linda, her whole family, and the wider black community. However, the quality of conventional womanhood that the
grandmother did not possess was submissiveness, and Linda Brent
was portrayed as having inherited her spirit. Her love for her
grandmother was seen to be tempered by fear; she had been
brought up to regard her with a respect that bordered on awe, and
at the moment when Linda Brent needed the advice of another
woman most desperately she feared to confide in her grandmother,
who she knew would condemn her. Out of the moment of her most
intense isolation Jacobs made her narrator forge her own rules of
behavior and conduct of which even her grandmother would disap-
prove.

Dr. Flint was characterized by Jacobs as the epitome of corrupt
white male power. He was a figure that was carefully dissected to
reveal a lack of the conventional qualities of a gentleman. His lack
of honor was established early in the text when he defrauded Linda
Brent's grandmother. Presented as a representative slaveholder,
Dr. Flint embodied the evil licentiousness that was the ultimate
threat to virtue and purity. He whispered foul suggestions into
Linda's ears when she was still an innocent girl and used his power
to deny her the experience of romance, preventing her from marrying her first, true love. In the chapter entitled "The Lover," a free-
born black carpenter was described as possessing the qualities that
were absent in Dr. Flint. Honor was posed against dishonor, respect for Linda's virtue against disrespect and insult. The lover
Jacobs described as both "intelligent and religious," while Dr. Flint
appeared as an animal watching a young girl as his prey. The "base
proposals of a white man" were contrasted with the "honorable
addresses of a respectable colored man" (40–41). But, despite the
fact that Dr. Flint was the embodiment of the corruption of the
slave system, as his prey Linda Brent was not corrupted by him, and
her struggle was an aggressive refusal to be sexually used and
compromised or to succumb to the will of the master.

Instead, hoping to gain a degree of protection from Dr. Flint,
Linda Brent decided to become the lover of a white "gentleman," a

Mr. Sands. She thought that in his fury Dr. Flint would sell her to her newly acquired lover and that it would be easier in the future to obtain her freedom from her lover than from her master. Linda's reasoning was shown to be motivated by consideration not only for her own welfare but also for improving the chances of survival for any children she might bear. From her experience she knew that Dr. Flint sold his offspring from slave women and hoped that if her children were fathered by Sands he could buy them and secure their future.

The struggle of Linda Brent to retain some control over her sexuality climaxed in a confession of her loss of virtue. It was at this point in the narrative that Jacobs most directly confronted conventional morality. In order to retain narrative authority and to preserve a public voice acceptable to an antebellum readership, Jacobs carefully negotiated the tension between satisfying moral expectations and challenging an ideology that would condemn her as immoral. Jacobs's confession was at once both conventional and unconventional in form and tone. The narrator declared in a direct address to her readers that the remembrance of this period in her "unhappy life" filled her with "sorrow and shame" and made no reference to sexual satisfaction, love, or passion, as such feelings were not meant to be experienced or encouraged outside of marriage and were rarely figured to exist within it.[18] Yet Jacobs refused to follow convention in significant ways. In contrast to the expected pattern of a confessional passage, which called for the unconditional acceptance of the judgment of readers, Linda Brent's act of sexual defiance was described as one of "deliberate calculation": the slave actively chose one fate as opposed to another. Jacobs attempted to deflect any judgmental response of moral condemnation through consistent narrative reminders to the reader that the material conditions of a slave woman's life were different from theirs. Readers were the "happy women" who had been "free to choose the objects of [their] affection." Jacobs, through Linda Brent, claimed the same right in her attempt to assert some control over the conditions of her existence: "It seems less degrading to give one's self, than to submit to compulsion. There is something akin to freedom in having a lover who has no control over you, except that which he gains by kindness and attachment" (55). Jacobs argued that the practice of conventional principles of morality was rendered impossible by the condition of the slave. Her own decision to take a lover was not described as immoral or amoral but as outside conventional ethical boundaries. In a key passage for understanding the extent to which Jacobs challenged ideologies of female sexuality, Linda Brent reflected, "in looking back, calmly, on the events of my life, I feel that the slave woman ought not to be judged by the same standard as others" (56). Within the series of "incidents" that Jacobs represented, this decision was pivotal to the structure of the text and to the development of an alternative discourse of womanhood. Previous events focused on the disruption to a normative journey through childhood, girlhood, and romantic youth; following incidents established the unconventional definitions of womanhood and motherhood that Jacobs, herself, tried to determine.

Linda Brent's decision as a slave, to survive through an act that resulted in her loss of virtue, placed her outside the parameters of the conventional heroine. Barbara Welter has described how heroines who were guilty of a loss of purity, in novels or magazines, were destined for death or madness.[19] According to the doctrine of true womanhood, death itself was preferable to a loss of innocence; Linda Brent not only survived in her "impure" state, but she also used her "illicit" liaison as an attempt to secure a future for herself and her children. Jacobs's narrative was unique in its subversion of a major narrative code of sentimental fiction: death, as preferable to loss of purity, was replaced by "Death is better than slavery" (63). *Incidents* entered the field of women's literature and history transforming and transcending the central paradigm of death versus virtue. The consequences of the loss of innocence, Linda Brent's (and Jacobs's) children, rather than being presented as the fruits of her shame, were her links to life and the motivating force of an additional determination to be free.

Linda Brent's second child was a girl, and the birth caused her to reflect on her daughter's possible future as a slave: "When they told me my new-born babe was a girl, my heart was heavier than it had ever been before. Slavery is terrible for men; but it is far more terrible for women. Superadded to the burden common to all, *they* have wrongs, and sufferings, and mortifications peculiarly their own" (79). The narrative that Jacobs wrote was assertively gender-specific and resonated against the dominant forms of the male slave narrative. But the sexual exploitation that Linda Brent confronted and feared for her daughter was, at the same moment, racially specific, disrupting conventional expectations of the attributes of a heroine. Death became the price that Linda Brent was prepared to pay to free her daughter from slavery: "I knew the doom that awaited my fair baby in slavery, and I determined to save her from it, or perish in the attempt." The slave mother made this vow by the graves of her parents, in the "burying-ground of the slaves," where "the prisoners rest together; they hear not the voice of the oppressor; the servant is free from his master" (92). Jacobs added the voice of her narrator to a history of slave rebels but at the same time completed a unique act. The transition from death as preferable to slavery to the stark polarity of freedom or death was made at this narrative moment. "As I passed the wreck of the old meeting house, where, before Nat Turner's time, the slaves had been allowed to meet for worship, I seemed to hear my father's voice come from it, bidding me not to tarry till I reached freedom or the grave" (93). Freedom replaced and transcended purity. Linda Brent's loss of innocence was a gain; she realized the necessity of struggling for the freedom of her children even more than for herself. Thus, the slave woman's motherhood was situated by Jacobs as the source of courage and determination.[20]

In order to save her children, Linda Brent apparently had to desert them. To precipitate a crisis and persuade Dr. Flint that he should sell the children to their father, Sands, Linda escaped and hid. The children were sold and returned to their great-grandmother's house to live, where, unknown to them, their mother was in hiding. However, Linda Brent's hopes for emancipation for her children were shattered when her daughter, Ellen, was "given" as a waiting maid to Sand's relatives in New York. After years in hiding, Linda escaped to New York and found employment. Her daughter was neglected, inadequately fed and clothed, and when Benjamin, her son, was finally sent north to join her, Linda realized that in order to protect her children she must own herself, freeing them all from the series of white people's broken promises that had framed her life.

Having obtained Ellen's freedom, Linda Brent confided her sexual history to her daughter as the one person whose forgiveness she desired. As opposed to the earlier confession, which was directly addressed to readers, Jacobs portrays Linda as in need of the unmediated judgment of Ellen. Ellen refused to condemn her mother and told her that she had been aware of her sexual relations with Sands, rejected her father as meaning nothing to her, and reserved her love for Linda. The motherhood that Jacobs defined and shaped in her narrative was vindicated through her own daughter, excluding the need for any approval from the readership. Jacobs bound the meaning and interpretation of her womanhood and motherhood to the internal structure of the text, making external validation unnecessary and unwarranted. Judgment was to be passed on the institution of slavery, not on deviations from conventions of true womanhood.

Jacobs gained her public voice and access to a sympathetic audience through the production of a slave narrative, a cultural form of expression supported and encouraged by the abolitionist movement. She primarily addressed the white Northern women whom she urged to advocate the abolition of the system of slavery. However, Jacobs's narrative problematized assumptions that dominated abolitionist literature in general and male slave narratives in particular, assumptions that linked slave women to illicit sexuality. Jacobs's attempt to develop a framework in which to discuss the social, political, and economic consequences of black womanhood prefigured the concerns of black women intellectuals after emancipation. For these intellectuals the progress of the race would be intimately tied to and measured by the progress of the black woman.

Black women writers would continue to adopt and adapt dominant literary conventions and to challenge racist sexual ideologies. Like Prince, Wilson, and Jacobs, they would explore a variety of narrative forms in the attempt to establish a public presence and continue to find ways to invent black heroines who could transcend their negative comparison to the figure of the white heroine. The consequences of being a slave woman did not end with the abolition of slavery as an institution but haunted the texts of black women throughout the nineteenth century and into the twentieth. The transition from slave to free woman did not liberate the black heroine or the black woman from the political and ideological limits imposed on her sexuality. In the shift from slave narrative to fiction, I will concentrate on the ways in which the novel was seen by black women authors as a form of cultural and political intervention in the struggle for black liberation from oppression.

4

"Of Lasting Service for the Race"

The Work of
Frances Ellen Watkins Harper

"I wish I could do something more for our people than I am doing. . . . I would like to do something of lasting service for the race."

"Why not . . . write a good, strong book which would be helpful to them? I think there is an amount of dormant talent among us, and a large field from which to gather materials for such a book."

"I would do it, willingly, if I could; but one needs both leisure and money to make a successful book. There is material among us for the broadest comedies and the deepest tragedies, but besides money and leisure, it needs patience, perseverance, courage, and the hand of an artist to weave it into the literature of the country."

"Miss Leroy, you have a large and rich experience; you possess a vivid imagination and glowing fancy. Write, out of the fullness of your heart, a book to inspire men and women with a deeper sense of justice and humanity."

"But who believes any good can come out of the black Nazareth?"

"Miss Leroy, out of the race must come its own thinkers and writers. Authors belonging to the white race have written good racial books, for which I am deeply grateful, but it seems to be almost impossible for a white man to put himself completely in our place. No man can feel the iron which enters another man's soul."

FRANCES ELLEN WATKINS HARPER, *Iola Leroy*

This self-referential passage comes from *Iola Leroy; or, Shadows Uplifted*, a novel published by Frances Harper at the age of sixty-seven in 1892.[1] Among the many other accomplishments of Harper's life, her novel is generally considered to be her least successful project.[2] Literary critics have dismissed it on the grounds of a lack of artistic merit. Historians have found the book interesting only for its "fascinating glimpses of black life among the freedmen, by the first black writer to deal with the Reconstruction South in fiction."[3] But the question which remains unanswered is why Harper chose to write a novel as a "lasting service to the race." I will argue in this chapter that, far from being an aberrant event in an otherwise successful life, the production of *Iola Leroy* was rooted in the authority of Harper's experience as abolitionist, lecturer, poet, teacher, feminist, and black woman.

Iola Leroy needs to be assessed not only in formal literary terms but also with close reference to its political intent, as a novel which was written to promote social change, to aid in the uplifting of the race. With these considerations in mind, I will examine the literary paternity and maternity of the novel in relation to other Afro-American writing as well as to the popular sentimental, or domestic, novels that preceded it. I will also reflect on Harper's novel as a vehicle for debate about the nature of black leadership and as a means for representing the relation of black intellectuals to the folk after the failure of Reconstruction. I reconsider the significance of the use of the figure of the mulatta in the late nineteenth century and argue against critics of Afro-American literature who dismiss the mulatta as a concession to a white audience. Far from being Harper's least successful project, the incorporation of her essays and speeches into her novel makes *Iola Leroy* the culmination of her career.

Sandra Gilbert and Susan Gubar, in their analysis of nineteenth-century women writers, argue that

the literary woman has always faced equally degrading options when she had to define her public presence in the world. If she did not suppress her work entirely or publish it pseudonymously or anonymously, she could modestly confess her female "limitations" and concentrate on the "lesser" subjects reserved for ladies as becoming to their inferior powers . . . [or] she could rebel, accepting the ostracism that must have seemed inevitable. . . . [s]he had to choose between admitting she was "only a woman" or protesting that she was "as good as a man." Inevitably . . . the literature produced by women confronted with such anxiety-inducing choices has been strongly marked not only by an obsessive interest in these limited options but also by obsessive imagery of confinement that reveals the ways in which female artists feel trapped and sickened both by suffocating alternatives and by the culture that created them.[4]

This cultural confinement, Gilbert and Gubar continue, was both a literal and a figurative entrapment in a male world:

[A]lmost all nineteenth-century women were in some sense imprisoned in men's houses. Figuratively, such women were . . . locked into male texts, texts from which they could escape only through ingenuity and indirection. It is not surprising . . . that spatial imagery of enclosure and escape, elaborated with what frequently becomes obsessive intensity, characterizes much of their writing.[5]

Iola Leroy does not conform to this analysis: neither did it confine itself to a female domain of concern nor was the novel dominated by a male textual framework. On the contrary, it addressed itself to a readership which was implicated in the disenfranchisement of blacks in the South and revealed and challenged the racist practices prevalent in the North.

As the title indicated, the protagonist was a heroine, Iola Leroy, who espoused feminist concerns within a structure more akin to the female-dominated domestic novel than to the realist, male-dominated novels of James and Howells. *Iola Leroy* was written to intervene in and to influence political, social, and cultural debate concerning the status of "the Negro" as "Jim Crow" practices threatened to extinguish the last hopes for a black political presence in the South. The compromise between the northern and southern states that had sabotaged Reconstruction in 1877 meant that recent black history was repressed, and slavery, as a topic, became unfashionable and unpopular. William Still noted in his introduction to the 1893 edition of Harper's novel that he had "doubts" about the choice of the "peculiar institution" as subject matter for Harper's story.[6] As an author, Harper did not confine her text to the limited options available either to women in the domestic domain or to blacks in the increasingly circumscribed and political context of the separation of the races. However, before analyzing either textual or figurative evidence, I wish to consider aspects of the literal or biographical level referenced by Gilbert and Gubar and examine to what extent Harper, as woman, was confined within a male world.

Frances Ellen Watkins was born in Baltimore, Maryland, on September 24, 1825, the only child of free black parents both of whom died while Frances was young, leaving her an orphan to be raised by her uncle, the Rev. William Watkins.[7] Watkins was a self-educated man involved in the abolitionist movement who ran a school for free black children. Frances attended this school until she was thirteen years old, when she left to live and work as a domestic in the house of a Baltimore bookseller named Armstrong. William Still documented that during this period of her life Frances Watkins published her first collection of poetry and prose, *Forest Leaves* (1845), of which no copy has survived. All biographers agree that Frances read assiduously in her free time while receiving training as a seamstress; in 1851, she left Baltimore to become a sewing teacher at Union Seminary, an African Methodist Episcopal (AME) church school near Columbus, Ohio. Apparently unhappy in this position, Frances left within a year and found another teaching post in Little York, Pennsylvania. In 1853, a law was passed in Maryland which made free blacks entering the state liable to be sold as slaves. This situation convinced Frances to commit herself full-time to the antislavery cause. She began her career as a lecturer, a career she was to follow for the major portion of her life.

Frances Watkins's first lecture in August 1854 was given to a public meeting in New Bedford, Massachusetts and was an address on the "Education and the Elevation of the Colored Race." By September she was engaged by the Antislavery Society of Maine and began to tour a circuit that was to take her throughout the eastern states and into Ohio and Canada. Frances Watkins was also working for and financially supporting the Underground Railroad, through which she began her long association with William Still and other activists.

On November 22, 1860, Frances Watkins married Fenton Harper, a widower and resident of Ohio. With the money from her lectures and publications, she invested in a farm near Columbus and temporarily retired from public life until the death of her husband only four years later on May 23, 1864. During this time Harper bore a daughter about whom there is little biographical information except that she died while still young. Freed from marital responsibilities and duties, Harper returned to full-time lecturing as an activist in the struggle to gain and maintain education and equality before the law for the freedmen. In 1871, she based herself in Philadelphia with her daughter and used her experiences of traveling to plantations, cities, and towns in the South in her speaking engagements at schools, churches, courthouses, and legislative halls.

Frances Harper fought for and won the right to be regarded as a successful public lecturer, a career not generally considered suitable for a woman, especially a black woman. But disabilities of gender and race were not automatically overcome. Still recorded that because she was so articulate and engaging as a public speaker, some audiences thought Harper must be a man, while others thought she couldn't possibly be black and had to be painted. *Christian Recorder*, official weekly of the AME church, printed a letter in 1871 under the heading "A Female Lecturer," which commented on Harper's performance as a lecturer:

> When persons come among us, who will not, at the peril of their lives, compromise our race, nor injure our common cause, they should have our healthy support. Mrs. Harper is evidently devoted to the interest of our race. . . . She has impressed many who were adverse to females entering the lecture field, that public speaking is her native element; the practical cast of her mind gives rare coloring and beauty to her lectures. Many more like Mrs. Harper are greatly needed, especially in the South, to remove the bad odor from the name "Negro."[8]

Public recognition of her abilities made no reference to any attempt on Harper's part to adopt masculine tones, gestures, or demeanor or to establish that she was "as good as a man." On the contrary, evidence indicates that her success was firmly based on her being a woman lecturer who refused to limit herself to issues considered suitable for women. White women commentators remarked on her performance as measured by contemporary conventional female qualities. Grace Greenwood wrote of Harper in *The Independent*: "she has a noble head, this bronze muse; a strong face, with a shadowed glow upon it indicative of thought and of a nature most femininely sensitive, but not in the least morbid."[9] In a rather patronizing eulogy, Phebe Hanaford praised Harper's talents in her book, *Daughters of America; or Women of the Century* (1882):

> Frances E. W. Harper is one of the most eloquent woman lecturers in the country. As one listens to her clear, plaintive, melodious voice, and follows the flow of her musical speech in her logical presentation of truth, he can but be charmed with her oratory and rhetoric, and forgets that she is of the race once enslaved in our land. She is one of the colored women of whom white women may be proud, and to whom the abolitionists can point and declare that a race which could show such women ought never to have been held in bondage.[10]

As a black woman and as a feminist, Harper had to confront the contradictions between advancing the cause of equal rights for her race and the predominantly white movement for women's suffrage. As a black Northern intellectual, she had to address the condition of the majority of black people in the South and assess the quality of alliances with white Northern intellectuals and movements. Harper regarded the South as "a great theater for the colored man's development and progress," but she did not view the Northern states as an example of progress and liberty. Harper was "glad that the colored man gets his freedom and suffrage together [in the South]; that he is not forced to go through the same condition of things here, that has inclined him to so much apathy, isolation, and indifference, in the North." The extent to which common cause could be made with white progressive movements had limitations, Harper believed, for while "between the white people and the colored there [was] a community of interests," she would not compromise where that community of interests meant "increasing the privileges of one class and curtailing the rights of the other."[11]

In 1869, Harper took a stand against the leaders of the American Equal Rights Association, Elizabeth Cady Stanton and Susan B. Anthony. As reported in two May 1869 issues of *The Revolution*, the Fifteenth Amendment caused the expression of dissent from support for black suffrage during the annual meeting of the association. Anthony took the position that "[i]f intelligence, justice, and morality are to be placed in the government, then let the question of

woman be brought up first and that of the negro last." Frederick
Douglass, always a supporter of female suffrage, responded to
Anthony and insisted on the need for urgency in mobilizing support
for the Fifteenth Amendment, which he saw as "a question of life
and death" for black people:

> When women, because they are women, are hunted down through the
> cities of New York and New Orleans; when their children are dragged
> from their houses and hung upon lamp-posts; when their children are
> torn from their arms, and their brains dashed out upon the pavement;
> when they are objects of insult and outrage at every turn; when they are
> in danger of having their homes burnt down over their heads; when their
> children are not allowed to enter schools; then they will have an urgency
> to obtain the ballot equal to our own.[12]

When asked if, surely, all this applied to the black woman, Douglass agreed and added, "not because she is a woman but because she
is black." Harper supported Douglass and found that, in this instance, the "community of interests" diverged between white and
black. She argued that when "it was a question of race we let the
lesser question of sex go. But the white women go all for sex, letting
race occupy a minor position." Harper concluded that in this particular situation gender was not sufficient grounds for solidarity.[13]
The history of the women's suffrage movement in the United States
proved Harper's analysis to be both perceptive and pertinent. Both
Anthony and Stanton eventually compromised with and acceded to
racist, exclusionary practices in order to court potential white female supporters in the Southern states. The encouragement of the
entry of white Southern women on terms which they dictated ensured that suffrage organizations became a white women's movement. However, Harper became increasingly active in later years in
the Women's Christian Temperance Union, which, while not being
exclusively a white organization, was mainly segregated. Temperance activity was regarded by Harper as an important arena in
which to develop the "community of interests" shared with white
women. She remained in the WCTU despite its ambivalence toward
racial issues and encouraged other black women to join.

During the years of Reconstruction, as a woman lecturer, Harper
felt that a crucial part of her duty was to give part of her lectures

privately to black women, for whom she never made any charge or took up any collection. "Now is the time," Harper argued, "for our women to begin to try to lift up their heads and plant the roots of progress under the hearthstone."[14] But Harper did not think that the role of black women in raising the condition of the race had to be limited to the domestic sphere. In an 1878 article entitled "Colored Women of America," she described the various roles of the black woman as worker, from field hand to property owner. Harper wrote not of women "imprisoned in men's houses" but of black women who were plowing, planting, and selling cotton in order to gain an education or to support a family, "working and managing plantations of from twenty to 100 acres," and organizing in mutual benefit groups. Even though not imprisoned within the sphere of the home, these women did not escape domestic violence, and Harper often found it necessary to preach "against men ill-treating their wives."[15]

Harper had a vision that women were potentially capable of transforming society, but although this vision was not limited to what women could achieve from the hearthstone Harper did regard the home as a crucial sphere of women's influence. At the World's Congress of Representative Women in Chicago in 1893, Harper encouraged her audience to see themselves on "the threshold of woman's era."[16] She charged her listeners to challenge a society that gave free rein to "brutal and cowardly men" to "torture, burn and lynch their [defenseless] fellow-men" and castigated legislators "born to an inheritance of privileges, who have behind them ages of education, dominion, civilization, and Christianity" but who oppose passage of a national education bill that would grant education "to the children of those who were born under the shadow of institutions which made it a crime to read." Women, Harper argued, should not be an influence in the domestic sphere only but should enter the "political estate":

> Today women hold in their hands influence and opportunity, and with these they have already opened doors which have been closed to others. By opening doors of labor woman has become a rival claimant for at least some of the wealth monopolized by her stronger brother. In the home she is the priestess, in society the queen, in literature she is power, in legislative halls law-makers have responded to her appeals, and for

her sake have humanized and liberalized their laws. The press has felt
the impress of her hand. In the pews of the church she constitutes the
majority; the pulpit has welcomed her, and in the school she has the
blessed privilege of teaching children and youth. To her is apparently
coming the added responsibility of political power; and what she now
possesses should only be the means of preparing her to use the coming
power.[17]

Harper was convinced that it was possible for women to formulate alternative aims for a society dominated by "the greed of gold
and the lust of power" but did not believe that women had a
"natural" claim to be the bearers of the highest aspirations of
humanity. She stated that she "was not sure that women are naturally so much better than men that they will clear the stream [of
political life] by virtue of their womanhood." How women would
use political power could not be predicted, Harper continued, but
she knew that "no nation can gain its full measure of enlightenment
and happiness if one half of it is free and the other half is fettered."
What Harper advocated was not an extension of "womanly influence," a feminization of society, but a total transformation of the
social order achieved through a unity gained in the "grand and holy
purpose of uplifting the human race."

Harper's respondent at the congress was Margaret Windheyer, a
representative of the Womanhood Suffrage League of New South
Wales, Australia, who voiced the popular objection that women
could have no political presence without the franchise. Though a
strong advocate of female suffrage, Harper was convinced that
women did not have to wait in silence until suffrage was granted;
she had been a public figure for nearly forty years and had claimed
her political presence without having gained the right to vote.
Harper was committed to a belief in the limitless, not confined,
areas in which women could, and did, legitimately intervene. Her
address to this international gathering adroitly linked the issue of
suffrage to issues of race: it was voters, stated Harper, who tortured,
burned, and lynched black people. Women's political perspective,
she insisted, would have to be wider than a focus on obtaining the
franchise.

This political and biographical context can provide the framework for understanding Harper's appeal to justice and humanity in

the passage from *Iola Leroy* quoted at the beginning of this chapter. Like Harriet Jacobs and Harriet Wilson, Harper told her readers that though black writers did not write out of situations where they had both money and leisure, they were determined to write books that could both take their place in "the literature of the country" and be "of lasting service for the race." These two desires were fused into a didactic novel. The desire to inspire her audience was confirmed in the authorial note appended to the concluding chapter:

> From the threads of fact and fiction I have woven a story whose mission will not be in vain if it awaken in the hearts of our countrymen a stronger sense of justice and a more Christlike humanity in behalf of those whom the fortunes of war threw, homeless, ignorant and poor, upon the threshold of a new era. Nor will it be in vain if it inspire the children of those upon whose brows God has poured the chrism of that new era to determine that they will embrace every opportunity, develop every faculty, and use every power God has given them to rise in the scale of character and condition, and to add their quota of good citizenship to the best welfare of the nation. (282)

Inspiration to political and social action was directed at two clearly defined audiences, white and black. This dual address was paralleled by the two major influences in the structure of the novel: women's fiction and the narratives written predominantly by Afro-American male authors. While the latter influence has been discussed by critics, especially the close relationship between *Iola Leroy* and William Wells Brown's *Clotelle* (1864), the former influence from women's fiction has been neglected. Hugh Gloster, in *Negro Voices in American Fiction* (1948), asserted rather than argued that "there is little question about the source of *Iola Leroy*: it is almost wholly the product of reading Brown's *Clotelle*."[18] In *The Negro Caravan* (1941), edited by Sterling Brown, Arthur P. Davis, and Ulysses Lee, this relationship was again asserted but also decried, for the "repetitions of situations" from Brown's text were regarded as "a forecast of a sort of literary inbreeding which causes Negro writers to be influenced by other Negroes more than should ordinarily be expected."[19]

If we move beyond a simple identification of the similarities in situation and character between the two novels, we should also recognize the shared aim of reaching a wide audience with a novelistic format. Brown's *Clotelle* (a revised edition of *Clotel, or, the President's Daughter: A Narrative of Slave Life in the United States*, which was published in London in 1853) was first published in the United States as a dime novel in a series entitled "Redpath's Books for the Campfires" and was intended for an audience of soldiers during the Civil War, a broad but primarily male audience. Harper wrote for black Sunday school readers, and her use of aspects of the sentimental, or domestic, novel is clearly an attempt to include an appeal to a female readership. Harper adapted and used these formulas from women's fiction in an attempt to reach a wide audience and entertain as well as teach.

Nina Baym has concluded that on the strength of the popularity of women's fiction "authorship in America was established as a woman's profession, and reading as a woman's avocation."[20] By the time Harper wrote *Iola Leroy*, she had been an author of poetry and short prose for forty-seven years.[21] Her work was popular and was sold at her public lectures. Harper's poetry and one short story, "The Two Offers," were, like her lectures, addressed to both white and black audiences of both sexes. Although Baym's analysis covers the period up to 1870, the dominance of a female readership for fiction remained a decisive factor for the rest of the century. Indeed, male authors like Howells and James recognized and responded to the demands of a female readership and told women's stories.[22]

Iola Leroy incorporated a miscellany of forms, but its unity relied on its presentation of a woman's story. The progress of Iola's life from childhood to marriage framed the major portion of the text, but her movement within the narrative landscape provided the occasions for a consideration of more general social events. As heroine and leading protagonist, Iola was also the narrative mechanism for transitions between the fictional and the didactic, the entertaining and the instructive. The various models for women's fiction in nineteenth-century North America which Baym describes can be compared to *Iola Leroy* to reveal the extent of Harper's use of the structure of novels by and about women from the middle of the century.[23]

Baym's initial model for women's fiction works from the premise that all the books with which she deals tell a single tale with variations. This tale is that of a young woman deprived of all support who has to win her own way in the world. The heroine negotiates her journey from adolescence to successful adulthood, a movement that often concludes with a happy marriage but always ends with an assertion of the feminine ego. Baym also argues that the protagonist is a comic heroine, that her displacement indicates social corruption and her triumph the reconstruction of a beneficent social order.

Baym's analysis prioritizes the concept of gender but ignores the racialization of characters and in this regard shares the limitations of contemporary feminist literary criticism. Contemporary Afro-American literary critics have used the concept of race to concentrate their analyses on Iola as an octoroon figure and her relation to other instances of the tragic mulatta in Afro-American narrative.[24] Literary history and criticism that focus entirely on the heroine as woman or on the heroine in her relation to blackness could benefit from the perceptions of each.

In its general characteristics Baym's model describes the skeletal structure of *Iola Leroy*. Iola was deprived of material and emotional support when her white father died and his cousin determined to return Iola, her mother, her sister, and her brother to the condition of slavery. Believing herself to be white, Iola had been educated at a Northern girls' school. The revelation of her blackness and her position as slave displaced her from a position within a privileged social order to that of exploited chattel. The removal of support from Iola was, however, more complex than Baym's model suggests. Not only Iola's gender but also the revelation of her race and transformation to the condition of slave contributed to her isolation from her former life. The "fall" of Iola was used by Harper to indicate the depths of social corruption represented by the institution of slavery; a woman who was socially accepted as white was, within the same society (and text), declared nonhuman and denied all protection and nurturance. This was not a mere adaptation of what had become the conventional or formulaic presentation of a heroine but, as I shall show, a transformation of the formulaic convention, for Harper did not graft a concern with race onto a form that primarily focused on questions of gender.

Baym has argued that (white) women authors "interpreted experience within models of personal relations, rather than classes, castes, or other institutional structures." These authors did not represent in their texts the institutionalization of patriarchal power; heroines negotiated their way between individualized fathers, brothers, and potential lovers. The consequence for women's fiction was that "the shape of human life was perceived not as determined by various memberships, but by various private interactions" (18). Harper, however, used her heroine as a means whereby a reader could identify the plight of a people and their struggles against the institutionalized hierarchies of racial power. The consequences of Iola's changed circumstances were not limited to the individual character but represented the circumstances of a race:

> Could it be possible that this young and beautiful girl had been a chattel, with no power to protect herself from the highest insults that lawless brutality could inflict upon innocent and defenseless womanhood? Could he ever again glory in his American citizenship, when any white man, no matter how coarse, cruel, or brutal, could buy or sell her for the basest purposes? Was it not true that the cause of a hapless people had become entangled with the lightnings of heaven, and dragged down retribution upon the land? (39)

This passage, wherein a Union general reflected on Iola's condition and meditated on the state of a people, indicates the structure Harper used to shift from the individual experiences of her characters to the experience of a race.

Harper constructed her heroine with regard for the conventional and unconventional aspects of literary heroines. Physically, Iola met the requirements of acceptable standards of womanhood. She was beautiful, fair, and virtuous yet not compliant or passive; her spark of defiance Harper often accented in terms such as "spitfire." Baym has described how a heroine expected to be protected by her guardians and accepted such nurturance as her right. The catalyst of events that heralded the failure to meet these expectations awoke the heroine to a sense of her own inner possibilities which developed into a strong sense of self-worth and conviction. What is important to Baym in the novels she analyzes is that

> the way women perceive themselves is a libel on their own sex . . . this false self-perception more than any other factor accounts for woman's degraded and dependent position in society. Although [the authors]

identify her treatment and training by society in the shape of powerful others as responsible for her damaged self-esteem and consequent impoverished personality, they separate cause from effect and insist that in nineteenth-century America women have the opportunity and responsibility to change their situation by changing their personalities. Hence these authors do blame women who make no effort, no matter how wronged such women may actually be. (19)

But in relation to the representation of the psychology of women, which Baym considers the subject of women's fiction, *Iola Leroy* disrupted conventional expectations and definitions. Certainly Iola was represented as a child and adolescent who expected the benefits of family and social privilege to continue uninterrupted. Her false self-perception was that she believed herself to be white. Harper, however, deepened the conflict that Iola had to eventually confront within herself by making her defend the system of slavery. When a "colored" girl arrived at Iola's Northern school, Iola responded sympathetically: "It is so hard to be looked down on for what one can't help" (98). But beyond the boundaries of the establishment of a personal relationship between them, Iola argued against her schoolgirl friend and against the abolitionists in favor of slavery. At this point in the novel, Harper used Iola to voice the mythology that slaves were happy and contented creatures who wouldn't want to be freed if they were offered the choice. The remand of Iola herself into slavery, therefore, caused more than a reassessment of self and self-worth: Iola had to confront a radical change in her own convictions in relation to the transformation of her position in the social structure. Iola accepted individual responsibility for change in herself when she acknowledged that "thoughts and purposes have come to me in the shadow I should never have learnt in the sunshine. I am constantly rousing myself up to suffer and be strong." But her future was perceived as social, a transformed individual committed to a definition of self in relation to community. Iola intended, when the Civil War was over, "to cast [her] lot with the freed people as a helper, teacher and friend" (114–15). Harper situated the source of Iola's individual strength in her response to the circumstances of a persecuted race.

The way in which Iola reacted to her changed circumstances contrasted dramatically with the response of her mother and her

sister. Iola refused to marry Dr. Gresham, a white doctor she met
when working as a nurse during the Civil War, on the grounds that
she would have to conceal her racial heritage in exchange for sexual
attraction and social acceptability. This action functioned as a
direct comment on her own mother's decision to marry a white man
for love and her compliance in concealing their black heritage from
her children. Iola's sister, Gracie, could not face the change in her
condition that followed the revelation of her blackness and
promptly died in a tearful and rather melodramatic manner, remi-
niscent of the sacrificial death of Little Eva in Harriet Beecher
Stowe's *Uncle Tom's Cabin*. The characterizations of Marie and
Gracie, as their names indicate, are close to the weak and passive
heroines who, once victimized, die graceful deaths. Iola was drawn
with no such trace of sentimentality in her character. While Marie
and Gracie literally "wasted away" when they heard they were to be
sold as slaves, the occasion caused Iola to increase her determination and strength to resist.

In Baym's analysis of literary convention, heroines were either
orphans or heiresses, starting poor and friendless or being reduced
to those circumstances. *Iola Leroy* combined both plots. Iola was
an heiress, her father a rich planter who planned that upon the
termination of Iola's education the whole family would move to
Europe and live a pampered life away from the fear of the slave
system. However, Iola's relation to her inheritance and such a
future was illegitimate as it was based on a lie, the concealment of
her true identity as black. As an heiress, Iola represented a threat to
a patriarchal system of inheritance, and her father's cousin, Alfred
Lorraine, restored the patriarchal order by returning the women—
Marie, Gracie, and Iola—and the son, Harry, to their rightful
inheritance, slavery. As slave, Iola could not inherit from her paternal ancestors but had to follow the condition of her mother. Iola
was, then, an heiress but also an orphan, for she had no legally
recognized father. The course of the novel was structured through
the search of Iola for her true family and true community. Though
a paternal orphan, Iola was also maternal heiress to a black family
from which she had previously been excluded. Her journey toward
finding her real self depended on finding and bringing together this
legitimate family; the search culminated in the knowledge of her
real community. The knowledge Iola gained and the familial ties

she found were her real, material inheritance and legitimated matri-
archal kinship over patriarchal kinship and bonds.

Baym's work on women's writing has established that when the
kin of a heroine failed her, a network of surrogate kin was developed which was institutionalized through marriage. But the family
that Iola discovered was not related to her through a husband but
belonged to her through a maternal lineage. During the Civil War,
Iola received a proposal of marriage at a point in the text when she
was friendless and alone, but the conventional option, the adoption
of a surrogate family, was firmly rejected. Instead, Iola found
paternal protection from a black soldier, Robert Johnson, who was
revealed to be Iola's uncle, her mother's "lost" brother.

The journey in search of family had a function in the structure of
the narrative in addition to the establishment of maternal kinship:
it allowed Iola to travel throughout the South and "discover" a
black community previously unknown to her. Harper, as a Northern intellectual, also went south to find this community, and certainly it was this experience that she drew on to delineate Iola's
passage into knowledge. Iola visited the plantation on which her
uncle was once a slave, and Harper used this visit to acquaint her
heroine and her audience with the "true" nature of black "folk"
characters as well as to define Iola's relation to the race. The
Gundover plantation appeared as a picture of utopian industrious-
ness transformed since emancipation. Harper used her representation of a plantation to illustrate what had been achieved by freedmen and to present her case for what had still to be reconstructed.
What was argued for most strenuously by a folk character named
Aunt Linda was the need for leaders, "who'll larn dese people how
to bring up dere chillen, to keep our gals straight, an' our boys from
runnin' in de saloons an' gamblin' dens" (161). It was this role of
intellectual leadership that Iola was created to fulfill and that
Harper, as author, felt was her duty.

If the journey of discovery united Iola with a community, it also
set her apart from the folk. She found a resting place and internal
calm which contrasted with an earlier unsettled agitation. Nevertheless, Harper carefully distinguished her heroine from the black
folk. Iola found a motherly warmth radiating from Aunt Linda that
made her nostalgic for "the bright sunshiny days when she used to
nestle in Mam Lisa's arms, in her own happy home" (169). The

maternal imagery and discovery of a homelike atmosphere did not function as an unqualified identification with the folk. Iola's act of remembrance of her own home and comparison between Aunt Linda and Mam Lisa served to remind the readers that when Iola nestled it was in the arms of a slave, her mammy. Iola was then the daughter of a slaveowner and a defender of the slave condition. What also distinguished Iola from the folk was that, like Harper, Iola could not share in the exchange of recollections of the days of slavery. Iola and Harper were not part of this history, and their perspective reinforced their social difference. The separate history prefigured how Iola's future was to be different from, though linked to, that of the folk. Iola was destined to be one of the "noble, earnest men, and true women" that she conceived to be "the greatest need of the race" (172).

The fact of Iola's education situated her in the role of intellectual and potential leader of the community. All the folk characters demonstrated their deference to Iola's opinions and their respect for her access to knowledge beyond their experience. Harper placed in the mouths of her folk characters a poorly written dialect that was intended to indicate their illiteracy.[25] The language Harper invented for them was based on an authorial sense of error and deviation from an assumed norm; it was not an attempt to describe the inherent qualities, cadence, and tone of the freedmen's speech. Aunt Linda's response to the suggestion that she should learn to read—"I think it would gib me de hysterics ef I war to try to git book larnin' froo my pore ole head" (156)—illustrated Harper's attitude toward her folk characters. Iola embodied the intellectual's response to the folk. She was "amused and interested at the quaintness of [Aunt Linda's] speech and the shrewdness of her intellect." Harper placed Iola as external observer to the ways of the folk, a position she herself must have occupied when she toured the Southern states and one we can find reflected in her poetry about the freedman in *Sketches of Southern Life*.

The evidence of the literary maternity of earlier women writers was particularly evident in Harper's treatment of her heroine. The passage of Iola from girlhood to womanhood was established at the moment when she was reunited with her brother, Harry, and her mother, Marie, both of whom commented on the vast change in Iola. As a woman, she was unrecognizable, a complete contrast to

"the most harum-scarum girl [Harry] ever knew—laughing, dancing, and singing from morning until night." Iola acknowledged that
she had "passed through a fiery ordeal of suffering" (195). Iola had
become a mature and sober woman, an intellectual whose independence and assurance were combined with feminist concerns.

Harper returned her characters to the North, where Iola decided
to work, not out of necessity but from a conviction that women
should work. She explained to her uncle that she had "a theory that
every woman ought to know how to earn her own living," believing
"that a great amount of sin and misery springs from the weakness
and inefficiency of women" (205). This decision allowed Harper to
espouse feminist concerns while simultaneously exposing the racist
employment practices prevalent in the North. Iola had to leave two
jobs as a saleswoman because she was "colored" and was also
rejected from a Christian boarding institution for working girls.
Her uncle attempted to persuade Iola to give up her search for work
and so avoid these experiences of racism, but Iola persisted, arguing
that she was convinced "every woman should have some skill or art
which would insure her at least a comfortable support. I believe
there would be less unhappy marriages if labor were more honored
among women" (210). Marriage was not presented by Harper as the
culmination and raison d'être of a woman's being. That a woman
should be able to provide for her own material prosperity was
advocated by her to be an advantage, not a disadvantage, in any
future relationships with men. Iola criticized attitudes that assessed
the qualities of a woman in terms of her suitability for becoming a
wife and attacked men who regarded women of ability as "flotsam
all adrift until some man had appropriated her" (242). For Iola,
each woman's life should be purposeful.

Harper described the romance and eventual marriage between
Iola and Dr. Latimer, a black male intellectual, in terms which
initially utilize romantic convention and then discard the romance.
To Iola, Dr. Latimer was her "ideal of a high, heroic manhood."
But this ideal existed on a spiritual rather than a material or
physical plane. Their union was not so base as to be formed
through sexual attraction; it transcended the passion of the body.
Sexual desire and its metaphorical figuration as the pulsing of
blood through veins was transformed, though not tempered, in
Harper's text. It was through Dr. Latimer's and Iola's "desire to

help the race [that] their hearts beat in loving unison." It was a "grand and noble purpose" that united them as a couple. When Latimer proposed that Iola "share his lot," she heard his words as "more than a tender strain wooing her to love and happiness, they were a clarion call to a life of high and holy worth" (265, 271). While such sentiment appears hard to digest for a contemporary reader, a historical reading should acknowledge the radical and unconventional nature of Harper's figuration of an egalitarian relationship. Iola had not found a protector to lift her into a life of security; security had already been achieved in other ways throughout the course of the novel. Harper wanted to conclude her novel with the proposition that the life of two young intellectuals would be based on a mutual sharing of intellectual interests and a common commitment to the "folk" and the "race." Of course, the novel was a romance and as such was not concerned with the actual progress of the marriage. An equality, a partnership, was projected rather than actually achieved within Harper's framework. Iola was shown to continue working after her marriage, and there was no patriarchal transfer of Iola, as property, from father to husband. Female and male sexuality were repressed and replaced by mental and spiritual kinship. "Kindred hopes and tastes had knit their hearts . . . and they esteemed it a blessed privilege to stand on the threshold of a new era and labor for those who had passed from the old oligarchy of slavery into the new commonwealth of freedom" (271).

"The people" for whom Iola and Latimer intended to dedicate their lives framed *Iola Leroy* as the subjects of both the opening and closing chapters. Initially they appeared as a series of concrete characterizations, but as the novel progressed the "folk" become a more abstract principle. Opening during the Civil War, the novel focused on the slaves who lived on the Gundover plantation. The influence of William Wells Brown's *Clotelle* on *Iola Leroy* has already been mentioned, but the inclusion of folk voices provides another occasion for comparison and contrast between the two texts. Folk elements and minstrel humor were an important aspect of the original novel titled *Clotel* and its various adaptations. The introduction to these black folk figures in *Clotelle* was through the character of Sam, a buffoon. Vain, pretentious, and pompous, Sam tried to outwit and outsmart not only his master but also his fellow slaves. Brown achieved his humor through descriptions of Sam's appearance ("his wool well combed and buttered, face nicely greased, and his ruffles extending five or six inches from his bosom") and of his actions, which were motivated by an attempt to "follow in the footsteps of his master."[26] Sam established a reputation as a "black doctor" on totally fraudulent grounds but finally gained his "comeuppance" when he was caught having stolen his master's clothes to "cut a fine figure" at a negro ball. Brown inflicted humor at the expense of his blackest character, whereas his mulatto characters were all treated seriously. Harper attempted no such buffoonery at the expense of her black folk characters. Like Brown, she signaled the presence of the folk through the use of dialect. Though lacking in verisimilitude, Harper's construction of folk dialect was a marginal improvement over Brown's rendering of such sentences as "dat's a werry unsensible remarkk ob yourn. . . . I admires your judgment werry much, I 'sures you. Dar's plenty ob susceptuble an' well-dressed house-serbants dat a gal ob her looks can git widout takin' up wid dem common darkies."[27]

Although the narrative presence of the folk was seriously weakened by Harper's flawed attempts to render dialect through direct speech, she was aware of the relationship between social power and the power of language. In the first chapter of *Iola Leroy*, Harper confronted the ways in which planters attempted to dehumanize their slaves through the process of naming them and then explored the various strategies that slaves used to resist such control. One character, Harper stated, "we shall call Thomas Anderson, although he was known among his acquaintances as Master Anderson's Tom" (7). The negation of the possessive case and of the term "master" had both a figurative and a literal value as Harper established that the plantation was owned by a dissolute planter who was also an absentee landlord. At the level of figuration, the removal of "master" was an indication of the absence of a determining authority controlling the ways in which Tom and his companion, Robert Johnson, thought and spoke. While masters and mistresses treated their slaves as animals, either pets or brute beasts, Robert and Tom revealed that they were in command of a secretly held body of knowledge expressed in the form of a coded language. Gay and humorous appearances were deceptive, a disguise for more furtive exchanges of news about the progress of the war. Attempts by whites to hide news of Southern defeats failed when faced by the concerted effort of the slaves to share skills of literacy with those who, though unable to read the written word, read through their owners' pretenses and disguised emotions. In contrast, then, to Brown's picture of jealousy, hypocrisy, and internally reinforced stratification among the folk, Harper dramatized organized group resistance. This drama Harper used to illustrate the potential basis of alliance between intellectuals and the folk, between the literate and the illiterate. Slaves recognized that they and their owners had very different interests in the social organization of the society they shared, whereas Harper showed white people attempting to establish that the interests between owners and owned were the same. Masters and mistresses had no knowledge of the hidden community of slaves, a community that gathered together in secret and possessed an autonomous means of communication. The united action of Harper's folk defeated white surveillance and control of black lives.

At an individual level, slaves were figured as manipulators of skills learned from their masters and mistresses, who were unable to conceive of these skills becoming weapons in the hands of their slaves. Robert Johnson, for example, was a good reader because Mrs. Johnson, his mistress, had taught him to read, but she had taught him "on the same principle she would have taught a pet animal amusing tricks. She had never imagined the time would come when he would use the machinery she had put in his hands to help overthrow the institution to which she was so ardently attached" (16). The same manipulation of the system was demonstrated by Iola, who was educated in the North on false grounds as a white girl but, as a black woman, used these skills to benefit those for whom they were not intended, the black community. The power gained through such knowledge by Harper's black folk was also accompanied by perceptive and sound judgment. The slaves recognized the mistake that Southern whites made in their consideration of their chattels and also knew that Northern soldiers were not about to acknowledge the unqualified humanity of the ex-slaves either. In a discussion of the consequences that would likely follow an escape to the Northern forces, Robert Johnson characterized the Union soldiers' reactions to black people in the animalistic terms employed by Southern whites. A slave who ran from the Secesh to the Union lines, he stated, would be considered "contraband, just the same as if he were an ox or a horse. They wouldn't send the horses back and they won't send us back" (16). This comment clearly reflected Harper's belief that black labor, slave and emancipated, was regarded as the labor of working beasts in both North and South.

Literacy, the power of the word, becomes in Harper's text a lesson for her black readership to learn, not fear. One man advised another that he "must not think because a white man says a thing, it must be so, and that a colored man's word is no account 'longside of his. . . . [I]f we ever get our freedom, we've got to learn to trust each other and stick together if we would be a people" (34). In Harper's legitimation of the "colored man's word," she was demystifying the ideological power of language and literacy to liberate as well as subordinate.

Providing a viable alternative to the racist images of blacks in the increasingly popular plantation novels, which dominated the field of literature which dealt with slavery, was a task no Afro-American author could afford to ignore. But Harper's appeal for mutual trust and unity in the face of increasing persecution acquired more sophisticated and complex layers of meaning than consideration of the text as contributing positive images of blacks would reveal. Robert Johnson's vision and dreams of a future of freedom were described by Harper as "rose-tinted and rainbow-hued" comments which echoed with authorial irony, for Harper wrote in 1892 with the knowledge of how short-lived those dreams had proved to be. Yet the pedagogic intent remained, and the key to understanding the lessons Harper wanted to teach lies in analyzing her presentation of the crucial significance of intellectuals of "the race."

Attempting to provide a coherent framework for understanding the development of black intellectual thought in the latter part of the nineteenth century, August Meier has argued that after the failure of Reconstruction there was a distinct shift in the attitudes of black intellectuals toward political activity. Indicative of this shift, Meier asserted, was that as disenfranchisement became a political reality increasing numbers of black people voiced their support for literacy and property qualifications to be attached to the right to vote. The rationale for qualifications was that they were thought to provide the motivation to achieve both wealth and education. To summarize and simplify a complex analysis, Meier has traced a growing emphasis by black intellectuals on the issues of achieving wealth through economic solidarity and self-help and a recognition of the crucial importance of education and racial solidarity. Meier's analysis has been a major influence in Afro-American cultural history, and his characterization of the major schism in black American intellectual practice as being between the competing ideas of W. E. B. Du Bois and Booker T. Washington has become a routine mechanism for the periodization of black intellectual history.[28]

It is not possible to consider Harper as an intellectual without being critical of Meier's definitive shaping of the contributions of Afro-American intellectuals. Certainly, Harper voiced support for voting qualifications. "What we need today," she argued, "is not simply more voters, but better voters. I do not believe in unrestricted and universal suffrage for either men or women. I believe in moral and educational tests."[29] But Harper's political attitudes were more complex and sophisticated than can be revealed by indicating a general shift toward conservatism among an intellectual elite. Harper's active intellectual life spanned the antebellum, Reconstruction, and post-Reconstruction periods, but, at present in Afro-American cultural analysis, links between these overarching histories and general periodizations exist only in biographical approaches to the male intellectuals who were Harper's contemporaries. Female intellectual activity at both an individual and a collective level has remained invisible, subsumed under the wealth of research into the ideas and actions of male leaders, thinkers, and activists.

W. E. B. Du Bois articulated the concept of "The Talented Tenth" to describe an exceptional group of intellectuals who would provide leadership for the race; he also argued for the need for a liberal arts education and the historical importance of the establishment of a black college-educated elite. The essay "The Talented Tenth" was published in 1903, but Du Bois formulated these ideas in his Harvard years, and they can be found in his manuscripts from 1894.[30] Harper's concept of a black intelligentsia as represented in *Iola Leroy* prefigured "The Talented Tenth." Iola and her brother, Harry, were presented as members of an intellectual elite: they were both educated in private secondary schools (though not colleges) in the North and were committed to devoting their skills to the moral and educational uplifting of the race. This commitment to the ideology of racial uplift was defined not as individual gestures by an educated hero and heroine but within the development of a community of intellectuals. This community, figured in the text through a doctor, a minister, and several teachers, was represented as being responsible for the formulation and articulation of the crucial aspects of contemporary issues about race.

A substantial proportion of *Iola Leroy* concerned the questions raised by these intellectuals, and two chapters were devoted to the presentation of debate between them. Chapter 26, "Open Questions," introduced the character of Dr. Latrobe, a Southerner and voice of white supremacist ideologies. Organized around a continuous dialogue, these racist views were carefully countered by two black male intellectuals, the Rev. Carmicle and Dr. Latimer, Iola's future husband. The structure of the dialogue closely followed the structure of Harper's public lectures, in which she would cite a prevailing Southern viewpoint and then gradually dismantle it. A large part of the content of the dialogue was taken from one of her lectures entitled "Duty to Dependent Races," delivered in 1891. In this lecture, Harper posed the following question:

> [I]s it not a fact that both North and South power naturally gravitates into the strongest hands, and is there any danger that a race who were deemed so inferior as to be only fitted for slavery, and social and political ostracism, has in less than one generation become so powerful that, if not hindered from exercising the right of suffrage, it will dominate over a people who have behind them ages of domination, education, freedom, and civilization, a people who have had poured into their veins the blood of some of the strongest races on earth?[31]

Having encapsulated one of the rationalizations for the disenfranchisement of the black voter, Harper continued by citing a related but more subtle justification offered by one of the originators of the concept of the "New South," Henry W. Grady, editor of the *Atlanta Constitution*, who argued:

> We do not directly fear the political domination of blacks, but that they are ignorant and easily deluded, impulsive and therefore easily led, strong of race instinct and therefore clannish, without information and therefore easily excited, poor, irresponsible, and with no idea of the

integrity of suffrage and therefore easily bought. The fear is that this vast swarm, ignorant, purchasable, will be impacted and controlled by desperate and unscrupulous white men and made to hold the balance of power when white men are divided.[32]

Harper transferred the text from her lecture to her novel when in "Open Questions" the Rev. Carmicle poses Harper's question to Dr. Latrobe, in the position of Grady:

> "Have you any reason," inquired Rev. Carmicle, "to dread that a race which has behind it the heathenism of Africa and the slavery of America, with its inheritance of ignorance and poverty, will be able, in less than one generation, to domineer over a race which has behind it ages of dominion, freedom, education, and Christianity?"

And Dr. Latrobe replied:

> "I am not afraid of the negro as he stands alone, but what I dread is that in some closely-contested election ambitious men will use him to hold the balance of power and make him an element of danger. He is ignorant poor and clannish, and they may impact him as their policy would direct." (221–22)

Part of the rebuttal of Grady's vision was Harper's mobilization of the popular and mythical specter of the anarchist to contrast with an image of the patriotism of the black population. In "Duty to Dependent Races," Harper had prefaced her conclusion with the statement, "Today the hands of the negro are not dripping with dynamite. We do not read of his flaunting the red banners of anarchy in the face of the nation, nor plotting in beer saloons to overthrow existing institutions, nor spitting on the American flag."[33] In "Open Questions," we can find the identical sentiments expressed when Dr. Latimer flings this taunt at Dr. Latrobe: "the negro is not plotting in beer-saloons against the peace and order of society. His fingers are not dripping with dynamite, neither is he spitting upon your flag, nor flaunting the red banner of anarchy in your face" (223). There are frequent and consistent examples of this close relationship between the text of *Iola Leroy* and the texts of Harper's lectures, a relationship that disproves the common belief in the dichotomy between the subjects of Harper's lectures and her novel.[34]

An important part of the function of *Iola Leroy* was to act as a forum for and advocacy of an educated elite. Chapter 30, "Friends in Council," was described as a "conversazione" at which were gathered "a select company of earnest men and women deeply interested in the welfare of the race" (246). The substance of the chapter was the presentation of a series of "papers": "Negro Emigration," "Patriotism," "Education of Mothers," and "Moral Progress of the Race." The text of the presentations was not included in the novel, but the titles were the "issues" that structured the dialogue, a dialogue that resembled the format of "Open Questions." The representation of such fictional discussions allowed Harper to present to her readership what she regarded as the key areas of concern for a black intellectual elite. For example, emigration to Africa was a subject dismissed as a practical or desirable option early in the discussion which focused instead on a consideration of patriotism which provided the initial occasion for a display of a series of educated judgments. Patriotism in relation to black people Harper defined within a historical perspective:

> I know of no civilized country on the globe, Catholic, Protestant, or Mohammedan, where life is less secure than it is in the South. Nearly eighteen hundred years ago the life of a Roman citizen in Palestine was in danger from mob violence. That pagan government threw around him a wall of living clay, consisting of four hundred and seventy men, when more than forty Jews had bound themselves with an oath that they would neither eat nor drink until they had taken the life of the Apostle Paul. Does not true patriotism demand that citizenship should be as much protected in Christian America as it was in heathen Rome? (250)[35]

Harper considered these subjects the most urgent issues that needed to be addressed by black intellectuals. She drew directly on the material from her lecture circuit, where she herself was trying to galvanize political concern and agitation; Harper lived the intellectual activity that she embodied in her fictional world. As an author, Harper used her novel as another platform to demonstrate to her readership as she demonstrated to her audiences the need for and effectivity of a reasoning and educated elite.

The final two "papers" of the chapter, "Education of Mothers" and "Moral Progress of the Race," were discussed in an atmosphere

of total consensus. All characters agreed that they were crucial
areas in which to concentrate their efforts. Harper's concerns are
clearly reflected in the voices of Iola, Marie, and Lucille Delany,
but her own experiences and observations of the Reconstruction
and post-Reconstruction South were most obviously present in the
concluding section of the chapter, a report from the Rev. Carmicle
on conditions in the South. This report was the narrative mechanism for the presentation of an abbreviated history of the progress
of blacks during the two decades following emancipation and
shared the concerns of Harper's earlier article, "Colored Women of
America" (1878), particularly in her response to the progress of
women in education.[36]

Harper's representation of an intellectual elite has been criticized
for being "idealized" and reliant on the figures of mulattoes as
black leaders:

> *Iola Leroy, Shadows Uplifted* describes the rise of a black middle class
> headed by mulattoes who feel the grave responsibility of defining for
> the black race what is best for it, who work within the context of moral
> Christian ethics, and whose faith in the country and its culture enables
> them to be conservative in all matters except race. Harper, then, re-
> sponded to charges that the Negro is and always will be a degenerate by
> idealizing this segment of the black community. At the center of this
> upward striving class is the mulatta, no longer tragic or melancholy but
> a source of light for those below and around her.[37]

This reading of the text is problematic as it conflates a complex
series of political and narrative issues and reduces them to one, the
question of the role of the mulatto.

If Iola is first analyzed as a heroine who appeared white, we can
begin to reconsider such conclusions. It has been generally assumed, and most recently articulated by Barbara Christian, that the
effectivity of the mulatta, octoroon, or quadroon heroine lay in
the appeal to a white leadership. Certainly, Iola did represent the
"quintessence of refinement" and approximated to what Christian
describes as an "upper-class white woman with privileges." Christian argues that a white female readership "could identify with the
beautiful woman who looked as white as they did, [and] who was
. . . more wealthy and privileged than they were."[38] The attempt of

black writers to counter negative images of black women, Christian concludes, meant that black authors relied on ideal images which conventionally referred only to white women. Christian's analysis depends on the assumption that social conventions totally determine the creation and use of literary conventions. However, the need to counter stereotypes and negative images is not the only or even the primary motivating force in the writing of *Iola Leroy*, and the figure of Iola was not only directed toward a white female audience. The dominance of the mulatto figure in Afro-American fiction during this period has too often been dismissed as politically unacceptable without a detailed analysis of its historical and narrative function. Afro-American literary and cultural history needs to reconsider the frequent use of the mulatto and to ask what the mulatto enabled black authors to represent before we can understand any particular use of the figure.

I would argue that historically the mulatto, as narrative figure, has two primary functions: as a vehicle for an exploration of the relationship between the races and, at the same time, an expression of the relationship between the races. The figure of the mulatto should be understood and analyzed as a narrative device of mediation. After the failure of Reconstruction, social conventions dictated an increasing and more absolute distance between black and white as institutionalized in the Jim Crow laws. In response, the mulatto figure in literature became a more frequently used literary convention for an exploration and expression of what was increasingly socially proscribed. Iola, as mulatta, allowed Harper to use the literary conventions of women's fiction and to draw on ideologies of womanhood in her heroine's fall from security. But the mulatta also enabled Harper to express the relationship between white privilege and black lack of privilege, for her heroine situated her advantages and social position in direct relation to a system of exploitation. When Dr. Gresham attempted to dissuade her from devoting her life to her race, Iola retorted: "It was . . . through their unrequited toil that I was educated, while they were compelled to live in ignorance. I am indebted to them for the power I have to serve them" (235). This comment was directed not only at an individual character but also at a white and a black readership. The white reader, who Christian argues would identify with Iola, Harper situated in a relation of exploitation as her, or his, position was acknowledged to be supported directly by the oppression of blacks. However, the black reader, a potential member of the black educated elite and privileged like Iola, could also not escape the recognition that he or she had benefited from the same system of exploitation.

In relation to the plot, the mulatta figure allowed for movement between two worlds, white and black, and acted as a literary displacement of the actual increasing separation of the races. The mulatta figure was a recognition of the difference between and separateness of the two races at the same time as it was a product of a sexual relationship between white and black. In Harper's text, the rigidity of Jim Crow laws in the South and the formation of ghettos in the North was displaced onto the narrative device of the mulatta. Iola was given a maternal and paternal history which delineated a specific aspect of the precarious relationships between white masters and their female slaves. From a variety of possible social and literary options, Harper selected a fictional relationship between Iola's father and mother that was determined ultimately not by the parameters of romantic love or romantic literary conventions but by references to the systemic limitations of slave society.

The progeny of relationships between masters and their female slaves likewise had a variety of possibilities of literary existence.[39] The first possibility was that the human product of the socially illicit relationship would attempt to deny his or her history through horror or lack of will. The fictional resolution to this possibility was annihilation, as represented by the death of Iola's sister, Gracie. The second possibility open to Iola and Harry was that both had the opportunity to "pass" into the white race. Their refusal to do so represented Harper's decision not to explore "passing" as a valid proposition either historically or metaphorically. Iola's and Harry's "choices" to be black were, however, followed by consequences that were gender-specific. In the army, Harry was offered the opportunity to enter white units; in choosing a black regiment, he automatically became a leader. He was exceptional and a member of an elite from the moment of his choice. Iola's decision not to pass was represented as having far more complex results. As a black woman, Iola's sexual autonomy was immediately threatened. Her refusal to accept the protection of white male patriarchy, in the form of Dr. Gresham's proposals that they marry and pretend Iola was white, was a prelude to a series of incidents in which Iola had to struggle as a woman as well as a black person to establish her independence.

As members of an educated elite and as mulattoes, Iola and Harry embodied these historical forces, but the text of *Iola Leroy* did not present either of them as the idealized representative of either a black middle class or an intellectual elite. Contrary to the implications of Christian's analysis, Harper did not assume that black intellectuals should appear acceptably white. In fact, Harper introduced two characters who were representative of both the progress and fruition of black education and the future intellectual leadership of the race, neither of whom was a mulatto figure.

Lucille Delany was introduced to the reader through an exchange between Harry and Iola which stressed the importance of her blackness:

> "She is of medium height, somewhat slender, and well formed, with dark, expressive eyes, full of thought and feeling. Neither hair nor complexion show the least hint of blood admixture." "I am glad of it," said Iola. "Every person of unmixed blood who succeeds in any department of literature, art, or science is a living argument for the capability which is in the race." "Yes," responded Harry, "for it is not the white blood which is on trial before the world." (199)

The Rev. Carmicle was also asserted to have "no white blood in his veins" (227). Both Carmicle and Delany had been educated to a level which surpassed that of Iola and Harry (and Harper) and should be regarded as archetypes of Du Bois's "Talented Tenth":

> The Negro race, like all races, is going to be saved by its exceptional men. The problem of education, then, among Negroes must first of all deal with the Talented Tenth; it is the problem of developing the Best of this race that they may guide the Mass away from the contamination and death of the Worst, in their own and other races. Now the training of men is a difficult and intricate task. Its technique is a matter for educational experts, but its object is for the vision of seers. If we make money the object of man-training, we shall develop money-makers but not necessarily men; if we make technical skill the object of education, we may possess artisans but not, in nature, men. Men we shall have only as we make manhood the object of the work of the schools—intelli-

gence, broad sympathy, knowledge of the world that was and is, and of the relation of men to it—this is the curriculum of that Higher Education which must underlie true life. On this foundation we may build bread winning, skill of hand and quickness of brain, with never a fear lest the child and man mistake the means of living for the object of life.[40]

I cite this passage at length to emphasize the many parallels between Du Bois's definition of the "Talented Tenth" and Harper's concepts of intellectual leadership evidenced in *Iola Leroy* and the texts of her speeches.

The Rev. Carmicle was a graduate of Oxford, while Lucille Delany graduated from an unspecified "University of A_____." Neither Iola nor her brother was a college graduate. Delany and Carmicle voiced the two cornerstones of Harper's contribution to the philosophy of racial uplift. Delany concentrated her energy on working with women, opening and running a school to train the actual and potential mothers of the race. Improvements in the condition of black women and a recognition of their crucial influence over every aspect of the lives of all black people were priorities in Harper's life and lectures. The Rev. Carmicle, on the other hand, voiced Harper's concern with a moral as opposed to a material uplifting. As I have already shown, Carmicle was frequently the voice of Harper's experience of the Reconstruction South. He also embodied Harper's antimaterialist and spiritual views which stressed the importance of religion and the necessity "to teach our people not to love pleasure or to fear death, but to learn the true value of life, and to do their part to eliminate the paganism of caste from our holy religion and the lawlessness of savagery from our civilization" (260). Both characters were concerned with the development of strength of character, the equivalent of Du Bois's use of making a "man" rather than prioritizing economic and material progress.

In Harper's portrayal of a group of intellectuals, therefore, she was engaged in the pursuit of establishing more than positive images of the race. The characters gained their representativeness or typicality from an engagement with history. They carried the past in their individual histories and were presented as a historical force, an elite able to articulate the possibilities of the future of the race. Harper's dramatization should be regarded both as an attempt to create a coherent vision of the relation of intellectuals to the race and as an extension of the world to which she as an intellectual belonged. She worked within the parameters of the division between mental and manual labor, symbolized as intellectuals and the folk, that became characterized during the next decade as the schism between Booker T. Washington and W. E. B. Du Bois.

The overall structure of *Iola Leroy* progressed increasingly toward a complete separation of the black community from the white world and thus implicitly accepted the failure of Reconstruction even though the novel appeared to end in the glow of its promise. What Harper acknowledged was the need to forge a new, alternative vision, a new role for black intellectuals. In this regard, *Iola Leroy* was a textbook for the educated black person in the crisis of disenfranchisement, lynching, and the Jim Crow laws. Iola's dismissal of the assistance of white patriarchal power was symptomatic of Harper's wider plea that the black community look toward itself for its future, not toward assistance and support from or alliance with the forces represented by the various white characters in the novel. By the final chapters of *Iola Leroy*, white characters had virtually disappeared; the group of black intellectuals had become self-sufficient, self-contained, and independent of the parameters of white intellectual debate. All were embedded within black communities and committed to the uplifting of the folk. Harper's novel was as much a part of that political program of uplift as her lectures and activism. Its didacticism was aimed at a black, not a white, community, though her moral condemnation was clearly designed to move, though not to depend on, white sympathies.

This overall movement toward self-sufficiency was sustained through Harper's own authentication of her book. The external referential world of the novel was to be found in the text of her lectures, speeches, and articles, in "The Great Problem" (1875), "Colored Women of America" (1878), "The Woman's Christian Temperance Union and the Colored Woman" (1888), "Duty to Dependent Races" (1891), and "Woman's Political Future" (1893).[41] The close relationship between Harper's lectures and *Iola Leroy* has already been discussed, but it remains to be stressed that what shaped her work was an assertion of what she saw to be female virtues, values, and actions to counteract rampant commercial and mechanistic interests. In contrast to Du Bois's plea to make men, not money-makers, Harper saw that for women

> Not the opportunity of discovering new worlds, but that of filling this old world with fairer and higher aims than the greed of gold and the lust of power, is hers. Through weary, wasting years men have destroyed, dashed in pieces, and overthrown, but today we stand on the threshold of woman's era, and woman's work is grandly constructive. In her hand are possibilities whose use or abuse must tell upon the political life of the nation, and send their influence for good or evil across the track of unborn ages.[42]

Harper was convinced of the power of women to exert influence over hegemonic material and commercial interests, not through the suffrage movement, though she fought for the women's vote, but through the Women's Christian Temperance Union.[43]

In conclusion, I wish to return to a consideration of the question with which this chapter opened: Why write a novel? Frances Ellen Watkins Harper produced *Iola Leroy; or, Shadows Uplifted* in an attempt to morally rearm the black intellectual and to contest the terrain of racist retrenchment. We may debate how effective her novel was in "the development of a national conscience,"[44] but we need to recognize that Harper intended to hand her readership a political weapon. Its dismissal or neglect by feminist or Afro-American literary critics leaves each tradition impoverished by its absence.

5

"In the Quiet, Undisputed Dignity of My Womanhood"

Black Feminist Thought
after Emancipation

Having examined some of the historical and political reasons why
black women like Frances Harper decided to write novels, it is
necessary to reflect on the conditions out of which black women's
fiction was produced. However, I am not going to situate authors
and their novels within a social or literary history as merely a
context for analysis. On the contrary, my basic premise is that the
novels of black women should be read not as passive representations of history but as active influence within history. In other
words, I am considering novels not only as determined by the social
conditions within which they were produced but also as cultural
artifacts which shape the social conditions they enter. As we have
seen, Harper intended that her writing should enter the arena of the
political struggles of Afro-American people in a period of crisis. In
Chapters 6 and 7 I will consider the novels of Pauline Hopkins, who
also hoped that fiction would become a tool in the struggle to
change the social, political, and economic conditions of black people. The novels of black women, like the slave and free narratives
that preceded them, did not just reflect or "mirror" a society; they
attempted to change it. Viewing novels as weapons for social
change, literary and cultural criticism needs to consider how these
novels actively structure and shape Afro-American culture and
political struggles. The novels of Harper and Hopkins became loci

of political and social interests, forming intellectual consituencies, not merely reflecting the interests of a preexisting intellectual elite.[1]

Frances Harper stood at the beginning of what she saw to be "a woman's era."[2] Though Afro-American cultural analysis and criticism have traditionally characterized the turn of the century as the age of Washington and Du Bois, the period was in fact one of intense activity and productivity for Afro-American women. In 1891, Emma Dunham Kelley published the novel *Megda*, and 1892 was the year of publication not only of *Iola Leroy* but also of Anna Julia Cooper's *A Voice from the South* and Ida B. Wells's *Southern Horrors: Lynch Law in All Its Phases*.[3] In 1893, at the Congress of Representative Women, Frances Harper, Fanny Barrier Williams, Anna Julia Cooper, Fanny Jackson Coppin, Sarah J. Early, and Hallie Q. Brown delivered addresses on various aspects of the progress of Afro-American women. In that same year Victoria Earle published *Aunt Lindy*, and in 1894 Gertrude Mossell published *The Work of the Afro-American Woman*.[4] The club movement among Afro-American women grew rapidly; in 1895, the first Congress of Colored Women of the United States was convened in Boston. The National Federation of Afro-American Women was an outgrowth of the conference, but in 1896 the National Federation and the National League of Colored Women united in Washington, D.C., to form the National Association of Colored Women (NACW). Thus, for the first time, Afro-American women became nationally organized to confront the various modes of their oppression.[5]

Within this ferment of black female intellectual activity, I am going to focus on the distinctive work of Anna Julia Cooper and Ida B. Wells. Both Cooper and Wells theorized the relationships among race, gender, and patriarchy in their writing, but each selected a different object of analysis. Cooper concentrated on the education of black women, on racism and imperialism, and on the inherent racism of white women's organizations; and Wells dealt with the political and economic significance of lynching and how it drew on and mobilized racist sexual ideologies. I will conclude with a brief account of the relation of black female intellectual work to the formation of the NACW.

I have chosen to concentrate on these women and these topics as examples of the ways in which Afro-American women were analyzing particular forms of oppression in an attempt to define the political parameters of gender, race, and patriarchal authority. But this is not to imply that Cooper and Wells were the only ones who articulated this concern; throughout the work of black women intellectuals there has been a consistent engagement with the interrelation of racial and sexual oppression in both fiction and nonfiction. The formation of the NACW provided a forum for the exchange of ideas among Afro-American women intellectuals within a structure that disseminated this information nationally. Consideration of the work of Cooper, Wells, and the NACW indicates this process of exchange and defines more clearly the constituency that Harper's and Hopkins's fictional writing drew on and addressed. In the black women's movement at the turn of the century, organizing to fight meant also writing to organize.

In her collection of essays, *A Voice from the South*, Anna Julia Cooper, like W. E. B. Du Bois a decade later, identified the conflict of race as being the central American dilemma.[6] It was the question of the "colored man's inheritance and apportionment" that Cooper saw as "the perplexing *cul de sac* of the nation." Cooper felt that the dominant white power structure existed in "sublime ignorance" of the needs or desires of blacks. She drew a parallel with the ignorance of men of the needs and desires of women which formed her initial premise and the occasion for the book. As white voices could not adequately speak to the black experience of oppression, "neither should the dark man be wholly expected fully and adequately to reproduce the exact Voice of the Black Woman" (i–iii). My intention is not to provide a detailed analysis of each of the essays that form *A Voice from the South* but rather to consider the overall trajectory of Cooper's argument, focusing on three areas: the social status of women and the importance of education, the nature of imperialism and racism as hegemonic ideologies, and the critique of the white women's movement.

Cooper referred to a number of historical definitions of womanhood, juxtaposed them with a political indictment of the oppression of blacks within the United States, and emerged with a particular analysis of the position of the black woman that effectively challenged the terms of contemporary debate about gender and about race. Cooper's initial argument was based on the assumption that a civilization should be measured by the way its women are treated. She dismissed ideologies of womanhood that had their source in codes of chivalry (as in the Southern states) as being elitist, applying only to an elect few. Cooper's apparent reference to the Middle Ages and feudalism in Europe was but a metaphorical disguise for the vaunted ideals of chivalry and elevated notions of womanhood of the South. She situated the possibilities for the "radical amelioration of womankind, reverence for woman as woman regardless of rank, wealth, or culture," in relation to the Gospel of Christ but was careful to separate what she regarded to be the radical potential of the Gospel from the actual achievement of the organized church that had done "less to protect and elevate woman than the little done by secular society" (14–15). Cooper interpreted the Gospel as a liberation theology, a set of ideals which argued for equality not only for women but also for the poor, the weak, the starving, and the dispossessed. It was these ideals of a radical Christianity that she felt could become the practices of American institutions, but her optimism clearly stemmed not from current social conditions but from the "possibilities and promise that are inherent in the system, though as yet, perhaps, far in the future" (12). The available possibilities for radical change and the future promise that Cooper heralded depended on her interpretation of the structural power of women; for within any society, Cooper asserted, the position of women determined "the vital elements of its regeneration and progress." This power to determine and shape the moral and ethical character of society, she stressed, came neither because of woman's reproductive role nor because woman was any "stronger or wiser than man"; rather, it had its source in the social influence that women were able to exert over the formation of men, shaping their adulthood in their childhood years (21). Thus, Cooper's argument was that women had an arena in which power could be exerted, but, as we shall see, Cooper also pointed to this early social influence as a critical factor in the perpetuation of racism for which white women could be brought to account.

Within the black community, Cooper indicted the practice of measuring the achievements and progress of black men as representative of the whole race while black women were still subject to the sexual abuse from white men that had been a central feature of their oppression as slaves. Indeed, the issue of black womanhood was central to Cooper's demand for the right of self-determination for all black people. She condemned the practice of taking the advancement of successful individuals as indicative of the advancement of a people as a whole and argued that only when black women had the power collectively to determine their future would the race be able to move forward. In a passage that reflected Cooper's attempt to represent this collective voice, she declared: "Only the Black Woman can say 'when and where I enter, in the quiet, undisputed dignity of my womanhood, without violence and without suing or special patronage, then and there the whole *Negro race enters with me*' " (31). For, despite their history of powerlessness, Cooper believed that it was black women who could be the agents for change. Cooper recognized that what was needed to confront Southern attempts to induce black passivity, "congregations of shiny faced peasants with their clean white aprons and sunbonnets catechised [sic] at regular intervals," was action in defense of rights, self-determination, and autonomy (39). Passivity she characterized as a living death in which the black community were the "recipients of missionary bounty" which had to be refused, for not even "the senseless vegetable is content to be a mere reservoir" (46).

Like Frances Harper, Cooper felt that women did not have to be confined to a domestic sphere of influence within the white or black communities, but she developed a more sophisticated analysis of the power that women could exert as intellectuals. Cooper strongly defended the need for the higher education of women and exposed the ways in which arguments against educating women were tied to ideologies of female sexuality which defined intellectual women as "less desirable" sexual objects for exchange in the marriage market. Cooper's analysis acknowledged that the education of women would radically change their social relations with men but replaced the patriarchal emphasis on how men regarded intellectual women with the assertion that higher education made women more demanding of men. It was a challenge that men, not women, had to face:

> The question is not now with the woman "How shall I so cramp, stunt, simplify and nullify myself as to make me eligible to the honor of being swallowed up into some little man?" but the problem, I trow, now rests

with the man as to how he can . . . reach the ideal of a generation of
women who demand the noblest, grandest and best achievements of
which he is capable. . . . If it makes them work, all the better for them.
(70–71)

Cooper's reflections on the consequent changes necessary in marriage relations were, like Harper's fictional representation, directed
toward the utopian possibilities for women of partnerships with
husbands on a plane of intellectual equality.

However, moving from observations that affected all women to
an analysis of the educational opportunities available to black
women, Cooper concluded that, while there appeared to be an
increase in social commitment to the higher education of white
women, obstacles were placed in the way of black women who
demanded education. Cooper corresponded with a number of universities and found that there were only a total of thirty black
women graduates from Fisk, Oberlin, Wilberforce, Ann Arbor,
Wellesley, Livingston, and Atlanta. She identified a failure in the
black community to provide or nurture "any special stimulus to
female development" and focused on black male attitudes as a
contributing factor in this neglect of black women's needs. A particularly pertinent negative influence against the education of black
women was the pressure to conform to the circumscribed limits of
the ideology of true womanhood:

[W]hile our men seem thoroughly abreast of the times on almost every
other subject, when they strike the woman question they drop back into
sixteenth century logic. . . . [T]hey actually do not seem sometimes to
have outgrown that old contemporary of chivalry—the idea that women
may stand on pedestals or live in doll houses, (if they happen to have
them) but they must not furrow their brows with thought or attempt to
help men tug at the great questions of the world. I fear the majority of
colored men do not yet think it worth while that women aspire to higher
education. . . . The three R's, a little music and a good deal of dancing, a
first rate dress-maker and a bottle of magnolia balm, are quite enough
generally to render charming any woman possessed of tact and the
capacity for worshipping masculinity. (75)

Drawing on her own educational experiences, Cooper illustrated
how such attitudes became instilled in black educational institutions. In a school that Cooper attended, she had to humble herself,

"as became a female member of the human species," to gain access
to knowledge that was designated for men only (77). Black women
students invariably supported themselves through work to pay their
fees, as scholarships were reserved for men; women were actively
discouraged from intellectual distinction and encouraged to direct
their ambition toward marriage with one of the male students.
Cooper agitated for the establishment of foundations that would
offer scholarships for black women at black universities and colleges to enable them to establish their independence of such sexual
discrimination.

But Cooper's analysis of the position of women, both white and
black, was more than a demand for female access to social institutions; it was also a complex analysis of social, political, and economic forces as being peculiarly masculine or feminine in their
orientation and consequences. Unlike Frances Harper but prefigur-
ing the concerns of Pauline Hopkins, Cooper identified the intimate
link between internal and external colonization, between domestic
racial oppression and imperialism. Her critique of imperialism and
racist attitudes is a particularly good example of how she developed
her theories of masculine and feminine practices and spheres of
influence. When considering this critique, it is important to recognize that Cooper's categories are not biologically dependent concepts referring to the physical differences between males and females, for she made it clear that women could conform to
masculinist practices and attitudes and men could display what she
called "womanly virtues."

Cooper recognized the imperialist or expansionist impulse, with
its ideology of racial hierarchies, as a supreme instance of patriarchal power and confronted her readers with a series of rhetorical
questions to force a reassessment of the history which produced

> the self-congratulation of "dominant" races, as if "dominant" meant
> "righteous" and carried with it a title to inherit the earth? Whence
> [came] the scorn of so-called weak or unwarlike races and individuals,
> and the very comfortable assurance that it is their manifest destiny to be
> wiped out as vermin before this advancing civilization? (51)

Cooper condemned the increasing imperialist expansion to Asia
and the Pacific with its contemporary appeal to a manifest destiny
to civilize the uncivilized as justification for consigning "to annihi-

lation one-third the inhabitants of the globe" (52). This impulse to conquer defined the predominant male influence, an influence which was compared to the beast from the Book of Daniel, devouring all before it and demanding its worship as an incarnation of power. The possible counteracting force, the female influence, was powerless to mollify or restrain "the beast," in Cooper's terms, and the pervasiveness of the rampant will to dominate and despise the weak was evident in the racist attitudes of women who were otherwise thinking beings. The example that Cooper used was a familiar one for black women and illustrated how the movement for women's rights was consistently compromised by racist attitudes and practices. For Cooper wanted to remind her readers that the women's movement and its leadership did not escape patriarchal influences or the "worship of the beast" (54–55). But, despite this knowledge, Cooper felt that the only counter to patriarchal abuse of power was the feminine factor, which had to be developed through the education of women. Education, she argued, would empower women so that they could shape an alternative course to a future society which would exercise sensitivity and sympathy toward the poor and oppressed. Power in the hands of women, however, Cooper knew was not in itself the answer, for, as she had experienced, the power that white women were able to gain was rarely exercised in sympathy with their black sisters.

One of Cooper's most vituperative essays, "Woman versus the Indian," was an attack on the exclusionary practices and discourse of white women's organizations which presumed to exist for and address the experiences of women. I am going to focus on what I consider to be the three most important aspects of her critique: an analysis of the nature of the power white women were able to exercise, an account of the dominance of Southern influence over women's activities, and a conviction that women's interests were advanced or secured at the expense of other oppressed groups.

Cooper was one of many black women, including Frances Harper, Ida B. Wells, and Mary Church Terrell, who were outspoken about the racism they found pervading organizations dominated by white women. All of them were well aware that as black women they had been the subject of a compromise in the formation of an alliance between Northern and Southern white women. Cooper explored the source of this racism and exposed the historical and ideological framework within which white women defended their own class and racial interests. She developed a theory that black women were in the position of being able to apply a unique perspective on racist and sexist oppression, a perspective which gave insight into the plight of all oppressed peoples.

Beginning with an anecdote of one of the many instances of the rejection of a black woman from a white women's club, Cooper moved from an individual racist instance toward a dissection of the hierarchical power structure among American women. Wimodaughsis was a woman's club whose name was made up of the first letters of the words *wives, mothers, daughters*, and *sisters*. The secretary of this association Cooper described as patronizing, the type of person who "would really like to help 'elevate' the colored people (in her own way of course and so long as they understand their places)." This woman was horrified and outraged to discover that a black woman wished to take advantage of the classes offered by the club. Cooper attacked, first, the definition of womanhood upon which such clubs operated and, second, their right to refer to their political orientation as progressive:

> Indeed, she had not calculated that there were any wives, mothers, daughters, and sisters, except white ones; and she is really convinced that *Whimodaughsis* would sound just as well, and then it would mean just *white mothers, daughters and sisters* . . . and this immaculate assembly for propagating liberal and progressive ideas and disseminating a broad and humanizing culture might be spared the painful possibility of the sight of a black man coming in the future to escort from an evening class this solitary cream-colored applicant. (81–82)

Black women, Cooper argued, could understand, "appreciate," and "even sympathize" with the dilemma of the leaders of the women's movement like Susan B. Anthony and Anna Shaw, who felt themselves to be caught in a difficult predicament between the black woman and the Southern white woman. But, Cooper asserted, it was possible for the American woman to wield a power that was felt throughout society; the hierarchical structure of white social organizations ensured that the "leading women" had an influence over men that touched "myriads of church clubs, social clubs, culture clubs, pleasure clubs and charitable clubs" (85). White American women, Cooper insisted, were responsible for American manners and moral code, "the oil of social machinery," she called it. The influence of these women, she argued, was not merely a surreptitious hold over men, for the women themselves were bound within a strict hierarchy ruled over by a few, an elite of "leading women." Cooper identified this elite as a central power, a governing core from which the intense concern with racial superiority spread throughout the society:

> [T]he working women of America in whatever station or calling they may be found, are subjects, officers, or rulers of a strong centralized government, and bound together by a system of codes and countersigns, which, though unwritten, forms a network of perfect subordination and unquestioning obedience. . . . At the head and center in this regime stands the Leading Woman in the principality. The one talismanic word that plays along the wires from palace to cook-shop, from imperial Congress to the distant plain, is *Caste*. With all her vaunted independence, the American woman of today is as fearful of losing caste as a Brahmin in India. (86–87)

Cooper's conclusions were that racism was perpetuated and transmitted to future generations by women who instilled it in their children with their first food and was an "injunction" laid on husbands and lovers.

Cooper was asserting that white women exercised a significant influence over the shaping of the social formation even though they could not hold legislative office. She characterized this influence as an ability to be the "teachers and moulders of public sentiment," a sentiment that, she argued, preceded and was the source of "all laws, good or bad," including the Jim Crow laws (95). In direct contrast to this form of influence, Cooper defined the unique position of the black woman, unique precisely because her femininity, her womanhood, was so consistently denied authenticity that it could not be used to gain social position or social influence. Cooper saw her as relegated beyond the pale and, simultaneously, as the touchstone of American manners and morals. Black women, she argued, could not retreat into an abstraction of womanhood dissociated from the oppression of their whole people; their everyday lives were a confrontation of the division between the inviolability of elitist conceptions of womanhood and that which it denied.

When a train stopped "in a dilapidated station," Cooper related, she saw "two dingy little rooms with 'For Ladies' swinging over one and 'For Colored People' over the other." Cooper encapsulated the Janus face of the conventional definition of womanhood as she reflected how she had to stop and think and wonder under which category she came (96).

Cooper called for a revolution in the attitudes and practices of women who would be leaders of reform, but the biggest stumbling block she conceived to be the Southern woman who was totally preoccupied with protecting herself from being forced to accept her ex-slaves as social equals. As Pauline Hopkins was to argue ten years later, Cooper stated that debates about social equality were fallacious; the concept was being misused by Southerners to imply a forced association which was not the social justice blacks demanded. Cooper aggressively reinterpreted forced association as the manacled black male and the raped black woman, as "association" which was more strenuously opposed in the black community than in the white. For Cooper it was black autonomy and the right of blacks to self-determination which were the central issues. She understood that behind the smoke screen of the controversy over social equality was a barrage of questions of heritage and inheritance which gained consensus in both North and South.

Cooper was convinced that the key to understanding the unwritten history of the United States was the dictation and dominance of Southern "influence, ideals and ideas" over the whole nation. The manipulative power of the South was embodied in the Southern patriarch, but its concern with inheritance and heritage, figured as "blood," was described by Cooper entirely in female terms, as a preoccupation that was transmitted from the South to the women of the North. The South, she stated, represented not red blood but blue:

> If your own father was a pirate, a robber, a murderer, his hands are dyed in red blood, and you don't say very much about it. But if your great great great grandfather's grandfather stole and pillaged and slew, and you can prove it, your blood has become blue and you are at great pains to establish the relationship. . . . [The South] had blood; and she paraded it with so much gusto that the substantial little Puritan maidens of the North, who had been making bread and canning currants and not thinking of blood the least bit, began to hunt up the records of the

Mayflower to see if some of the passengers thereon could not claim the
honor of having been one of William the Conqueror's brigands, when
he killed the last of the Saxon kings and, red-handed, stole his crown
and his lands. (103–4)

The ridicule with which Cooper undermined the search for an
aristocratic heritage and biological racial superiority was accompanied by a very serious critique that Pauline Hopkins was to adopt
and develop in her fiction a decade later. Cooper used her juxtaposition of red with blue blood as a political indictment of the narrative of national heritage, a narrative which disguised a history of
unrestrained murder and theft. Cooper's work provided the framework for an alternative reading of this history which exposed the
piratical methods of expansionism inherent in the colonization of
the Americas and in American imperialist ventures. Hopkins used
this framework to develop an alternative narrative in her fiction
which demystified the mythological pretensions of the American
story of origins.

Cooper also reinterpreted the history of Northern compromise to
the demands of the South as the courting of a petulant "Southern
belle" who was finally allowed to keep her "pet" institution, slavery,
under another name. The suffrage movement was described as
"courting the Southern lady" in much the same manner. Cooper
differentiated between Southern ladies (white) and Southern
women (black), whose interests remained fundamentally opposed
(108). Cooper pointed to the courting of the lady at the expense of
the woman as the direct cause of a constrained, restricted, and
provincial outlook in the constituency of the white women's movement. She took the title of her essay, "Woman versus the Indian,"
from a paper delivered by Anna Shaw to the National Woman's
Council, convened in Washington in February 1891. Cooper indicted the framework of polarity of the paper, the same polarity
that in the context of the Women's Equal Suffrage Association led
Frances Harper and Frederick Douglass to oppose Anthony's proposal to agitate for the vote for white women instead of black men.
Cooper attacked the suffrage movements for becoming what she
characterized as the plaintiff "Eye" in a suit "Eye vs. Foot" (123).
This polarity was dependent on a negative portrayal of Indians and
Afro-Americans as "ignorant and gross and depraved" and there-

fore unworthy to cast a vote while the "intelligent and refined, the pure-minded and lofty souled white woman" was denied the franchise. Cooper addressed a challenge to white suffragists to revolutionize their thinking and to transform their arguments from a provincial determination to secure their own gender and class interests at the expense of the denial of rights to the oppressed:

> Is not this hitching our wagon to something much lower than a star? Is not woman's cause broader, and deeper, and grander, than a blue stocking debate or an aristocratic pink tea? Why should woman become plaintiff in a suit versus the Indian, or the Negro or any other race or class who have been crushed under the iron heel of Anglo-Saxon power and selfishness? If the Indian has been wronged or cheated by the puissance of this American government, it is woman's mission to plead with her country to cease to do evil and to pay its honest debts. . . . [L]et her rest her plea, not on Indian inferiority, nor on Negro depravity, but on the obligation of legislators. (123–24).

Cooper understood and exposed the divisive tactics of the American suffrage movements and redefined a woman's cause as not that of "the white woman, nor the black woman nor the red woman, but the cause of every man or woman who has writhed silently under a mighty wrong" (125). Cooper intended to expand the rubric of the concerns of women to include "all undefended woe, all helpless suffering" and to encompass an ideal and set of practices that could become a movement for the liberation of all oppressed peoples, not remain a movement for the defense of parochial and sectional interests in the name of "woman."

Cooper used the occasion of the World's Congress of Representative Women to repeat this appeal for a transformed women's movement.[7] The congress, part of the World's Columbian Exposition, gave women a forum and a platform from which they could address not only an American but an international audience. Five black women lectured at the congress, but Ida B. Wells did not. Instead, she was engaged in protesting the exclusion of Afro-Americans from participation in the World's Fair and edited and sold a pamphlet which detailed the oppression of blacks in the United States.[8] The contrast between the direction of Wells's protest and the publication of *The Reason Why the Colored American Is Not in the World's Columbian Exposition* and the target of Cooper's speech at the World's Fair indicated the distance between their respective objects of analysis and critique.

Wells has been characterized as a leader without a movement, "a lonely warrior," a spokesperson for protest in "the age of accommodation," whose life's work can be considered "a limited success."[9] She has been measured by historians and declared a dwarf in relation to the giants of Du Bois and Washington; subject to such comparison, her political ideas, strategies, tactics, and analyses have been totally subordinated to and understood only in relation to the achievements of these men.[10] Wells did not entirely agree with the political philosophy of Washington or Du Bois and should not be considered an imitator of either. No men found her easy to work with, for she was a woman who refused to adopt the "ladylike" attitudes of compromise and silence. Nine years before the exposition, in May 1884, one year after the U.S. Supreme Court ruled the Civil Rights Act unconstitutional, a train conductor tried to remove Wells from a ladies' car and insisted that she move to the smoking car in the rear. Wells fought, physically against the conductor and then in court after she was ejected from the train. Initially she won her suit against the Chesapeake and Ohio Railroad and was awarded damages, but the decision was reversed by the supreme court of Tennesse and illustrated how black people were at the mercy of the interpretations of justice as they were defined by individual states. Wells was a public schoolteacher, like Cooper, but she found her vocation in protesting with the pen and became a militant journalist. She was, to put it bluntly, an "uppity" black woman with an analysis of the relationship among political terrorism, economic oppression, and conventional codes of sexuality and morality that has still to be surpassed in its incisive condemnation of the patriarchal manipulation of race and gender. The influence of her work can be found in the writing of black women from Pauline Hopkins to June Jordan and Alice Walker who, like Wells, have struggled to consider the interrelation of rape and lynching as weapons of political, social, and economic oppression.

Frances Harper was convinced that the moment of her political awakening, her "call to duty," was the passing of the Fugitive Slave Act and the subsequent kidnapping of escaped slaves in Northern territory. She recalled that occasion as being a catalyst which defined exactly who, why, and for what she should fight. Wells determined to be a journalist, but the cause to which she would be committed for the rest of her life was likewise determined by one particular event. Wells was working full-time for a Memphis newspaper, *Free Speech*, in March 1892. She had proved to herself that she could make a living writing articles and had resolved not to return to teaching, when "there came the lynching in Memphis that changed the whole course of [her] life."[11] Thomas Moss, Calvin McDowell, and Henry Stewart, close friends of Wells, owned and operated the People's Grocery Company, which was popular and competed with the white grocery store that had previously had a monopoly on the trade of the black suburb. The People's Grocery was attacked, its owners defended themselves, and they were arrested; they were taken from jail by a mob and lynched, and the grocery was destroyed. White mobs scoured the town, shooting into any groups of blacks they could find on the orders of a judge of the criminal court. Subsequently encouraged by editorials in *Free Speech*, about two thousand inhabitants of the black community left Memphis and migrated west, while others organized boycotts of stores and streetcars. The economic boycott, which nearly bankrupted the streetcar company, made Wells realize the formidable protest power that blacks could exercise.

In May of the same year, Wells left Memphis to attend an AME conference in Philadelphia and to stay with Frances Harper. She left behind her an editorial due for publication on May 21 that reflected the tentative beginnings of her political analysis of the causes of lynching. As she stated in her autobiography, *Crusade for Justice*, she too had previously concurred in the logic of lynching, that it was spontaneous outrage at the crime of rape. The murder of her friends made her understand that lynching was "an excuse to get rid of Negroes who were acquiring wealth and property" and a political tactic to create an atmosphere of terror to "keep the nigger down."[12] In her editorial, Wells traced the causes of recent lynchings over a three-month period and concluded that the supposed crime of rape, for which lynching was regarded as suitable punishment, was linked to consensual sexual relations between black men and white women. Her editorial accused the Memphis community as follows:

> Eight Negroes lynched since the last issue of the *Free Speech*. Three were charged with killing white men and five with raping white women. Nobody in this section believes the old thread-bare lie that Negro men

assault white women. If Southern white men are not careful they will
over-reach themselves and a conclusion will be reached which will be
very damaging to the moral reputation of their women.[13]

The response of the white community of Memphis to Well's editorial was the destruction of *Free Speech* and the threat to burn the
author at the stake. Wells did not return to Memphis but instead
accepted a position with T. Thomas Fortune on the *New York Age.*
Her immediate response to the destruction of her paper was to
consider the violent reaction as a retaliation in defense of the
reputation of white womanhood, but Wells quickly realized that her
editorial was used as the pretext to accomplish what the white
community had long determined to do: close the black newspaper
permanently.

In June, the *New York Age* carried an article which enlarged
upon and substantiated the editorial from *Free Speech.* The material was then published as a pamphlet, *Southern Horrors,* with a
preface by Frederick Douglass. The pamphlet circulated widely,
and Wells was asked to make her first public speech to a gathering
of black women from Boston and Philadelphia. This lecture inaugurated her career in antilynching activism, for which Wells would
travel not only throughout the United States but also to Britain.
Southern Horrors was followed by two other pamphlets, *A Red
Record: Tabulated Statistics and Alleged Causes of Lynching in the
United States, 1892–1894* (1895) and *Mob Rule in New Orleans*
(1900).[14]

Southern Horrors was dedicated to the Afro-American women of
New York and Brooklyn, whose contributions had made the publication of the pamphlet possible. The *Free Speech* editorial was
reprinted along with an account of the threats from the leading
businessmen of the town which had been published throughout the
white press. But in addition *Southern Horrors* provided the opportunity for Wells to develop her analysis. She argued that the association of lynching and rape was a contemporary phenomenon, as
"the crime of rape was unknown during the four years of the Civil
War, when the white women of the South were at the mercy of the
race which is all at once charged with being a bestial one" (SH, 5).

Wells's analysis of lynching was multifaceted: she situated the
murder of black men historically within the whole spectrum of

black and white social, political, and economic relations. But at its core, what was and has remained unique about Wells's theorizing is its dissection of sexual ideologies and mores. Early in her work, Wells indicted the miscegenation laws which, in practice, meant that black women were the victims of rape by white men who had the power to terrorize black men under the pretense of the protection of white womanhood. Wells asserted that there were "many white women in the South who would marry colored men if such an act would not place them at once beyond the pale of society and within the clutches of the law" and that the miscegenation laws only operated "against the legitimate union of the races" (SH, 6). Wells supported her assertions by quoting reports from the white press of black male and white female sexual relationships that were encouraged by white women. Wells increasingly used evidence from the white press in her publications and speeches; she eventually drew all her statistics from respected white newspapers, not only to avoid accusations of exaggeration or falsification of the numbers of lynchings that had occurred but also because Wells believed that "out of their own mouths shall the murderers be condemned" (RR, 15).

Southern whites appealed to Northern whites to understand and sympathize with the circumstances of lynching. Northerners did sympathize, Wells thought, because the South claimed that any condemnation of lynching was a public display of indifference to the plight of white womanhood. Thus, black disenfranchisement and Jim Crow segregation had been achieved, shielding the South behind "a screen of defending the honor of its women (SH, 13–14). An effective black political presence had been annihilated. In order to expose the underlying political intentions of the South with regard to its black population, Wells culled figures from the *Chicago Tribune* and demonstrated that accusations of rape were made in only one-third of the cases of lynching but that the cry of rape was an extremely effective way to create panic and fear. Lynching, Wells argued, had become an institutionalized practice supported and encouraged by the established leaders of the Southern community and the press they influenced. Northern sentiment concurred that lynching was a direct response to the rape of white women and that concession to lynching for a specific crime, Wells was sure, acknowledged the right to lynch anyone for any crime: the charge became the excuse.

An atmosphere of political terror was effectively created, spread, and maintained in newspapers, and Wells indicted the white press for being malicious and untruthful in their creation of a moral panic, a fear of black men.[15] Memphis papers, for example, were unable to give an account of one Afro-American male who had been charged with sexual assault, but they ran a series of articles entitled "More Rapes, More Lynchings" which actively created a picture of a white community unable to protect itself from the unrestrained and unquenchable lust of the Negro male (SH, 16). The press was accused by Wells as being accomplices in the ideological work of teaching the black community political and economic subordination. Also named as accomplices were those who remained silent and only secretly disapproved of the methods of lynching; Wells condemned them as being equally guilty with the actual perpetrators of lynching.

Reflection on the events of Memphis after the lynching of Moss, McDowell, and Stewart taught Wells a lesson in political strategy, a strategy that would not be fully utilized until the 1950s. The black community needed to become aware of its economic power. The South, Wells argued, owed its rehabilitation to Northern capital on the one hand and Afro-American labor on the other. Those black people who left Memphis and those who remained behind and practiced a boycott stagnated white business interests. Wells was convinced that "by the right exercise of his power as the industrial factor of the South, the Afro-American can demand and secure his rights." But economic power was not the only potent force in Wells's consideration of the possibilities of active resistance. She concluded: "a Winchester rifle should have a place of honor in every black home" (SH, 23). Any potential lyncher, she thought, would have a greater respect for Afro-American lives if an attack risked the loss of his or her own life.

By 1895, when *A Red Record* was published, Wells had an increasingly sophisticated analysis of lynching. She had compiled statistics for a period of three years, 1892 through 1894, and situated this evidence within a historical framework. The emancipation of the slaves represented the loss of the vested interests of white men in the body of the Negro, Wells maintained, and lynching should be understood as an attempt to regain and exercise that control. Wells gave an account of the three main strands of excuses that whites used to justify the murder of black people. First was the often cited necessity to repress "race riots," a reason Wells identified as lacking any evidence of injured whites or any massacres or any proof offered of planned insurrections. The second reason, Wells argued, was a product of the social relations of Reconstruction when, under the rallying call of a refusal to be dominated by Negroes, organized mobs, the Ku Klux Klan and Regulators, massacred blacks for attempting to exercise their right to vote. Wells understood this history of condoned murder as a direct consequence of blacks having been granted a political right, the franchise, without being given the means to protect or maintain that right. For the American black, a concept of both manhood and citizenship was embodied in the right to vote, Wells stated, and therefore the loss of the vote was both a political suffocation and an emasculation. The third strand in Wells's formulation was the mobilization of racist sexual ideologies through the cry of "rape," a plea for revenge and an attempt to place blacks "beyond the pale of human sympathy." Rape had come to mean "any mesalliance existing between a white woman and a colored man" (RR, 11), and the much vaunted Southern chivalry, Wells agreed with Cooper, was an empty gesture that confined itself "entirely to the women who happen to be white," though even Northern white women, she asserted, had been placed outside the chivalric code when they went south to educate blacks after the Civil War (RR, 13). Wells had a bleak vision that Pauline Hopkins was to come to share, a vision of the annihilation of the black community in the United States being accomplished without protest. Wells's hope was based on the possibility that the murder of blacks would be recognized and publicly condemned for what it was: murder. Her aim, therefore, was to deconstruct the myriad of Southern claims and pretenses to which otherwise progressive forces in the North acceded.

Wells's analysis of lynching and her demystification of the political motivations behind the manipulation of both black male and female and white female sexuality led her into direct confrontation with individuals who considered themselves progressive. Frances Willard, president of the Women's Christian Temperance Movement, after a tour of the South in 1890, had been reported in the *New York Voice* as saying: "The colored race multiplies like the locusts of Egypt. The grogshop is its center of power. The safety of woman, of childhood, the home is menaced in a thousand localities at this moment, so that men dare not go beyond the sight of their own roof-tree." Willard cited as her source of information "the best white people" (RR, 59). Wells attacked Willard for what appeared to be a condoning of lynching and for her refusal to publicly condemn the practice. In Willard's address to the WCTU in Cleveland in November 1894, she in turn condemned Wells for her implications that white women encouraged sexual liasons with black men and objected to "an imputation upon half the white race in this country" (RR, 80). Willard was quite prepared to believe that the vast majority of Southerners felt nothing but good will toward blacks and that they were justified in taking action to protect themselves, including the denial of the black vote; she disapproved also of the "alien illiterates" who "rule our cities today." Willard failed to see that lynching was an institutionalized practice and preferred to believe that lynching and intimidation occurred only because of a "rough class of whites" (RR, 83).

Willard's attitude and Wells's conclusion that she was "no better or worse than the great bulk of white Americans on the Negro question" (RR, 85) was indicative of the racism that Cooper also condemned in white women's organizations. Frances Harper, too, had publicly condemned the leadership of the WCTU because there had not been a single black woman admitted to its Southern organizations. What Cooper called the white woman's concern with caste was also made evident in Wells's exposure of the assumption of "progressive" white women that rape actually was the crime to which lynching was the response.[16]

Cooper's essays demanded changes within both the black community and organizations dominated by white women. The way in which she interrelated the practices of racism and sexism with the practices and consequences of imperialism produced an analysis which attempted to reveal a common oppression shared by all under U.S. domination. Patriarchal power, for Cooper, was embodied in these forces of aggressive violence. The trajectory of Cooper's arguments was toward a transformed women's movement as an instrument for structural societal change. Wells, on the other hand, in her analysis of lynching provided us with a more detailed dissection of *how* patriarchal power manipulates sexual ideologies to effect political and economic subordination. Cooper failed to address what was central to the thesis of Wells, that white men used their ownership of the body of the white female as a terrain on which to politically oppress the black male. White women who felt that caste was their protection aligned their interests with the patriarchal power that ultimately confined them. Cooper identified this link between patriarchal power and the white women who practiced racist exclusivity, but she did not examine and analyze what forged that link. Cooper believed that what men taught women could be unlearned if women were educated, that female complicity in racist and imperialist oppression was a symptom of ignorance. Wells, however, was able to reveal how a patriarchal system which lost its total ownership over black male bodies used its control over women to attempt to completely circumscibe the actions of black male labor. As black women were designated as being outside the "protection" of the ideology of womanhood, both Cooper and Wells used their position of marginality to criticize the role of white women in the maintenance of a system of oppression. Black women responded to these issues by organizing to achieve a national political presence, but the work of Cooper and Wells had little effect on organizations dominated by white women. Cooper was right to argue that a transformed women's movement, purged of racism, would have been a liberating experience not only for black women but also for the white women themselves. But racism led to segregated organizations and, outside the antilynching movement itself, to a resounding silence about and therefore complicity in the attempt to eliminate black people politically, economically, and literally as a presence in North America.

It is important to recognize that black women like Frances Harper, Anna Julia Cooper, and Ida B. Wells were not isolated figures of intellectual genius; they were shaped by and helped to shape a wider movement of Afro-American women. This is not to claim that they were representative of all black women; they and their counterparts formed an educated, intellectual elite, but an elite that tried to develop a cultural and historical perspective that was organic to the wider condition of black womanhood. What each of them wrote and lectured about influenced and was influenced in turn by a wider constituency. Wells said that the meetings to organize her first antilynching lecture and the forum itself were "the real beginning of the club movement among the colored women" in the United States.[17] The meeting on one particular issue, lynching, was a catalyst in the establishment of clubs and a movement that would extend far beyond any one single issue. In 1892, the Women's Loyal Union was formed in New York, the Colored Women's League in Washington, and the Women's Era Club in Boston. In 1893, the Ida B. Wells Club was established in Chicago. As Mary Church Terrell has indicated, there had long been a sophisticated and complex network of black women organized within the black church, but in the early years of the nineties "secular organizations among them were very rare."[18] This existing network was mobilized to its fullest extent in cities and suburbs in the formation of local autonomous women's clubs.

In 1895, Josephine St. Pierre Ruffin, president of the Women's Era Club of Boston, called the First National Conference of the Colored Women of America. It convened from July 29 until July 31.[19] A national convention had been planned for some time, but the particular occasion for the appeal to attend this conference was to protest the actions of the president of the Missouri Press Association, who had made indecent accusations "reflecting upon the moral character of all colored women." Copies of a letter from him to organizations in England were issued with each appeal to attend accompanied by warnings to use the letter discreetly as it was thought "too indecent" for publication. The invitations were "extended to all colored women of America, members of any society or not."[20]

Issues surrounding and linked to the representation of black female sexuality provided both the occasion for and the substance of the conference. As Josephine St. Pierre Ruffin complained, the question of sexuality affected the relationship of black women to white women's organizations: "Year after year southern women have protested against the admission of colored women into any national organization on the ground of the immorality of these women, and because all refutation has only been tried by individual work the charge has never been crushed."[21] Cooper's concern to break silence and give expression to a black female experience was transformed in the process of this convention from the raised voices of individual women to a recognition of the importance of an organized and united voice. Ruffin used the occasion to stress the right of women to organize autonomously and also appealed for the support of black men. It is "fitting," she said, "that the women of the race take the lead in this movement, but for all this we recognize the necessity of the sympathy of our husbands, brothers and fathers." Ruffin agreed with Cooper's thesis that a women's movement should not be directed solely toward women's issues and declared that "our woman's movement is a woman's movement in that it is led and directed by women for the good of women and men, for the benefit of all humanity."

A major consideration for the women who attended the conference was the issue of exclusivity, for many had experienced being excluded from white women's organizations and did not intend to practice discrimination themselves. Consequently, the convention refused to define itself as an organization defined by race or color; those who attended asserted that they gathered together as American women who had to organize in order to be recognized as a significant social and political force. No women were prohibited from membership who could share the aims and ideals of the movement. Ruffin asserted: "We are not drawing the color line; we are women, American women, as intensely interested in all that pertains to us as such as all other American women; we are not alienating or withdrawing, we are only coming to the front." It was essential, she concluded, that they all be "workers to the same end," to achieve the elevation and dignity of all black women of the United States, aims that could be achieved only through the establishment of a national organization.[22] By the time the Nashville Convention was held in 1897, the National Association of Colored Women had a membership of fifty thousand women.[23]

In a pamphlet which celebrated the decision of black women to form a national movement, Victoria Earle Matthews appeared to favor total independence from white women and their organizations. She argued that no other women knew the needs of black women, who were solely responsible for the re-creation of their own history and future: "she has done it almost without any assistance from her white sister; who . . . has left her to work out her own destiny in fear and trembling."[24] *The Awakening of the Afro-American Woman* addressed all black women, from farm laborers to house servants, as co-breadwinners in their families who reared and educated their daughters and were the "arch" of the Afro-American church. Earle Matthews established a direct line of cause and effect

between the experiences of the ex-slave women and the members of
NACW who "have aroused themselves to the necessity of system-
atic organization for their own protection, and for strengthening
their race where they find it weak." However, despite the apparent
plea for the autonomous organization of black women as black
women, Earle Matthews, like Cooper, Wells, and Harper, knew
that in order to transform the social and political condition of black
women alliances with white women were important, if not crucial.
But the recognition of the need for allies was not the signal for
compromise; an alliance would work only if white women's organizations made the black woman's cause their own:

> We need them. We have always needed them . . . in the work of religion,
> of education, of temperance, of morality, of industrialism; and above all
> we need their assistance in combating the public opinion and laws that
> degrade our womanhood because it is black and not white; for of a
> truth, and as a universal law, an injury to one woman is an injury to all
> women.[25]

Black women intellectuals were advocates of a transformed wom-
en's movement and an alliance with white women, but at the same
time they knew they had to forge a culture of black womanhood out
of a history in which sisterhood had only rarely existed and most
white women had betrayed, abandoned, or excluded most black
women from their lives. As an elite, black women intellectuals
could only maintain a representative black female voice if they
weighed the advantages of forming an alliance against the knowledge that for the mass of black women white women were not
potential allies but formidable antagonists.

Earle Matthews embodied in her life many of the contradictions
of the fictional heroines of black women's novels. She went south
and exposed the exploitation of young black girls by employment
agencies which served the prostitution trade. But Earle Matthews
was able to be so effective in her political work in the South because
she did not look "black." As Elizabeth Lindsay Davis, in her history
of the NACW, described Earle Matthews in a direct circumlocution
of the issue of blackness: "It was her personality and natural en-
dowment, physically, which gave her entry to places, and conditions in the south not accessible to many of our women."[26] The

woman who moved across the chasm that existed between white womanhood and assertion of black womanhood was not only a metaphorical figure. Adella Hunt Logan was an officer of the Tuskegee Woman's Club and a member of the National American Woman Suffrage Association; only a few suffage leaders knew she was black. When Logan applied to Susan B. Anthony in 1897 to speak at an NAWSA convention as a black woman on behalf of black women, she was rejected. Anthony's reply was typical of the patronizing attitudes that dominated the suffrage movement; she felt that she should control the access of black women to a public forum for the good of the black community: "I would not on any account bring on our platform a woman who had a ten-thousandth part of a drop of African blood in her veins, who should prove an inferior speaker . . . because it would militate so against the colored race." Anthony was worried that allowing Logan to speak would be like bringing "right out of the South a woman who would almost be an ex-slave." As Logan's granddaughter, Adele Logan Alexander, has pointed out, Anthony's description was hardly accurate of "the former lady principal of Tuskegee."[27] If the American suffrage movement was unable to accommodate without a crisis a woman who was part of the minority black elite, who embodied upper-class habits of gentility and could pass for white, there was little reason to expect an alliance with the majority of black women.

Black women intellectuals did not focus all their energies on transforming white women's organizations but helped to create and maintain black cultural institutions. Earle Matthews delivered an address on the importance of race literature at that first national conference of black women in 1895.[28] On the one hand she praised the energetic columns of *The Women's Era* but on the other expressed regret at the lack of the abundance of weekly black publications that had existed thirty years earlier and bitterly complained of members of the black community who

> strain their purses supporting those white papers that are and always will be independent of any income derived from us. . . . [I]t is even hard to prove to them that in supporting such journals, published by the dominant class, we often pay for what are not only vehicles of insult to our manhood and womanhood, but we assist in propagating or supporting false impressions of ourselves or our less fortunate brothers.[29]

The cultural production of "race literature," Earle Matthews argued, would ensure the recording and preservation of black achievements, "thus saving from destruction and obliteration what is good, helpful and stimulating."[30] Earle Matthews concluded her address with a plea for black scholars to focus on and explore African history and the African ancestry of black Americans so that this knowledge could be transmitted by writers to a future generation.[31]

Earle Matthews directed the attention of black women to a series of specific cultural and historical needs that could be addressed by black literature, and it was precisely this absence that the *Colored American Magazine*, which published its first issue five years later, intended to fill. The Colored Co-operative Publishing Company was an attempt to attain both financial and editorial control in a publishing enterprise, to found a race literature, and to preserve the history of black Americans. Pauline Hopkins, the subject of the next two chapters, was associated with both organizations and with the Women's Era Club. When she published her fiction, she was part of this wider awakening of Afro-American women. Her writing had its source in this constituency and was supported by it; she read extracts from her first novel, *Contending Forces*, to other women of the club before it was published.

The movement of black women was able to give birth to and support the particular practices of individual women, and the individual practices in turn shaped and transformed the movement. Hopkins was able to draw on the insights and analyses of Harper, Cooper, Wells, and others, not only as individual black women but also as cultural producers who shaped and were shaped by a movement of women. Hopkins drew the material from her fiction from this discourse, but she also created a fiction which she intended to act back upon its source, urging and inspiring all black Americans to political action.

6

"Of What Use Is Fiction?"

Pauline Elizabeth Hopkins

In September 1900, the fourth issue of the *Colored American Magazine* carried an announcement for a new novel, *Contending Forces*, a romance written by Pauline E. Hopkins.[1] Published by the Colored Co-operative Publishing Company of Boston, which also published and housed the *Colored American Magazine*, *Contending Forces* was the first of Hopkins's four novels; the following three were serialized within the magazine and never published in book form. The prospectus for *Contending Forces* posed a rhetorical question, a question that indicated the intellectual concern of the journal and the novel: "Of what use is fiction to the colored race at the present crisis in its history?"[2] This issue of the social value and function of literature will be central to this consideration of the writing of Hopkins between 1900 and 1904, the period of her association with the *Colored American Magazine*.

Born in Portland, Maine, in 1859, Pauline Hopkins grew up in Boston. Her father and subsequent stepfather were Virginians, but her mother was from an established New England family.[3] As a mature writer, Hopkins re-created an idealized concept of her New England heritage in an image of the city of Boston when it was a center of abolitionist agitation. The history of abolition was a consistent reference point for Hopkins; the possibility of the revival of such a force for political change was the source of her political optimism. But as a young woman it was the influence of the temperance movement that provided the first occasion for a demonstration of Hopkins's creative writing skills. William Wells

Brown, in association with the Congregational Society of Boston, ran a competition for the black students in the Boston school system for the essay that best described the "Evils of Intemperance and Their Remedy."[4] Pauline Hopkins, aged fifteen and a student at the Girl's High School, won the prize of ten dollars in gold. Sixteen years later, a musical drama by Hopkins, "Escape from Slavery" (1880), was produced and ran through five performances.[5] Hopkins was not able to make her living as an author and worked throughout the nineties as a stenographer, first for Republican politicians and then for the Massachusetts Bureau of Statistics. When Hopkins died in 1930, she was working as a stenographer for the Massachusetts Institute of Technology.

Hopkins became a published author of narrative fiction when she was forty years old. On November 15, 1899, she read passages from her recently completed first novel, *Contending Forces*, to the Women's Era Club in Boston.[6] Hopkins's debut as novelist coincided with her becoming a founding member of the staff of the *Colored American Magazine*. It is difficult to determine exactly the extent of Hopkins's influence over the journal, but textual analysis would indicate that it was considerable. She exerted a powerful influence on every issue of the first six volumes, up until editorial control was lost to Booker T. Washington in 1904 and the journal moved to New York.[7] I am going to concentrate on this period of abundant activity and creativity in Hopkins's life and argue that any attempt to gain a comprehensive understanding of her fiction must begin with an analysis of all her work for the *Colored American Magazine*.

An editorial statement which appeared in the first issue of the *Colored American Magazine* clearly outlined the policy of the journal and the cultural and political need for its existence:

American citizens of color, have long realized that for them there exists no monthly magazine, distinctively devoted to their interests and to the development of Afro-American art and literature. Many American magazines have liberally and kindly treated such individuals and subjects, as have by virtue of remarkable ability, or absorbing interest, become of national importance, but as a rule, the Anglo-Saxon race, fails to sufficiently recognize our efforts, hopes and aspirations. The Colored American Magazine proposes to meet this want, and to offer the colored people of the United States, a medium through which they can demonstrate their ability and tastes, in fiction, poetry, and art, as well as in the arena of historical, social and economic literature. Above all it aspires to develop and intensify the bonds of that racial brotherhood, which alone can enable a people, to assert their racial rights as men, and demand their privileges as citizens. . . . A vast and almost unexplored treasury of biography, history, adventure, tradition, folk lore poetry and song, the accumulations of centuries of such experiences as have never befallen any other people lies open to us and to you.[8]

This collective statement of intent reflected not only the general ambition of the magazine but also the particular contributions that Hopkins made. Her writing for the journal included historical and social literature, asserted the bonds of racial brotherhood, and used biography, history, adventure and tradition in an attempt to render into words the unique experience of a people. Hopkins authored two major biographical series—"Famous Men of the Negro Race" and "Famous Women of the Negro Race"—and a miscellany of shorter biographical sketches, including a reflection on the nature of heroism, "Heroes and Heroines in Black."[9] But Hopkins's reflections on history and tradition were not confined to the biographical; she wrote numerous essays of political and social commentary, including analyses of the relation of blacks to the labor and suffrage movements.[10]

The *Colored American Magazine* should be regarded as a product of the magazine "revolution" that had been taking shape since the 1880s, when journals first began to establish a mass audience and large advertising business. In the 1890s, low prices, mass circulation, and advertising revenues became the cornerstones of the magazine industry. The *Colored American Magazine* tried to sell at a competitive price, fifteen cents, and to make enough money to cover the rest of the cost of production from advertising; the first six half-page advertisements appeared at the end of the second issue, in June 1900.[11] At the end of the first year of publication, the *Colored American Magazine* had pages of advertisements both back and front and regular full- and half-page patrons. Subscription was encouraged at $1.50 a year and various inducements offered, including a year's free subscription for two years paid in advance and "A Beautiful Watch Free!" for anyone who returned subscriptions for eight people. A system of agents was established. Initially there were twenty-four agents for twenty cities in sixteen states. At the beginning of the second year, there were eight branch offices for the *Colored American Magazine* in Baltimore, New York, Chicago, Nashville, Philadelphia, Pittsburg, St. Louis, and St. Paul, housing general agents as well as appointed subscription and advertising agents. Below these were eighty-three agents in thirty-three states and one in Liberia. At the end of a year, the following assessment was made:

> From a handful of readers in May, 1900, to one hundred thousand readers at the present time; from a weak and halting existence then, to a vigorous and healthy growth now; from early criticism and prejudice to broad and increasing usefulness; from what seemed certain defeat to a goodly success, with a most auspicious future, such, in brief, is the story of the first year's life of the Colored American Magazine.[12]

No report was made in the pages of the journal regarding the percentage of readership that actually subscribed. Agents were constantly encouraged to place early orders as the journal regularly fell well short of demand. This would indicate that most copies were bought one at a time and that the subscription list was not large enough to provide a secure basis of advance capital. This insecurity culminated in a transfer of management on May 15, 1903. The new administration purchased "the copyright, title and all bookrights, records, plates, cuts and other property of the Colored Co-operative Publishing Company" and printed emphatic assurances that the journal would, in future, be ready for delivery on time, that they would publish "the best known colored authors," and that "the entire management and office force will consist of colored Americans of high standing in the community."[13] Following the transfer, Hopkins appeared for the first time on the masthead as "literary editor."

Two aspects make the *Colored American Magazine* different from other magazines of the period. It was part of a cooperative publishing venture: readers could become members for an investment of cash over five dollars, and authorial contributions were granted a cash evaluation of their articles that would also entitle them to certificates of deposit. Both groups were entitled to full membership and dividends. However, what clearly differentiated the journal from other monthly magazines was its target audience. As the first editorial stated: "American citizens of color, have long realized that for them there exists no monthly magazine, distinctively devoted to their interests and to the development of Afro-American art and literature." The *Colored American Magazine* was an attempt to define as well as create the boundaries of a black magazine-reading public and was therefore a pioneer of the contemporary black magazine market. It aimed

> to meet this want, and to offer the colored people of the United States, a medium through which they can demonstrate their ability and tastes. . . . The Colored American Magazine awaits its success or failure, on the proposition that there is a demand for such a magazine, and the ability to make it a just and adequate exponent of Afro-American Literature.[14]

However, in any consideration of the potential readership of popular magazines, Richard Ohmann has warned, we have to exercise care, for even if addressed to the "people of the United States,"

> the readership was not "people," not the entire population (magazines were not a universal medium like television). It was not the 20% who were immigrants or children of immigrants; not the 12% who were black; not the poorest Anglo-Saxon farmers and workers; but probably a full half of the white "native" stock and something like a third of all the people.[15]

It may appear contradictory to consider the *Colored American Magazine* in relation to mass magazines as its audience lay within the 12 percent of the population that was black. But the argument remains illuminating, for even within this small percentage of the total market the journal did attempt to reach a wide spectrum of readers. In general, the aim was "the introduction of a monthly magazine of merit into every Negro family"[16] with the purpose of "develop[ing] and intensify[ing] the bonds of that racial brotherhood, which alone can enable a people, to assert their racial rights as men, and demand their privileges as citizens."[17] By 1903, the period of the transfer of ownership, the staff considered that the journal was "not only National but International in character," reaching correspondents and patrons in "China, Hawaii, Manila, West Indies and Africa."[18]

Despite the apparent exclusivity of the address to "men of the race," women were considered by the staff of the *Colored American Magazine* to be an integral part of the potential audience. Hopkins edited a "Women's Department," which started in the second issue, and women were represented in biographical articles and sketches. The *Colored American Magazine* was a serious attempt to reach a comprehensive black readership, and it is important to define its constituency because the journal did reach a significant proportion of the potential black readership which, however, was a small part of the black population.

In 1900, out of a total black population of 6,415,581 in the U.S., 45 percent aged ten years and over were illiterate.[19] Regional statistics reveal that 18.2 percent of the black population of the North were illiterate, while in the three Southern regions the figures ranged between 47 percent and 49 percent.[20] As would be expected, the figures for urban illiteracy were much lower than for rural illiteracy; in 1910, the figures were 17.6 percent and 36.1 percent, respectively.[21] Consequently, agents for the journal were situated in major cities, and there were many more in the North than in the South, which reflected where most readers were. Gross literacy figures, however, are not very useful in trying to determine who read what, especially when it is difficult to determine what constituted the definition of literacy used in these surveys.

It is most interesting perhaps to speculate about the readership of the *Colored American Magazine* in terms of occupation. Between 1900 and 1910, 50 percent of all black males and up to 28 percent of black females who were employed worked in agricultural production. In nonagricultural employment,

More than one-third of the total number of Negro women returned as gainfully employed in 1910 were returned in two occupational groups, as either "servants" or "laundresses not in laundries," and for both males and females not employed in agriculture some form of unskilled or semiskilled labor in the various lines of service, trade, and industry was returned in a large majority of cases as the gainful employment. Skilled trades, such as molders, plumbers, machinists, chauffeurs, painters, blacksmiths, masons, barbers, and carpenters, are, however, represented in each case by some thousands of workers, as are also such professional groups as physicians and surgeons, trained nurses, and teachers.[22]

The investigations of W. E. B. Du Bois revealed that between 1826 and 1899 there were approximately 2,500 black college graduates, so any assessment of readership cannot be limited to a black college-educated elite. The readership of the *Colored American Magazine* would have included those in professional service, the majority of whom were teachers or clergy[23] and the literate among those Du Bois categorized as "negro artisans."[24] Artisans included both male and female tobacco factory operatives, male blacksmiths, wheelwrights, boot and shoe makers, butchers, carpenters and joiners, cotton and textile mill operatives, machinists, masons, miners and quarrymen, printers, and railroad workers, as well as female dressmakers, milliners, seamstresses, and tailoresses.[25] Domestic servants, however, although excluded by Du Bois from the skilled and semiskilled category of workers, should be considered as potential readers who could wield a powerful influence in black urban communities, especially in the South.[26]

The pedagogic role of the journal was considered by the staff as a significant aspect of its function; the possibility of being able to "educate" and expand the horizons of its audience was fully exploited. Hopkins, in particular, was described by a colleague as regarding fiction as a particularly effective way of gaining a wide audience for the instructive by being entertaining: "Her ambition is to become a writer of fiction, in which the wrongs of her race shall be so handled as to enlist the sympathy of all classes of citizens, in this way reaching those who never read history or biography."[27] Under her own name and that of her mother, Sarah Allen, Hopkins published three serialized novels in the pages of the *Colored American Magazine*—*Hagar's Daughter. A Story of Southern Caste Prejudice*; *Winona. A Tale of Negro Life in the South and Southwest*; *Of One Blood. Or, the Hidden Self*[28]—and many short stories, including "The Mystery Within Us," "Talma Gordon," "General Washington. A Christmas Story," "A Dash for Liberty," "Bro'r Abr'm Jimson's Wedding. A Christmas Story," "The Test of Manhood," and "As the Lord Lives, He Is One of Our Mother's Children."[29]

Hopkins created fictional histories as experiences which could explain the present and which had a pedagogic function for both her characters and her audience. Her narratives rewrote contemporary versions of the relationship between the races during slavery in order to challenge contemporary racist ideologies. The social relations of the separation of the races in which Hopkins's fiction was produced—disenfranchisment, lynching, and the institutionalization of Jim Crow—were displaced by her alternative fictional history of close blood ties through miscegenation. Social Darwinism and the discourse of racial inferiority were replaced by an attack on the barbarity of the practices of rape and lynching.

Hopkins's first novel, *Contending Forces*, was the source of figures and narrative devices that developed throughout her later work; her use of history to rewrite an American heritage and question the boundaries of inheritance was important in her fiction and shaped her political perception. The actions and destinies of Hopkins's characters were carefully related to the condition and actions of their ancestors; the consequences of events initiated at some specific moment in history constituted a significant aspect of Hopkins's fictional strategy.

Hopkins dedicated *Contending Forces* to "the friends of humanity everywhere." In her preface she stated her motivation for writing to be "to raise the stigma of degradation from my race" and to gain the public's "approval of whatever may impress them as being of value to the Negro race and to the world at large." There were many forms through which Hopkins could have expressed such sentiments, but she felt that, among all intellectual pursuits, it was "the simple, homely tale, unassumingly told, which cements the bond of brotherhood among all classes and all complexions." Her pedagogic and political intent was that her fiction enter "these days of mob violence" and "lynch-law" and directly intervene in and help transform the state of relations between the races (13).

Hopkins spoke with such confidence of the possibility of narrative intervention in the political and social formation because she believed that fiction, as a cultural form, was of great historical and political significance:

> Fiction is of great value to any people as a preserver of manners and customs—religious, political, and social. It is a record of growth and

development from generation to generation. *No one will do this for us: we must ourselves develop the men and women who will faithfully portray the inmost thoughts and feelings of the Negro with all the fire and romance which lie dormant in our history*, and, as yet, unrecognized by writers of the Anglo-Saxon race. (13–14)

Her narrative voice was situated in the North and addressed *our* "hard struggles . . . to obtain a respectable living and a partial education" but concentrated on what the readership could learn from a re-creation of the history of the South in a causal relation to the present. Current oppression, Hopkins urged, should be understood in the context of past oppression. "Mob-law is nothing new. Southern sentiment has not been changed. . . . The atrocity of the acts committed one hundred years ago are duplicated today, when slavery is supposed no longer to exist." But what Hopkins was afraid of was that what had been distinctively Southern sentiments, "the old ideas close in analogy to the spirit of the buccaneers," in their reemergence as mob rule and lynch law would become acceptable practices for the whole of the republic (15).

The political activity that Hopkins wanted to revive or encourage was that of the New England antislavery societies of the antebellum period, "the memory of New England men who had counted all worldly gain as nothing if demanding the sacrifice of even one of the great principles of freedom." But she had to negotiate the racism of her beloved Boston, where "the descendants of the liberty-loving Puritans" virtually closed every avenue of employment and business against the Negro (83, 86). Thus, in order to use the mythology of a regional tradition of liberty in New England in her fiction, Hopkins made the inheritors of the love of liberty not the descendants of the founding fathers but the black inhabitants of the North, who "reflected the spirit of [their] surroundings" in the creation of an "intelligent, liberty-loving community" within the "free air of New England's freest city" (114–15).

Through her reconstruction of the "spirit" of abolitionism, Hopkins hoped that her fiction would encourage among her readership a resurgence of the forms of political agitation and resistance of the antislavery movement. This political strategy was also evident in her essays, for it was not only fictional black characters who were represented as the heirs of the New England reform tradition. In an article on black women educators, Hopkins situated Northern black intellectuals in general as being the descendants of the antebellum radicals. But the attempt to negotiate the contradictory aspects of a tradition that clearly no longer existed was a difficult task which led to a vacillation between severe critiques of the position of blacks in the North and moments of unashamed sycophancy:

> Intermarriage between Northern and Southern white families, the introduction of Southern teachers into the schools, and a natural feeling of kinship between the Northern and Southern Anglo-Saxon, may cause happenings in New England which smack of prejudice towards us as a race. But such things are as nothing when we remember that New England principles gave us a free Kansas way back in 1857; that New England blood was first shed in the streets of Baltimore when the tocsin of war sounded the call to save the union; that New England cemented the Proclamation of Emancipation in the death of Col. Shaw; and greater than all, stern New England Puritanism in the persons of Garrison, Sumner, Phillips, Stearns, Whittier, Francis Jackson, and others, gave the black man the liberty that the South would deny even to-day, if possible; gave to the Negro all over this broad land his present prosperity, no matter how inconsiderable it may appear to us; gave us Douglass and Langston, Robert Elliot and Bruce, and Booker T. Washington. . . . May my tongue cleave to the roof of my mouth and my right hand forget its cunning when I forget the benefits bestowed upon my persecuted race by noble-hearted New England.[30]

The blatant dismissal of racism in this passage indicated the extent of Hopkins's failure to negotiate the contradiction between her belief in a tradition of Northern radicalism and the fact of Northern racism, a contradiction which was reproduced in the preface to *Contending Forces*, which concluded with a plea "for that justice of heart and mind for my people which the Anglo-Saxon in America never withholds from suffering humanity" (15).

Contending Forces was a novel about the period in which it was written, but it opened with a chapter entitled "A Retrospective of the Past." This first story was set in the decade between 1790 and 1800: the years of political agitation in Britain for the abolition of slavery in the West Indies. Hopkins reproduced the history of the British abolitionists in the interests of being "instructive" as well as "interesting" (18) and to preface the story of Charles Montfort, a

West Indian planter who had moved his family and estate of slaves from Bermuda to North Carolina to avoid emancipating them. Hopkins delineated the "instructive" aspect of this decision as the perversion of morality in favor of commercial interest and profit:

> Nature avenges herself upon us for every law violated in the mad rush for wealth or position or personal comfort where the rights of others of the human family are not respected. If Charles Montfort had been contented to accept the rulings of the English Parliament, and had allowed his human property to come under the new laws just made for its government, although poorer in the end, he would have spared himself and family all the horrors which were to follow his selfish flight to save that property. (65)

It was the economic profitability of the system of slavery which was established as being the cause of the events and conditions of the rest of the novel.

Hopkins used the move to North Carolina to establish a series of contrasts between the British and U.S. slave systems, a romanticized vision of the former set against the human misery within the latter. Montfort was criticized for his "liberality" as a master and his intention to free his slaves after he had made his fortune and could afford to retire to Britain. The local vigilante group decided to put an end to his bad example. Montfort's supposed liberality was used to set into relief the uncivilized and savage aspects of the American slave system, but the focus of the text quickly became the suspicion and subsequent rumor that the blood of Grace Montfort was "polluted" by an African strain. Hopkins made it clear that it was irrelevant whether Grace Montfort was a black or a white woman. Her behavior was a representation of "true womanhood," but her skin was a little too "creamy." The readers were left to guess her actual heritage; what was important was that the suspicion of black blood was enough cause for the ostracism of the whole family and Grace Montfort's transition from the pedestal of virtue to the illicit object of the sexual desire of a local landowner, Anson Pollock. The possibility that Grace might be black was responsible for the murder of Charles Montfort, the "rapes" of Grace and her black foster sister, Lucy, and the enslavement of the two sons, Jesse and Charles.

Grace Montfort rejected the sexual advances of Anson Pollock, who planned his revenge and the satisfaction of his sexual obsession. Under the pretense of an imminent rebellion by Montfort's slaves, Pollock and the vigilante group, "the committee on public safety," raided the Montfort plantation. Montfort was quickly dispatched by a bullet in the brain, leaving Grace prey to Pollock's devilish intentions. In a graphic and tortured two-page scene, Hopkins represented the brutal rape of Grace in the displaced form of a whipping by two of the vigilantes. Her clothes were ripped from her body, and she was "whipped" alternately "by the two strong, savage men." Hopkins's metaphoric replacement of the "snaky, leather thong" for the phallus was a crude but effective device, and "the blood [which] stood in a pool about her feet" was the final evidence that the "outrage" that had been committed was rape (68–69).

Grace committed suicide to escape Pollock and was replaced as his mistress by her black maid and slave, Lucy. The actual and figurative ravishing of "grace" at the hand of Southern brutality established the link that Hopkins believed existed between the violent act of rape and its specific political use as a device of terrorism. Both Charles and Grace Montfort suffered because they threatened to break the codes that bound the slave system. The possibility that Grace Montfort was black represented the ultimate violation of the position of the white woman which necessitated the degradation of her and her offspring to use as chattel. Charles Junior was eventually bought from Pollock by an English mineralogist; Jesse escaped as a young man when on an errand to New York and made his way to Boston and eventually New Hampshire, where he was absorbed into the black community. One grew up "black" the other "white," which emphasized Hopkins's political intent of blurring the lines between the races.

This first tale took the first eighty pages of *Contending Forces* and acted as an overture to the main story which was set at the end of the nineteenth century, but it also contained all the narrative elements that eventually resolved the crises of the relations between the main characters. At the end of the novel the characters were finally made aware of the history which had shaped their lives; the Smith family inherited a tale which appeared remote from their everyday lives and retained significance only in the naming of children. Ma Smith, her husband dead, ran a lodging house with her son, William Jesse Montfort, and her daughter, Dora Grace Montfort. Two other main characters were lodgers, John P. Langley, engaged to Dora, and Sappho Clark, a woman with a mysteriously hidden past. The future of each of these characters was tied to and dependent on a revelation of their personal histories. These fictional histories were Hopkins's narrative displacement of the increasing separation of the races; issues of inheritance, heritage, and culture dominated the text, and blood lines between the races were so entangled that race itself became a subordinated concern. Crucial to the construction of this narrative was the historical importance of rape; because of the rapes of Grace and Lucy, white and black shared an interdependent destiny. John Langley was revealed to be the descendant of Anson Pollock and Lucy, and he was destined to repeat and relive his ancestor's sexual obsession.

However, the initial tale of slavery had a second important narrative function which situated the personal histories within a history of the relations between imperialist nations and their colonies, between colonizers and colonized. Hopkins wrote *Contending Forces* at a moment of intense debate concerning the consequences of acquiring and colonizing overseas territories. The Spanish-American War of 1898 had led to the secession of the Philippines, Puerto Rico, and Guam to the United States, and the Filipino resistance was brutally repressed. In 1899, Germany and the United States divided Samoa, and a year later the United States annexed Hawaii. By end of the nineteenth century the United States had acquired the basis of its empire, an empire that was and would continue to be "composed primarily of darker peoples, people of African, Indian, Polynesian, Japanese and Chinese extraction."[31]

Both imperialist and anti-imperialist argument derived their problematic from the history of the internal colonization of native American Indians and Africans. The question of the citizenship of both the internally and externally colonized was a major issue. At the same moment that black Americans were again being systematically excluded from participation in social institutions, the status of the people who lived in what the United States now deemed to be its "possessions" was an integral component of the contemporary discourse on race. Those who argued against expansionist policies failed to "challenge the central assumption of imperialist thought: the natural inequality of men."[32] On the one hand, the impulse to colonize was supported by an appeal to a version of manifest destiny: "the newer, post-Darwinian idea that it was the manifest *duty* of higher civilizations to displace lower ones, either through outright elimination (as the white man had eliminated the Indian) or through a process of uplift and 'Christianization.'"[33] On the other hand, anti-imperialists feared the possibility that Asian aliens could become citizens. Benjamin R. Tillman, a senator from South Carolina, typified how the imperialist discourse drew upon home-grown racist categories of thought: "we understand and realize what it is to have two races side by side that cannot mix or mingle without deterioration and injury to both and the ultimate destruction of the civilization of the higher. . . . I would save this country from the injection into it of another race question which can only breed bloodshed."[34] The fear of "mixing blood" was not confined to Southern bigots. In the Northern states these attitudes were shared; the temperate zone, higher civilization, and a pure Anglo-Saxon stock were seen as being interdependent social elements. The policy of expansionism that had resulted in the genocide of the Native American was, within this discourse, regarded as successful social policy precisely because it had protected the purity of the Anglo-Saxons, their institutions and society. There was almost universal acquiescence to the first stringent immigration laws and to the right of the South to implement the total separation of the races, including those "who called themselves liberals—survivors of the antislavery crusade and the battles of the sixties on behalf of the Negroes."[35]

This was the shared discourse of imperialism that Hopkins attempted to enter and disrupt. She represented an alternative historical interpretation of the relationship between white and black through an engagement with the concepts that structured the racist discourse. In her fictional history the degradation of a race was not the result of degeneration through amalgamation but a consequence of an abuse of power; it was the use of brutality against a subordinate group that was defined as and equated with savagery. Hopkins quoted Emerson on her title page and again in the body of the text: "The civility of no race can be perfect whilst another race is degraded." In *Contending Forces*, Hopkins used the relationship between Britain and the West Indies to make visible a colonial relationship that applied equally to North American imperialist ventures and to represent blacks as a colonized people.

In order to fully understand the significance of imperialism in *Contending Forces*, we can refer to a short story that Hopkins wrote and published at the same time. Her most concentrated revision of an imperialist history occurred in "Talma Gordon," which appeared in the *Colored American Magazine* in October 1900. The story was set in an elite male club where a small group was discussing "Expansion; Its Effect upon the Future Development of the Anglo-Saxon throughout the World." The major aspects of contemporary debate were summarized for the reader, and then conversation focused on the participants' fears of amalgamation. The one voice that argued in favor of intermarriage was the voice that Hopkins adopted to be the narrator of the rest of the story. As an illustration of his assertion that "the law of heredity . . . makes us all one common family," the narrator reconstructed the tale of the Gordon family, who were presented as being a part of the mythology of the founding of North America. The Gordons were descended from New England Puritans who arrived on the *Mayflower*. Captain Gordon's money had been accumulated through his and his ancestors' imperialist adventures as sea captains and enabled him to establish cotton mills when he retired from the sea. It was this interpretation of the history of an established New England heritage that Hopkins then undermined and rewrote in the rest of the story.

The first revelation made about the Gordon family history was that upon the birth of a black baby the first Mrs. Gordon was discovered to be an octoroon. She and the baby died, but her two older daughters were designated black and disinherited. Gordon remarried in an attempt to produce a male heir, but he, his wife, and child were murdered. Because they were the only family members left alive, suspicion fell on the "black" Gordon daughters as they inherited the estate, but their guilt remained unproven and they lived in exile in Europe. However, the second revelation situated the personalized family history within a wider imperialist history. The actual murderer of the Gordons was found to be an East Indian named Cameron, who sought revenge for Gordon's murder of his father. The history that Cameron told transformed Gordon from a heroic member of the "founding families" into "no better than a pirate." Cameron's individual revenge became one instance of "the many soul[s] crying in heaven and hell for vengeance on Jonathan Gordon. Gold was his idol; and many a good man walked the plank, and many a gallant ship was stripped of her treasure, to satisfy his lust for gold" (289). Cameron as East Indian was placed by Hopkins as a representative of those oppressed and murdered in that first moment of European mercantilist expansion. The history of the Gordon family as it was representative of the history of the founding families was revealed as mythology: their dynasty and the American nation were founded through acts of piracy. The narrator of the tale, who was established as being one of the powerful men who controlled the destiny of the nation, was revealed to be married to Talma Gordon, the surviving "black" Gordon daughter. This third and final revelation was Hopkins's device to authenticate the narration, the narrator's assertion of the existence of a "common family," and his prediction that intermarriage was, indeed, the consequence of colonial expansion.

In "Talma Gordon" and *Contending Forces*, Hopkins reconstructed an interdependent history of the colonized and their colonizers as a narrative of rightful inheritance in which lynching and rape were the central mechanisms of oppression. Commercial interests and a desire for profit motivated Montfort to keep his slaves and move to the United States. The consequence in Hopkins's fictional world was that a debt needed to be paid on two levels: the debt that accrued within the family history of the Monforts and, by implication, a debt that was owed to the whole black community from the profits of the slave trade.

The search for and establishment of kinship is a recurrent Afro-American literary metaphor. It had its source in slave narratives but recurred throughout the nineteenth century and expanded to become a figure for the dispersion of blacks throughout the diaspora. But Hopkins's particular use of this narrative device crossed racial boundaries. Ma Smith told the family tale to the British Charles Montfort-Withington, who then revealed himself to be a direct descendant of Jesse's brother, Charles. From Britain, Charles had successfully sued the U.S. government, and money had been left in trust for the heirs of Jesse, who were, of course, the Smith family. The rights of inheritance were established, and Ma Smith received $150,000. Lucy was found in Bermuda, with her granddaughter who identified John Pollock Langley as her son. Withington invested "a small annuity" on them both as they lived in total poverty, but Lucy, the only living witness to the original tale, died within days of being found. The fictional kinship network of the Montforts included an aristocratic British family, who acknowledged their intimate relation and paid the debt of history to their "American cousins." In relation to the Pollock kin, however, inheritance and heritage were given a negative emphasis. The young John Langley inherited none of the characteristics of his black family but was represented as being a carbon copy of his evil white grandfather, Anson Pollock. Hopkins repeated the story of the Montforts and the Pollocks in the story of the Smiths, John Langley and the mysterious Sappho Clark.

Sappho arrived at the Smith lodging house as a typist who had to work at home, for while her boss was willing to employ her he could not allow a black woman to work for him on his premises. She was represented as a tragic mulatta, and all members of the household fell in love with Sappho. Will formed a romantic attachment, while Langley, engaged to Dora, grew increasingly sexually obsessed with her. Langley, a lawyer ambitious to succeed politically, was a person in whom the "natural instinct for good had been perverted by a mixture of 'cracker' blood of the lowest type on his father's side" (221). He accepted bribes from white Northern politicians to be an acquiescent and malleable black representative who exercised control over his community to prevent any form of organized political demonstration against lynching or any other form of outrage perpetrated on blacks in the South. Langley perceived Dora to be the most suitable choice of wife to further his ambitions, but he desired Sappho as his mistress. Sappho's need to hide her sexual history provided the occasion for Langley to blackmail her.

In preparation for the denouement which linked the personal history of Sappho to the history of black persecution in the South, Hopkins assembled all her characters for a meeting of the American Colored League, called in response to the increased number of lynchings in the South. Langley, as a white man's puppet, urged that no action be taken, but his conservative platitudes were countered by a new character, Lycurgus (Luke) Sawyer, who addressed the audience by defining the "contending forces" of Hopkins's title:

> I want to tell the gentlemen who have spoken here tonight that conservatism, lack of brotherly affiliation, lack of energy for the right and the power of the almighty dollar which deadens men's hearts to the suffer-

ings of their brothers, and makes them feel that if only *they* can rise to the top of the ladder may God help the hindmost man, are the forces which are ruining the Negro in this country. It is killing him off by thousands, destroying his self-respect, and degrading him to the level of the brute. *These are the contending forces that are dooming this race to despair!* (255–56)

Luke had two tales to tell. In the first a lynching was the central focus, in the second a rape. Both tales confirmed the primacy of these two violent acts in Hopkins's thesis of "contending forces." The first history was about Luke's father, whose success in trade resulted in competition with white traders, threats to his life, and eventually a mob attack on his house and family. Because Luke's father attempted to defend himself, he was lynched, and his wife and daughter were whipped and abused until they died. Luke's two baby brothers were seized by the mob, who "took them by the heels and dashed their brains out against the walls of the house" (257).

The second tale followed from the first. Luke escaped into the woods, was found and rescued by a black, Beaubean, who took Luke into his home to raise as a son. Beaubean's white father had been his owner, and he had a wealthy and politically influential white half-brother who assumed a stance of paternal friendship toward Beaubean's daughter, Mabelle, which was a disguise for his real intention to rape her. When fourteen years old, Mabelle was kidnapped by her uncle, raped, and left a prisoner in a brothel. After weeks of searching, Beaubean found his daughter and confronted his brother with his crime. In his defense, the brother stated, "What does a woman of mixed blood, or any Negress, for that matter, know of virtue? It is my belief that they were a direct creation by God to be the pleasant companions of men of my race" (261). He then offered Beaubean a thousand dollars. Beaubean threw the money back at his brother and threatened legal action in the federal courts. This threat was met with mob action; Beaubean's house was set alight and the family shot. Luke escaped with Mabelle and placed her in a convent.

At this point in the text, Hopkins tried to mold Sappho's history into a paradigm of the historical rape of black women. At the conclusion of the story, Sappho fainted, and Langley correctly identified her as Mabelle Beaubean. Armed with this information, he confronted Sappho and tried to blackmail her into being his mistress. Sappho at first misunderstood his intention and declined what she thought to be a proposal of marriage, but his response was clear: "who spoke of marriage? Ambitious men do not marry women with stories like yours" (320). Hopkins molded Langley as an archetype, an embodiment of the cultural myth of the rise of the poor child to success and power. She re-created in this individual character what she understood to be a representative figure of the "Gilded Age," manipulating and monopolizing unbridled power:

> He had prospered. He had accomplished the acquisition of knowledge at the expense of the non-development of every moral faculty. He did not realize that he was a responsible being, or that morality was obligatory upon him. With him, might was right. . . . John had given no thought to the needs of his soul in his pursuit of wealth and position. (335–36)

Langley embodied what Hopkins represented as the dominant characteristics of the South, which she felt needed "nothing less than a new moral code." In alliance with the white politicians who bought his allegiance, he was implicated in the social structure of "Southern arrogance, trusts, political bossism, and every other abuse waged against God's poor" against which Hopkins urged organized opposition.[36]

Hopkins used the history of Anson Pollock, as representative of the oppressive power of slaveholders, with the contemporary characteristics of political, social, and economic opportunism, and produced a John Langley. The social forces that these two males, white and black, reproduced had particular consequences for the patriarchal control of women. Langley placed the responsibility for her rape on Sappho's own shoulders and could envision no possible future for her other than as concubine. Yet it was Langley and the patriarchal oppression he represented that had no future in Hopkins's fictional world. Langley was given a choice; he was offered an alternative path of action, much as the text itself attempted to pose alternative relations between dominant and subject peoples. A fortune-teller, Madame Frances, warned Langley that if he persisted in his machinations he would die in utter desolation and desperation surrounded by the wealth he so desired but which would be useless to him. The warning was disregarded, and Langley died in the final pages of the novel, in the middle of the Klondike gold fields, in a storm of snow and ice, surrounded by an immense fortune and the twenty-nine bodies of his companions.

Langley and the histories of Luke Sawyer and Mabelle Beaubean formed the story of the colonization of a people within the United States. But their stories were also a part of Hopkins's critique of the racism that structured the imperialist enterprise:

> there were strangely contradictory sides to the Social Darwinist and imperialist positions . . . but . . . [t]he thread that unified these disparate positions was the ideology of white supremacy. No matter how the prevailing arguments for and against Social Darwinism and imperialism were manipulated, adherence to white supremacy stands out as a consistent theme which ran through most of them. The turn of the century was a time of excited debate and agitation, and although white supremacy shaded and slanted every debate, it was so intrinsic to white thinking that it was seldom itself the subject of debate.[37]

Hopkins tried to make visible this intrinsic framework of thought and reproduced through her characters and their histories of oppression the consequences of both the assertion of white supremacy and acquiescence in white supremacist practices.

The dominance of characterizations of mulattoes and octoroons in *Contending Forces* has been interpreted as an intention to glorify the possibilities of the black race if only it would integrate with and eventually lose itself within the white.[38] But the presence of "mixed" characters in the text did not represent an implicit desire to "lighten" blacks through blood ties with whites. Hopkins wanted to emphasize those sets of social relations and practices which were the consequence of a social system that exercised white supremacy through the act of rape. Her use of mulatto figures engaged with the discourse of social Darwinism, undermining the tenets of "pure blood" and "pure race" as mythological, and implicitly exposed the absurdity of theories of the total separation of the races. But Hopkins also attempted to demonstrate the importance of social, political, and economic interests in determining human behavior in order to negate contemporary propositions of the danger of the degeneracy of a social group through its amalgamation with another. Hopkins addressed accusations that miscegenation was the inmost desire of the darker races of the earth, a conspiracy to weaken and debilitate the white race. Her response was to reconstruct miscegenation as white male rape and to deny that the black community wanted intermarriage. The character of Will Smith, who most frequently made political statements similar to the political opinions of Hopkins, stated categorically to the American Colored League, "Miscegenation, either lawful or unlawful, we do not want" (264).

Hopkins used *Contending Forces* to demonstrate that the political issue behind the violence of lynching was not the threat of black sexuality but the potential power of the black vote: "Which race shall dominate . . . south of Mason and Dixon's line? The negro if given his full political rights, would carry the balance of power every time. This power the South has sworn that he shall never exercise" (264). Her presentation of rape and lynching as tactics of political terror to repress any attempt at black political, social, or economic advancement drew on the arguments and indictments of Ida B. Wells. The act of rape, Hopkins argued, had to be totally separated from the issue of violated white womanhood and situated as a part of the social, political, and economic oppression of black people:

> Lynching was instituted to crush the manhood of the enfranchised black. Rape is the crime which appeals most strongly to the heart of the home life. . . . *The men who created the mulatto race, who recruit its ranks year after year by the very means which they invoked lynch law to suppress*, bewailing the sorrows of violated womanhood! no; it is not rape. If the Negro votes, he is shot; if he marries a white woman, he is shot or lynched—he is a pariah whom the National Government cannot defend. But if he defends himself and his home, then is heard the tread of marching feet, as the Federal troops move southward to quell a "race riot." (270–71)

In Hopkins's fictional representation of the social relations between white and black, she reconstructed a generational history across a century to situate the contemporary reassertion of the doctrine of white supremacy within a framework that demythologized the American story of origins. Democracy was exposed as an imperialist slavocracy. Hopkins's characters were created not as holistic individuals but as the terrain on which the consequences of her authorial interpretation of history were worked through, making the whole Smith family the bearers of the history of colonization and slavery. But perhaps Hopkins's political intention was at its clearest in the construction of the two identities of Sappho Clark.

The disguise in which history was hidden was Sappho, the poet of Lesbos, who was admired and loved by men and women, though her erotic poetry was addressed to women. The Sappho of Hopkins's text was the focus of admiration of all the occupants of the boardinghouse, indeed of everyone she met, men and women. To Dora, who occupied domestic space running the boardinghouse, Sappho was the independent woman who in their intimate moments together talked of the need for suffrage and the political activity of women. Sappho disrupted Dora's complacency with her existence that led her to "generally accept whatever the men tell me as right" (125) and made her reassess the importance of friendships with women:

> There was a great fascination for her about the quiet, self-possessed woman. She did not, as a rule, care much for girl friendships, holding that a close intimacy between the two of the same sex was more than likely to end disastrously for one or the other. But Sappho Clark seemed to fill a long-felt want in her life, and she had from the first a perfect trust in the beautiful girl. (97–98)

The feelings that Sappho created in Dora contrasted dramatically with Dora's emotional response to John Langley, her betrothed, who, she complained to Sappho, made her feel "unsexed" (122).

But Sappho as an ideal embodiment of womanhood did not exist. In order to function, to work and survive, Mabelle Beaubean, a product of miscegenation and the subject of rape, had to bury her violated womanhood and deny her progeny. For, like Sappho of Lesbos, Sappho Clark had a child, "Whose form is like gold flowers."[39] Sappho Clark fled the accusations of John Langley and returned south to New Orleans, telling no one of her whereabouts. Her journey to retrieve her own identity and understand and accept the consequences of her womanhood meant that she also had to acknowledge her position as mother and to accept the child she had denied, a child that represented her rape. In a chapter entitled "Mother-love," Harper exposed the consequences of rape: "the feeling of degradation had made her ashamed of the joys of mother-hood, of pride of possession in her child" (345). The passage toward acceptance of her motherhood retrieved and combined the elements of Sappho and Mabelle. This necessary transition preceded the final transformation into wifehood and marriage with Will. "Mother-love" was present in the text as a process of purification, a spiritual revival that could purge the circumstances of birth and that prepared Sappho for the future, "fitting her perfectly for the place she was to occupy in carrying comfort and hope to the women of her race" (347).

The most significant absence in the network of social forces through which Hopkins delineated her characters was the black father. The father was a narrative figure who mediated patriarchal control over women. In Hopkins's text, as in texts by most nine-teenth-century black women, patriarchal control was exercised by and mediated through the figures of white men who denied politi-cal, social, and economic patriarchal power to black men. Henry Smith was present only as a memory; his story was recounted as a life circumscribed by racism in every activity he undertook. Though the struggle of his life was constant, "he had no desire to contend with the force of prejudice" (83). He had no active part in Hopkins's text, having died years before her contemporary tale began. His absence thus confirmed the denial of patriarchal power to black men, but in this space Hopkins created alternative figures of black men constructed in peer relations, as brothers or as potential partner/husbands. The black heroines did not become the subject of an exchange between black men in marriage; they are not trans-ferred from father to husband in a passage from daughter to wife. As did Frances Harper's *Iola Leroy*, *Contending Forces* posed but did not explore the possibility of utopian relations between men and women.

What Hopkins concentrated on instead was a representation of the black female body as colonized by white male power and practices; if oppositional control was exerted by a black male, as in the story of Mabelle's father, the black male was destroyed. The link between economic/political power and economic/sexual power was firmly established in the battle for the control over women's bodies. Hopkins repeatedly asserted the importance of the relation between histories: the contemporary rape of black women was linked to the oppression of the female slave. Children were destined to follow the condition of their mothers into a black, segregated realm of existence from where they were unable to challenge the white-controlled structure of property and power. Any economic, political, or social advance made by black men resulted in accusations of a threat to the white female body, the source of heirs to power and property, and subsequent death at the hands of a lynch mob. A desire for a pure black womanhood, an uncolonized black female body, was the false hope of Sappho's pretense. The only possible future for her black womanhood was through a confrontation with, not denial of, her history. The struggle to establish and assert her womanhood was a struggle of redemption: a retrieval and reclaiming of the previously colonized. The reunited Mabelle/Sappho was a representation of a womanhood in which motherhood was not contingent upon wifehood, and Will was a representation of a black manhood that did not demand that women be a medium of economic exchange between men. The figure of Mabelle/Sappho lost her father when he refused to accept that his daughter was a medium of cash exchange with his white stepbrother. Beaubean had his fatherhood denied at the moment when he attempted to assert such patriarchal control and was slaughtered by a white mob. Instead of representing a black manhood that was an equivalent to white patriarchy, Hopkins grasped for the utopian possibility that Will could be a husband/partner to Mabelle/Sappho, when he accepted her sexual history, without having to occupy the space of father to her child.

Contending Forces was the most detailed exploration of the parameters of black womanhood and of the patriarchal limitations of black manhood in Hopkins's fiction. In her following three novels, Hopkins would adopt the more popular conventions of womanhood and manhood that defined heroes and heroines as she produced a magazine fiction that sought a wide audience. Hopkins continued to write political fiction at the same time as she adopted popular fictional formulas and was the first Afro-American author to produce a black popular fiction that drew on the archetypes of dime novels and story papers.

7

"All the Fire and Romance"

The Magazine Fiction of
Pauline Hopkins

We must ourselves develop the men and women who will
faithfully portray the inmost thoughts and feelings of the
Negro with all the fire and romance which lie dormant in our
history.

PAULINE HOPKINS

In March 1901, Pauline Hopkins's serialized fiction was published
for the first time in the *Colored American Magazine*. *Hagar's
Daughter. A Story of Southern Caste Prejudice* appeared under the
pseudonym "Sarah A. Allen," the name of Hopkins's mother.
Though structural similarities to *Contending Forces* can be found
in Hopkins's magazine serials, what is more intriguing is the notice-
able shift to incorporate some of the strategies and formulas of the
sensational fiction of dime novels and magazines. Hopkins made a
distinct move away from, though she did not abandon, the novel of
ideas in order to emphasize the elements of suspense, action, adventure, complex plotting, multiple and false identities, and the use of
disguise. There was a more frequent use of physical action and
confrontation in her fiction alongside her representation of social
and intellectual conflict.[1] These changes in the narrative structure
of Hopkins's fiction were an indication of her attempt to combine
elements of popular fiction with a more didactic intent to create
stories of political and social critique. The physical action of *Hag-*

145

ar's Daughter included murder, kidnappings, and escapes, if not the
actual fights often found in dime novels and story papers, and
concluded with a spectacle, a confrontation in open court which
brought together the entire community of the text.[2] However, this
use of a more popular format was a consequence not only of
authorial intent but also of the demands of serial publication. Each
episode ended in a cliff-hanging suspense that was not resolved
until the next issue, which in its turn ended in a state of suspense.
Resolutions came thick and fast in the concluding episode only.

Unlike *Contending Forces*, Hopkins's serialized fiction was situated within a white community rather than a black social order.
The Smith family boardinghouse and the local black church provided the loci for the entry and exit of Hopkins's major figures in
Contending Forces. But in *Hagar's Daughter* and *Winona*, the
white world was represented directly through individual white villains who symbolized the power of white society to oppress and
embodied greed and rapaciousness. In *Contending Forces*, white
society was a systemic set of forces portrayed indirectly through
accounts of the experiences of Hopkins's black characters. In *Hagar's Daughter*, the three primary female characters existed within
the context of a white community and were thought to be white.[3]
Their blackness was a secret which made them victims, and the
process of victimization was the mechanism of the plot.

Like *Contending Forces*, *Hagar's Daughter* had an introductory
plot and a main plot that were interdependent. The first story was
an imitation of a section of William Wells Brown's *Clotelle* (1864).
Hagar, an orphan, happily married to Ellis Enson, a slave and
plantation owner, gave birth to a daughter. This birth displaced
St. Clair Enson, brother to Ellis, as heir to their estate outside of
Baltimore. Following *Clotelle*, Hopkins incorporated an evil slave
trader named Walker, who sought to profit both himself and
St. Clair by revealing Hagar to have been a slave who was adopted
by the people she thought to be her parents. Walker claimed both
Hagar and her daughter as his property. Ellis disowned her and
then left. A disfigured body was found on the estate, and Hagar
accused St. Clair of fratricide but was unable to stop him from
claiming his inheritance; Walker took Hagar and her daughter to a
slave pen in Washington.[4] Hagar's subsequent escape from the pen
and her rush for a bridge from which to throw herself and her child

into the Potomac were a duplication of the famous incident in *Clotelle* and ended the initial part of the story.

The main body of the tale took place twenty years later and was situated within Washington's high society. The drama involved various levels of disguise, from the apparently simple changes of names to more complex uses of the device. Hagar became "Estelle Bowen," the second wife of Senator Bowen, a working-class man with an aptitude for making millions, who needed Estelle's education and cultivated tastes to ensure his political position. St. Clair Enson was disguised as a "General Benson," who, with his partner, "Major Madison" (Walker), conspired to gain control over Bowen's money. Ellis Enson reentered late in the tale as "Mr. J. Henson," a detective. The changes in names were accompanied by change in appearance: all characters were older, and the disguises cloaked the evil intentions of the villains from their potential victims. While the villains attempted to manipulate their victims through knowledge of their secret pasts, the victims remained ignorant of the true identities of their blackmailers until the end of the story. At a more complex level of hidden identity, the three major female characters, Estelle, her stepdaughter, Jewel, and Major Madison's daughter, Aurelia, were disguised as white when they were actually black. Each reverted to her original position as a black woman by the end of the story, and the occasions of the public revelation of their blackness enabled Hopkins to address the social and moral implications of being defined as a black woman. The use of disguise worked at the level of appearance; the nature of the character did not change. Benson (St. Clair) and Madison (Walker) were consistently immoral and criminal, and the revelation of their identities resulted in a punishment delayed only as long as their disguise was effective. Estelle (Hagar) and Jewel were consistently "good," and they suffered only when they were punished for being black; their actions were beyond repute.

The disguise of whiteness was a prerequisite for being able to write a story about the Washington elite of the period if black characters were to be included as more than servants. The device that allowed a white character to darken his skin and move about the black community in popular fiction[5] had no equivalent that would allow black characters equal access to white society, which could be accomplished only by the creation of a narrative of "passing." The "whiteness" of Hopkins's major female figures should be analyzed in relation to these formal prerequisites, because Hopkins was drawing on and using popular fictional formulas and conventions in her use of disguises and double identities; this "whiteness" enabled an identity to be hidden. Consideration of the formal aspects of "whiteness" as disguise problematizes interpretations which consider the representation of white-looking black characters as an indication of acquiescence in dominant racist definitions of womanhood and beauty. Certainly, this interpretation would be difficult to apply to *Hagar's Daughter* because, in addition to the formal demands of the text, the character of the third black woman, Aurelia, could not be so simply dismissed. Though beautiful in conventional terms, Aurelia was not created to be an embodiment of noble womanhood. On the contrary, Aurelia was a female character who compromised her sexuality in two ways: she used her charms to lure men to gamble and lose their money to her father, and she adopted masculine characteristics. The use of Aurelia as a woman with masculine traits was further evidence of the influence of popular fictional forms on Hopkins. The masculinized female in popular novels first appeared in the 1860s and was found in many nineteenth-century popular novels.[6] What Benson admired about Aurelia was her ability to be like a man: "It's a relief to be with a woman who can join a man in a social glass, have a cigar with him, or hold her own in winning or losing a game with no Sunday-school nonsense about her" (3: 118).

Aurelia existed as, but was not condemned for being, a villain. Her role was to entice and then marry Jewel's fiancé, Cuthbert Sumner, at the same time as her father and Benson gained control of Bowen's financial fortune. Unlike the two male villains, Aurelia was not punished for her role in the conspiracy but instead displayed courage and defiance. Her complicity was attributed to her social position as quadroon, for "debauched white men [were] ever ready to take advantage of their destitution." As the daughter of Madison's slave mistress, she had become "a willing tool" in her own downfall (3: 348, 349). Sumner's physical repulsion when he discovered Aurelia's black heritage revealed the limits of his liberalism and sparked a dramatic confrontation in which Aurelia's courage dwarfed his racism. Unlike Estelle and Jewel, Aurelia was not a mere victim but a fighter:

"If the world is to condemn me as the descendant of a race that I abhor, it shall never condemn me as a coward!" Terrible though her sins might be—terrible her nature, she is but another type of the products of the accursed system of slavery—a victim of "man's inhumanity to man" that has made "countless millions mourn." There is something too, that compelled admiration in this resolute standing to her guns with the determination to face the worst that fate might have in store for her. (4: 190)

Aurelia's "masculinity" and her courage disguised her "feminine" weakness, a weakness that led her to love the man who was also her prey. Aurelia was a perfect representation of the popular figure of the "adventuress" who used her sexuality for her own ends and threatened men with her ambition.[7]

Like the white and apparently white characters, the black characters continued from the first story into the second, and from slaves they were transformed into servants. In this shift, they gained their own community space and no longer had to live in the midst of the white community that Hopkins created; consequently, they were not disguised from each other or from the reader. Henny, Marthy, and Isaac retained their own names; Marthy and Isaac were married with a son and a daughter, Oliver and Venus. These black characters were aware of the disguises of other characters in correspondence to their proximity to the action. Isaac was man-servant to General Benson, as he was slave to St. Clair, but he kept the secret of his master's double identity from his wife and mother-in-law. Like Aurelia, he was complicit as a "willing tool." Isaac's daughter, Venus, worked as a maid to Jewel and supported her brother, Oliver, in college. Hopkins extended her application of the masculinized female to Venus, who evolved into a heroine of the story. Venus made the transition from minor character to heroine when she determined to find Jewel's kidnapper. Disguised as a man, "Billy," Venus was employed as Henson's assistant detective. Billy and another black male detective, Henry, were responsible for discovering Jewel, and Venus secured the escape of her mistress and her grandmother, Henny.

The figure of the detective was a relatively new character in popular fiction. The first dime-novel series that was entirely detective fiction was the Old Cap. Collier Library, which started in the

1880s.[8] The first detective agency in the United States was the Pinkerton Agency founded by Allan Pinkerton, who became famous for foiling an assassination plot against Abraham Lincoln. Hopkins used both this history and the fictional heroic status of the detective in *Hagar's Daughter*. Both Benson and Madison were implicated in an assassination attempt against Lincoln, attaching to the character of Henson the dimensions of both Pinkerton and the popular fictional detective hero. In the classic dime-novel detective story, the detective had no family background, which separated

> the detective both physically and psychically from his cases and from the individuals whose destinies he corrects. The objectivity allows him to work unhindered while the dispassionate approach may be the key to his success. He is the only one who can read the riddle because he is never personally involved. When he allows himself to become involved with his clients he is unable to function as a detective.[9]

Hopkins used and adapted this convention of the detective as lone hero. When Henson was brought into the story by Jewel to help Sumner fight a false accusation of murder, he appeared as a character who had no apparent relation to any of the other characters and was outside the society in which they moved. The discovery of the real murderer, Benson, was also the moment of discovery of his brother, St. Clair. The revelations of filial relationship led directly to Estelle's declaration that she was his wife, Hagar. The transformation of the client-detective relationship into a familial involvement ends Henson's days as a detective; his function in the narrative had to change, as he was renamed as landowner, husband, and eventually father.

The most magical of all the resolutions of *Hagar's Daughter* was the discovery that Jewel, far from being Hagar's stepdaughter, was actually her own daughter. Senator Bowen's last words before he died were "The little hair trunk," the meaning of which was left unresolved while murders and kidnappings occurred and were solved. But after Ellis and Hagar were reunited, Hagar remembered these words and opened the trunk that was Senator Bowen's most treasured possession. The trunk contained the story of the child's eventual discovery and adoption by Bowen and the baby clothes and locket that Hagar's daughter was wearing when she fell into the

Potomac with her mother. The rediscovery of a lost child through a locket or other magical sign was a common popular fictional strategy for restoring an orphan to his or her true parents.

Conventional use of disguise and double identities indicated a disruption of the natural order of events, whereas the revelations and resolutions of popular fiction signaled the reestablishment of order in the moral and social fabric of the characters' lives. However, the resolutions in Hopkins's story revealed the contradictions inherent in the attempt to use popular forms that entertained and were easily accessible to question the morality of, rather than restore faith in, the social order. St. Clair and Walker represented immorality and rampant greed, but their imprisonment did not return society to happiness. Neither were the heroes and heroines secured in their social positions when what appeared to be the prime threat was removed. Ultimately, the political forces that Hopkins wanted to indict could not be embodied in individually good or bad characters. The character of Cuthbert Sumner was an example of this dilemma.

Hopkins combined a New England background and heritage with a family history of abolitionism to situate Sumner's professed sympathy for blacks and black equality. But he was also a figure Hopkins used as a representation of the limits of white liberalism and New England philanthropy, an illustration of the inherent and disguised racism below the professed sympathy for black people. When Estelle revealed her true identity as Hagar and as a black woman, Sumner, who had secretly married Jewel in jail, told his wife that she could no longer have any contact with her stepmother. Hopkins described the contradictory aspects of his attitude and actions:

> Cuthbert Sumner is born with a noble nature; his faults were those caused by environment and tradition. Chivalrous, generous-hearted—a manly man in the fullest meaning of the term—yet born and bred in an atmosphere which approved of freedom and qualified equality for the Negro, he had never considered for one moment the remote contingency of actual social contact with this unfortunate people. He had heard the Negro question discussed in all its phases during his student life at "Fair Harvard," and had even contributed a paper to a local weekly in which he had warmly championed their cause; but so had he championed the

cause of the dumb and helpless creatures in the animal world about him. He gave large sums to Negro colleges and on the same principle gave liberally to the Society for the Prevention of Cruelty to Animals, and endowed a refuge for homeless cats. Horses, dogs, cats, and Negroes were classed together in his mind as of the brute creation whose sufferings it is his duty to help alleviate. (4: 283)

Hopkins's searing indictment of "the limits of New England philanthropy" had narrative consequences that revealed the limits of her use of conventions of popular fiction: there would be no happy endings. The last revelation, Jewel's blackness, was aimed directly at the punishment of Sumner and the hypocrisy of his philanthropy. The focus was not on the consequences for Jewel, for she was quickly removed from the text and rapidly died off-stage. The spotlight was entirely on Sumner. His racist attitudes were, at this point in the story, well established, and he was destined to repeat the desertion of Hagar by Ellis in the first story. By the time Sumner had reflected on his relation to Jewel, changed his mind, and searched for her a year later, she was dead. The tragic aspects of the tale, however, were not individual. At the moment of Sumner's realization of regret, Hopkins shifted the attention of her reader from individual to nation, from the acts of particular characters to systemic oppression, and rejected the possibility of a simple return to an acceptable moral order that a conventional "happy ending" would have indicated:

Cuthbert Sumner questioned wherein he had sinned and why he was so severely punished. Then it was borne in upon him: the sin is the nation's. It must be washed out. The plans of the Father are not changed in the nineteenth century; they are shown us in different forms. The idolatry of the Moloch of Slavery must be purged from the land and his actual sinlessness was but a meet offering to appease the wrath of a righteous God. (4: 291)

Hopkins's refusal to resolve the drama of *Hagar's Daughter* within the terms of the popular formal conventions that structured her narrative was symptomatic of the tension between her political and didactic intent and the desire to write popular stories. The shift into a direct authorial address to emphasize the social implications of the tale returned the reader to a consideration of the contemporary meanings of the separation of the races and should prompt the literary critic to reflect on the problematic nature of Hopkins's representation of fictional, imaginary resolutions.

The conclusion was dominated by biblical references. In the book of Genesis, Hagar was an Egyptian slave who was given by Sarah, her mistress, to her husband, Abraham, to conceive the children that Sarah could not have. But once Hagar produced an heir, she was brutally treated and tried to escape. When Sarah eventually had a son of her own, Hagar and her son, Ishmael, became a threat to the established order and were cast out to die. Saved from the desert by God, Hagar was promised that in time her son would be the founder of a nation.[10] Jewel, as Hagar's daughter, not a son, compared herself to Miriam, who spoke against Moses for marrying an Ethiopian woman. Miriam's punishment was to be struck with leprosy which turned her "white as snow."[11] Jewel's whiteness was likewise cursed, for it caused her to commit the sin of racism: "My sin, for it is a sin to hold one set of God's creatures so much inferior to the rest of creation simply because of the color of the skin, has found me out. Like Miriam of old, I have scorned the Ethiopian and the curse has fallen upon me, and I must dwell outside the tents of happiness forever" (4: 290). Unlike Miriam's situation, there was nowhere Jewel could return to: because she hated what she had become, her whiteness was literally the curse of death. Jewel had little existence outside of being an access to wealth, the "white" heiress to be sought and won. Her usefulness as a foil ceased with the end of her desirability as a commodity of exchange for her father's fortune. Unlike Aurelia, who was granted a dramatic exit, determined in her own words, Jewel faded in an awkward authorial dispatch: death in Europe from some indeterminate "fever."

Hopkins's use of Old Testament stories and prophecies was not accompanied by an optimistic view of the beneficent influence of institutionalized religion. On the contrary, in *Winona*,[12] she inserted an explicit narrative intervention criticizing the failure of organized religions to temper the brutality of human behavior:

> If Christianity, Mohammedanism, or even Buddhism, did exercise the gentle and humanizing influence that is claimed for them, these horrors would cease now that actual slavery has been banished from our land;

because, as religion is the most universal and potent source of influence upon a nation's action, so it must mould to some extent its general characteristics and individual opinions. Until we can find a religion that will give the people individually and practically an impetus to humane and unselfish dealing with each other, look to see outward forms change, but never look to see the spirit which hates and persecutes that which it no longer dare enslave, changed by any other influence than a change of heart and spirit. The liberties of a people are not to be violated but with the wrath of God. Indeed, we tremble for our country when we reflect that God is just; that His justice cannot sleep forever; that considering natural means only, a revolution of the wheel of Fortune, an exchange of situation is among the possibilities. (5: 264)

The theme of revenge was pivotal to *Winona*, which contained Hopkins's first aggressively active black male hero, Judah, who was described as "a living statue of a mighty Vulcan" (5: 101). An orphaned son of an escaped slave, he grew up in "a mixed community of Anglo-Saxons, Indians and Negroes" (5: 29). Despite Judah's stoicism, which enabled him to bear his punishment as slave "without a murmur," each beating stimulated the desire for vengeance (5: 103). Hopkins created Judah as "the true expression of the innate nature of the Negro when given an opportunity equal with the white man" (5: 106), and she used him as a figure of mediation for her own reflections on structures of subordination:

But is there such a thing as social equality? There is such a thing as the affinity of souls, congenial spirits, and good fellowship; but social equality does not exist because it is an artificial barrier which nature is constantly putting at naught by the most incongruous happenings. Who is my social equal? He whose society affords the greatest pleasure, whose tastes are congenial, and who is my brother in the spirit of the scriptural text, be he white or black, bond or free, rich or poor. (5: 260–61)

Judah became a warrior who achieved his individual act of revenge while fighting with John Brown. His heroism was rewarded in the text by his removal from the United States to Britain, where he became an honored soldier and citizen.

The story of *Winona* used the historical landscape of slavery to represent the contemporary social order. Situated against the background of John Brown and the Free Soil movement in Kansas, the tale concentrated on organized and individual acts of resistance and self-defense against oppression. *Winona* was transparently a call for organized acts of resistance against contemporary persecution displaced to a fictional history. It was Hopkins's only long piece of fiction set entirely before the Civil War. But, in order to see the ultimate trajectory of her fiction, we need to consider the last serial Hopkins published in the *Colored American Magazine*, *Of One Blood. Or, the Hidden Self*.[13]

Of One Blood returned to a theme of Hopkins's first short story, "The Mystery within Us," published in the first issue of the magazine. The "mystery" involved spiritualistic phenomena and the power of magnetism, which enabled the protagonist to experience visions of and communion with the soul of another after the body had died. In *Of One Blood*, Hopkins placed these references to supernatural powers within an elaborate framework that drew on the thematic structure of her previous fiction, inheritance and heritage, and utilized popular convention in her most extensive revision of black history.

The male hero, Reuel Briggs, was a medical student at Harvard, an acclaimed scientific genius among his peers. His origin was a mystery, but he was assumed by his fellow students to be Italian or Japanese. Poor, intensely serious, and isolated, Reuel had one friend, Aubrey Livingston, a Southern aristocrat and hedonist. Early in the narrative, Hopkins contrasted their personalities and appearance and began to disturb her readers' expectations of conventions of archetypal hero figures. Reuel was an unlikely candidate for heroism, and his position as outsider was confirmed by his features. Aubrey appeared as a classical hero, "a tall man with the beautiful face of a Greek God," but his stature was immediately undermined by the authorial comment, "the sculpted features did not inspire confidence" (6: 32).

Reuel was an expert in "magnetism," and his reputation was secured when he publicly restored to life a Fisk Jubilee singer named Dianthe Lusk. His spiritual powers were aroused when he realized that the apparently dead singer was the actual embodiment of a woman of his dreams whom he believed he was destined to help. While Reuel honorably loved and planned to marry Dianthe, Aubrey, already engaged to another, experienced an uncontrollable

lust and sexual desire that was given the historical reverberations of
the power dynamic between a white plantation owner and his black
mistress. Surreptitiously, Aubrey used his knowledge of Reuel's
black heritage to ensure that all Reuel's applications for medical
positions were rejected while he persuaded him to accept the only
job he was offered which would take him out of the country. The
contradictory aspects of appearance, disguise, and secret motives
were an important aspect of the text as access to the knowledge of
hidden origins granted power. Dianthe assumed the disguise of a
white woman, "Felice Adams," and was accepted into Aubrey's
society, but the knowledge that she was black gave him the power to
blackmail her. Aubrey, who appeared as a devoted friend, was
revealed to be a mortal enemy. On the eve of his departure, Reuel
married Dianthe and placed her in the care and under the power of
his "friend." This first section of the tale established motivations for
later character actions but was very different from the second tale in
both structure and theme.

The journey of Reuel, as a doctor on an archeological expedition
to Africa, was the journey into Hopkins's vision of black history
and her challenge to the mythology of the superiority of European
civilization. In June 1902, five months before the publication of the
first installment of *Of One Blood*, Hopkins outlined, in an article
on Afro-American women educators, the basic premise of the serial:

> Rome got her civilization from Greece; Greece borrowed hers from
> Egypt, thence she derived her science and beautiful mythology. Civiliza-
> tion descended the Nile and spread over the delta, as it came down from
> Thebes. Thebes was built and settled by the Ethiopians. As we ascend
> the Nile we come to Meroe the queen city of Ethiopia and the cradle of
> learning into which all Africa poured its caravans. So we trace the light
> of civilization from Ethiopia to Egypt, to Greece, to Rome, and thence
> diffusing its radiance over the entire world.[14]

Reuel was transposed from Boston, "the modern Athens" (6: 425)
to the Athens of Africa.[15] Hopkins drew on her own classical
education and cited Herodotus as a source for her description of
Meroë, actually a Kushite city. Hopkins followed Herodotus in his
references to Kushite civilization as Ethiopian.[16]

The character of a historian of ancient civilizations and leader of the expedition was the authenticating device to establish for the reader that Meroë was the original source of civilization and "the primal existence of the Negro as the most ancient source" of all that is valued in modern life, "even antedating Egypt." The question and the challenge of Hopkins's fiction was how "the Anglo-Saxon world [could] bear the establishment of such a theory" (6: 270). Hopkins melded her classical referent with biblical sources and integrated them both into the magical elements of popular fiction to mellow the highly abstract nature of much of her prose.

A series of magical signs was the mechanism for the revelation of disguise. The expedition was led to Meroë by a parchment which acted both as a map and as a series of prophetic warnings. Letters to Reuel from Dianthe were withheld by a member of the team in the pay of Aubrey Livingston, but their contents were revealed to him in a vision. Two false signs of the death of his wife caused Reuel to despair and risk his life in an attempt to discover the secret passageways into Meroë. Hopkins developed in *Of One Blood* a unique variation on the Afro-American convention of the search for and discovery of family. Entering through a pyramid, Reuel found not death but a rebirth as the direct descendant of a line of African kings and fulfilled an ancient legend which prophesied the return to Meroë of a king who would "restore the former glory of the race" (6: 343). Unconscious, Reuel was carried by the descendants of the city of Meroë to their hidden city of Telassar, a utopian echo of the city of Eden after which it was named. Protected from discovery by mountains and swamps, the remnant of an ancient civilization awaited the arrival of Reuel. The high priest, Ai, whose office had directly passed from father to son for more than six thousand years, initiated Reuel into the mysteries of not only his family heritage but also the heritage of all blacks in the diaspora.

Hopkins's descriptions of the fantastic Telassar re-created the mythology of an ancient civilization more advanced in knowledge, science, and art than the world outside. Certain members of its ruling council traveled outside the city, and Hopkins used their "experiences" to construct a dialogue about the "uncivilized" aspects of contemporary American society, epitomized by its treatment of blacks. That contemporary black Americans were Ethiopians was not only asserted within the text of *Of One Blood* but also reinforced externally by a series of documentary articles that ran concurrently with the fiction: "Ethiopians of the Twentieth Century" by A. Kirkland Soga.

Reuel was the mediator of the meaning of the historic link to Ethiopia for Afro-American readers. Revelation occurred in stages. The first was through a magical sign: the lotus birthmark on the breast of all the descendants of the royal family. The second was the identity with Pan-Africanism: the peoples of Telassar represented the spectrum of African nations. The establishment of Ethiopia as the source of all civilization at whose feet "the mightiest nations have worshipped, paying homage to our kings," seeking "the honor of alliance with our royal families because of our strength, grandeur, riches and wisdom" (6: 431), allowed Hopkins to eliminate from her fiction any significance attached to an Anglo-Saxon heritage on which so many of her stories depend for their denouements. In *Contending Forces*, it was a source of pride to the Smith family that they were related to British ancestors. In *Of One Blood*, the discovery of Reuel's heritage was the discovery of Pan-Africanism. To also establish a pride in this heritage required a reassessment of Reuel's previous denial of being African.

In the *Colored American Magazine* of December 1902, the same issue that ran the second installment of *Of One Blood*, Hopkins published a short story, "The Test of Manhood," in which she directly confronted the consequences of "passing" for the first time in her fiction. There was a clear distinction in Hopkins's writing between "passing" as a social practice and her conventional use of disguise. "Passing" involved the conscious decision to use a white appearance to hide a black heritage for social advancement; disguise was used by the author as a narrative mechanism, not a narrative subject. In "The Test of Manhood," the protagonist purposefully and deliberately determined to "become" white, and this formed the subject of the entire narrative. His material success, including the acquisition of a white woman as his betrothed, was dependent on the denial of a black mother; the climax and the title of the story derive from a willingness to renounce the rewards that white society has bestowed on him, including its prize, a white wife.[17] In *Of One Blood*, Reuel was confronted by Ai to explain his isolation from his race, and Hopkins used this moment to condemn the denial of an African heritage: "Reuel bowed his head in assent, while over his face passed a flush of shame. He felt keenly now the fact that he had played a coward's part in hiding his origin. What though obstacles were many, some way would have been shown him to surmount the difficulties of caste prejudice" (6: 430–31).

Concomitant with Hopkins's desire to advocate an identification with an African heritage was the need to confront Western ideologies of beauty. In the initial pages of the tale, Hopkins undermined Aubrey Livingston's heroic appearance but delayed defining standards of a black beauty until the Telassar sequence. As "King Ergamenes," Reuel was pledged to marry the descendant of the line of queens, Candace, who appeared as a reincarnation of Dianthe but was "bronze," not white. Their union was intended to "give to the world a dynasty of dark-skinned rulers, whose destiny should restore the prestige of an ancient people" (6: 496), but Hopkins extended her concept of black beauty beyond her hero and heroine. Later in the tale, Ai contradicted the logic of American racism by asking a rhetorical question which also defined Hopkins's choice of title:

> And yet, ye are all of one blood; descended from one common father. Is there ever a flock or herd without its black member? What more beautiful than the satin gloss of the raven's wing, the soft glitter of eyes of blackest tint or the rich black fur of your own native animals? Fair-haired worshippers of Mammon, do you not know that you have been weighed in the balance and found wanting? that your course is done? that Ethoapia's [sic] bondage is about over, her travail passed? (6: 581–82)

The idealization of black beauty within the text was classic in its pretensions rather than African. Hopkins selected black skin, eyes, brows, and "crisp" black hair for particular praise, but profiles and bone structure remained Athenian. This attempt to reconstruct a classic form of black beauty within her fiction was externally authenticated by an anonymous article, which could have been written by Hopkins herself, in the May/June 1903 issue of the magazine. "Venus and the Apollo Modelled from Ethiopians" asserted scientific proof that "the most famous examples of classic beauty in sculpture . . . were chiselled from Ethiopian slave models."[18] The network of these relations between *Of One Blood* and other, nonfic-

tional, articles in the *Colored American Magazine* indicated the
extent of an intertextual coherence, achieved under Hopkins's literary editorship, which aimed at the reconstruction of a sense of pride
in an African heritage.[19]

Using the advanced but ancient technology of Telassar, Hopkins
shifted the focus of her story from Meroë civilization back to the
United States. Reuel and Ai consulted a disk capable of revealing
the past and the present in which Reuel saw that his wife, Dianthe,
was alive and married to Aubrey. A series of revelations about
Reuel's family history confirmed the immediate meaning of the
title, *Of One Blood*, and linked it to a more abstract concept of the
family of man. From the dying lips of Jim Titus, the man Aubrey
intended should kill Reuel, Reuel learned that Dianthe was actually
his sister and Aubrey his half-brother. Reuel cursed his relation to
the Anglo-Saxon race and swore revenge. Reuel was motivated not
by personal satisfaction but in defense of all women of the race.
Dianthe became the mediating figure for Reuel's first action of
identification with all black people and, as sister, was the means for
Reuel to identify with all Afro-American women as his "sisters": "in
Reuel's wrongs lay something beyond the reach of punishment by
the law's arm; in it was the accumulation of years of foulest wrongs
heaped upon the innocent and defenceless women of a race"
(6: 643).

Dianthe, meanwhile, had found her grandmother in a cabin on
Aubrey's plantation. Famous as a "voodoo" practitioner, Hannah
was also described as looking like an African princess. Hannah told
Dianthe the family history, which revealed that Reuel and Dianthe's second husband, Aubrey, were her brothers. In order to
accomplish this second revelation, Hopkins used the popular fiction convention of the switching of babies at birth. Hannah's extraordinary history was confirmed through signs; each member of
the family bore a lotus birthmark on his or her breast. The havoc
wrought to social relations by the institution of slavery was represented at its most extreme in *Of One Blood*, which offered no
possibility of the fictional restoration of a social and moral order
within the United States. The double nature of this incestuous
relationship between two brothers and their sister was Hopkins's
vision of a hell in which "The laws of changeless justice [bound]
Oppressor and oppressed" in the most literal way possible.

Interrupting the narrative, Hopkins directed the attention of her reader to the interdependence among the family, the nation, and all of humanity and to make clear her didactic intent:

> The slogan of the hour is "Keep the Negro down!" but who is clear enough in vision to decide who hath black blood and who hath it not? Can any one tell? No, not one; for in His own Mysterious way He has united the white race and the black race in this new continent. By the transgression of the law He proves His own infallibility: "Of one blood have I made all nations of men to dwell upon the whole face of the earth," is as true to-day as when given to the inspired writers to be recorded. No man can draw the dividing line between the two races, for they are both of one blood! (6: 729)

In order to satisfactorily end an incestuous relationship, Aubrey and Dianthe die in picturesque fashion. Aubrey forced Dianthe to drink the poison she intended for him, and in the tradition of the kings of Ethiopia, Aubrey became his own executioner. Reuel returned to rule Telassar with Queen Candace and to worry about the consequences of the latest phase of European imperialist penetration into the African continent. He viewed, "with serious apprehension, the advance of Mighty nations penetrating the dark, mysterious forces of his native land. 'Where will it stop?' he sadly questions. 'What will the end be?'" (6: 807).

This question was Hopkins's own. Writing at a time when she was convinced that the Negro was threatened with annihilation, Hopkins argued that the "voice of history is the voice of God."[20] The history that Hopkins wanted to rewrite and reclaim was a history that could challenge theories of black inferiority. It was evident that Hopkins was an idealist; she believed that a transformation of racist ideas, attitudes, and ideologies were the prerequisite of a subsequent transformation in the social relations between blacks and whites. Her political perspective was Pan-African; she addressed herself to "all Negroes, whether Frenchmen, Spaniards, Americans or Africans," to rediscover their history as one weapon in the struggle against oppression.[21]

Perhaps the most apt word to describe Hopkins's writing is *testimony*. Biographical and political essays, short stories, novels, and serials, all testified to an aspect of black presence in history.

She challenged her audience to bear witness to her testimony that
all black peoples faced an international crisis:

> The dawn of the Twentieth century finds the Black race fighting for
> existence in every quarter of the globe. From over the sea Africa
> stretches her hands to the American Negro and cries aloud for sym-
> pathy in her hour of trial. England, at this late day, begins to doubt the
> wisdom of her course in acknowledging the equality of the Negro race.
> In America, caste prejudice has received fresh impetus as the "Southern
> brother" of the Anglo-Saxon family has arisen from the ashes of seces-
> sion, and like the prodigal of old, has been gorged with fatted calf and
> "fixin's."[22]

Within the context of the *Colored American Magazine*, Hopkins
utilized her various capacities as journalist, editor, and author of
fiction to validate black figures in history. The political trajectory
of the history that she re-created and re-presented developed from
an assertion of the presence of Afro-Americans within an Anglo-
Saxon context, in *Contending Forces*, toward the classical reinter-
pretation of their own heritage in Africa.

The establishment of an African genealogy was the climax to
Hopkins's consistent concern with questions of inheritance and
heritage. Her definition of history was "an account of the deeds of
men who have been the models and patterns for the great mass of
humanity in past centuries even from the beginning of the world."
Hopkins hoped that her writing could be such a model, a pattern to
inspire political resistance and agitation against the threat of annihilation. Hopkins called for "a wild courage" and a "stoicism of the
blood"; she was a black intellectual who considered her writing as
part of, not separate from, the politics of oppression. "As a race,"
she stated, "we need the stimulus of books and tales of this 'cathartic virtue' more than any other literature we can mention."[23] For
Pauline Elizabeth Hopkins, her fiction was a cathartic response to
the pessimistic vision of the limited possibilities of black existence
on the western shores of the Atlantic.

8

The Quicksands of Representation

Rethinking Black Cultural Politics

The term *renaissance* in Afro-American cultural history has been almost exclusively applied to the literary and artistic production of intellectuals in Harlem in the years between the end of World War I and the depression.[1] But definitions of the Harlem renaissance are notoriously elusive; descriptions of it as a moment of intense literary and artistic production, or as an intellectual awakening, or as the period of the self-proclaimed "New Negro" are concepts that are not applicable only to Harlem or to the twenties.[2] This particular cultural moment has come to dominate Afro-American cultural history and overshadow earlier attempts of black intellectuals to assert their collective presence. However, the more assertive we try to be as cultural critics and cultural historians about what the Harlem renaissance was, what it was not, and when it occurred, the less sure we become about what made this moment of Afro-American cultural history unique. The staff of the *Colored American Magazine* considered their journal to be a tool in the creation of a black renaissance, an inspiration for "Theologians, Artists [and] Scientists" whose theories had grown dormant for lack of a channel of communication,[3] but no comparative cultural study has been undertaken to reveal the relationship between the intellectual activity of Boston at the turn of the century and Harlem in the twenties. Indeed, the Harlem renaissance is frequently conceived as a unique, intellectually cohesive and homogeneous historical moment, a mythology which has disguised the contradictory impulses of the Harlem intellectuals. I do not intend to argue the case that the Harlem

163

renaissance is purely an invention of the literary and cultural historian, although to a large extent this is the case; rather, I want to indicate the shift in concerns of the intellectuals of the twenties as opposed to the previous two decades by stressing the discontinuities and contradictions surrounding issues of representation.

I use the word *representation* in two distinct but related ways: as it is formally understood in relation to art and creative practices, and as it applies to intellectuals who understand themselves to be responsible for the representation of "the race," defining and constructing in their art its representative members and situating themselves as representative members of an oppressed social group. The relation of the black intellectual elite to the majority of black people changed drastically as a result of the migration north of Southern blacks. Before World War I, the overwhelming majority of blacks were in the South, at a vast physical and metaphorical distance from those intellectuals who represented the interests of the race. After the war, black intellectuals had to confront the black masses on the streets of their cities and responded in a variety of ways.

At the turn of the century in Boston, Pauline Hopkins and the staff of the *Colored American Magazine* assumed that their relation to the majority of black people was entirely unproblematic and unmediated. The *Colored American Magazine* unashamedly asserted that it could speak for and represent the unique historical experience of "the black people" and addressed them in these all-encompassing terms. These intellectuals did not doubt or question their position of leadership as members of the "Talented Tenth" speaking from the North to the majority of blacks who lived outside it. But after World War I, the large-scale movement of black people into the cities of the North meant that intellectual leadership and its constituencies fragmented. No longer was it possible to mobilize an undifferentiated address to "the black people" once an urban black working class was established.

This movement of masses of rural black Southern workers destined to become an urban proletariat was not immediately represented in fiction, but there was a distinct shift in who was represented as "the people." One possibility, in fiction, was that "the people" were represented as a metaphorical "folk," which in its rural connotations avoided and ignored the implication of the presence of black city workers. Zora Neale Hurston, for example, who felt concerned that whites just did not know who blacks were, chose to reconstruct figures of "the folk" in her novels. Most literary criticism acknowledges this representation of the folk as "the people" but does not question the historical significance of Hurston's choice. On the contrary, the representation of "the folk" is usually regarded as an ahistorical literary convention that is a natural expression of the Afro-American experience.[4] But we need to recognize that the "folk" was neither an inevitable nor a natural selection. Many intellectuals, including Jessie Fauset, registered the gap between the immediate and disconcerting presence of the black masses and being a member of a black elite by representing this difference in class terms.

The concept of the "New Negro" of the Harlem renaissance has become a conventional way of referring to these literary and artistic intellectuals, but this limited contemporary application of the term has emptied it of the radical working-class meaning that was established by the group of intellectuals, leaders, organizations, and journals which were devoted to "economic radicalism." For radical intellectuals like Asa Philip Randolph and Chandler Owen, editors of the *Messenger*, the "New Negro" was "the product of the same world-wide forces that have brought into being the great liberal and radical movements that are now seizing the reins of political, economic and social power in all the civilized countries of the world."[5] The editorial continued to assert that the "'New' Negro 'unlike the old Negro' was not to be 'lulled into a false sense of security with political spoils and patronage.'"[6]

This issue of patronage provides another point of contrast between the literary intellectuals of the twenties and their predecessors in Boston. The young black artists in the Harlem of the twenties were acutely aware of a high degree of reliance on the patronage of white individuals and organizations.[7] But the staff of the *Colored American Magazine*, like the economic radicals of the twenties, made specific attempts to avoid such a situation of dependency. As they stated after the first year in print, "there has been no attempt to seek the aid of philanthropists, although we feel that there have been many less deserving projects which have been lavishly supported in that way."[8] The issue of the acceptability of patronage and its role in defining and limiting what could be represented was of intense concern to the intellectuals of both

cultural moments. But what differentiated most clearly the crisis of
representation of the twenties from the intellectual assurance of the
turn of the century was the relation of the intellectual to "the
people."

In 1900, Pauline Hopkins and the staff of the *Colored American
Magazine* assumed a hegemonic position as representatives of black
people, calling themselves "the mouth-piece and inspiration of the
Negro race throughout not only this country, but the world."[9] After
World War I and the migration, the role of intellectuals became
problematic in two ways: there was no longer a unitary "people"
who could be represented, and the variety of intellectual practice—
literary, political, and cultural—became increasingly separated.
The Colored Co-operative Publishing Company was a collective
attempt to hold together the practices of literature, art, and political agitation for social change. But, by the twenties, black writers
sought artistic autonomy for their cultural practices and products
and separated themselves from the task of writing for the uplifting
of the race as a whole. From the point of view of the urban black
worker in the twenties, he or she could look toward a range of other
representatives which included black union organizations, economic radicals, or Marcus Garvey and the Universal Negro Improvement Association.

Within this increasingly fragmented discourse of "the people"
and intellectual leadership, I want to situate an analysis of Nella
Larsen's *Quicksand*, published in 1928.[10] Traditional Afro-American literary and cultural criticism has failed to adequately consider
the significance of the work of Larsen and Jessie Fauset.[11] Both
writers have at times been dismissed as minor figures, mere background to a major event, the Harlem renaissance. In contrast, Zora
Neale Hurston has been seen as a distinct literary figure.[12] Hurston,
as I have indicated, epitomized the intellectual who represented
"the people" through a reconstruction of "the folk" and avoided the
class confrontation of the Northern cities. Fauset and Larsen, however, wrote more directly out of this urban confrontation, though
each developed strategies of fictional representation that indicated
their very different responses to their class, racial, and sexual position as black female intellectuals.

Fauset responded to an emerging black urban working class by a
mediation of her authorial position as a class perspective. She

represented in her fiction a middle-class code of morality and behavior that structured the existence of her characters and worked as a code of appropriate social behavior for her readers.[13] Fauset's intellectual contribution was the development of an ideology for an emerging black middle class which would establish it as being acceptably urbane and civilized and which would distinguish it from the rural influx.[14] Unlike earlier women novelists, Fauset did not consider the aftermath of slavery and the failure of Reconstruction as a sufficient source of echoes and foreshadowings for her representation of the emergent black middle class who needed a new relation to history. Fauset represented this new history through a generational difference, a difference figured as a recognition of the need for the protagonists to revise the irrelevant history of their parents, a history tied to the consequences of slavery.

Deborah McDowell, in her introduction to the new edition of Fauset's *Plum Bun*, pleads for a sympathetic consideration for the progressive aspects of Fauset's novels, especially in relation to her implicit critique of the structures of women's romance.[15] However, I would argue that ultimately the conservatism of Fauset's ideology dominates her texts. In *The Chinaberry Tree*, for example, which focused on two women, the movement of the text is away from the figures of isolated unmarried mothers and daughters supporting themselves through their own labor, toward the articulation of a new morality and community in which black women were lifted from the abyss of scandal and gossip, which threatened to overwhelm them, by professional black men who reinserted them into a newly formed and respectable community as dependent wives. The individual and collective pasts of the female characters led them to flounder in the waters of misdirected desires; their history was anarchic and self-destructive. The future, within which the women could survive, was secured when they were grounded, protected, and wrapped around by decent men. In order to represent a new, emergent social group, Fauset by necessity had to sever ties with the past; the characteristics of the new class were those of individual success and triumph over ties to and previous interpretations of history. To signal the depth of this new fictional strategy, consider Pauline Hopkins's use of history to raise questions of inheritance and heritage that were crucial to her political perception. Who Hopkins's characters were and what they were to become was to be understood in relation to their ancestors. The quality of these ancestors and the nature of their past actions had specific ramifications for the present: the consequences of history were Hopkins's fictional future. In stark contrast, in *The Chinaberry Tree*, Fauset constructed a chaotic and irrelevant history to which the heroes, not the heroines, brought a new order and meaning. The new middle class both emerged from and changed previous history and its interpretations; the forces of previous history alone could not provide a basis for its future. Fauset adapted but did not transcend the form of the romance. It is important that her work did reveal many of the contradictory aspects of romantic conventions of womanhood, but her imaginary resolutions to what were social contradictions confirmed that women ultimately had to be saved from the consequences of their independence and become wives.

In stark contrast, Nella Larsen in *Quicksand* refused the resolutions offered by this developing code of black middle-class morality at the same time as she launched a severe critique against the earlier but still influential ideology of racial uplift. The *Quicksand* of 1928 did not just explore the contradictory terrain of women and romance; its sexual politics tore apart the very fabric of the romance form.

At the beginning of the novel, Helga Crane, the protagonist, was a teacher at Naxos, a black school in the South which appeared to be a combination of Atlanta, Fisk, and Tuskegee. Dissatisfied with what she saw to be a process of repression, the stunting of intellectual growth and creativity, Helga resigned her job in a stormy interview with the new president, a Dr. Anderson. She returned to Chicago, where she had grown up, but was unable to find a job and eventually traveled to Harlem as secretary to a famous "spokeswoman for the race." In Harlem, she lived with a woman called Anne Grey, worked in a black insurance company, and was an observor of the renaissance. Helga was disdainful of the ideology of racial uplift, critical of Anne's continual preoccupation with the problems of the race, and disparaging of the hypocrisy of the emerging black middle class. This class, she felt, condemned white racism while imitating white middle-class behavior and adopting their values and moral codes. Feeling that she was again being stifled, Helga determined to leave Harlem and used a legacy from a white uncle to visit her Danish aunt in Copenhagen. Helga lived in

Europe for two years, where the appreciation she had so desired was lavished on her. However, though pampered, Helga realized that she was being treated like an exotic object, admired only as a representative of the primitive and sensual. Experiencing a desperate need to be again among black people, she sailed to Harlem for the wedding of Anne and Dr. Anderson, intending to make only a temporary visit but staying long after the wedding. Helga recognized a long-repressed sexual attraction for Anderson, and in response to his encouragement determined to finally acknowledge her sexuality and sleep with him. Anderson's awkward rebuff shattered Helga's new acceptance of her sexual self, and when she accidentally met a hedonistic Southern preacher in a storefront church, she slept with him. She returned to the South as the wife of Rev. Mr. Pleasant Green, blind to all except the sensual aspect of their relationship. Helga planned to uplift the women and instruct the children of this community of Southern folk, but instead repeated childbirth degraded and oppressed her. She nearly died giving birth to her fourth child, and the novel ends with her fifth pregnancy which means her certain death.

In *Quicksand*, Larsen embodied the major aspects of what I have referred to as the crisis of representation of the period. She was unable to romanticize "the people" as the folk or to accept the world view of the new black middle class. Helga explored the contradictions of her racial, sexual, and class position by being both inside and outside these perspectives. Larsen was able to represent such duality by making her protagonist an alienated heroine. She was, at various points in the text, alienated from her sex, her race, and her class. Alienation is often represented as a state of consciousness, a frame of mind. Implied in this definition is the assumption that alienation can be eliminated or replaced by another state of consciousness, a purely individual transformation unrelated to necessary social or historical change. Helga does question the possibility that her recurrent dissatisfaction with her life could be due to her state of mind and that if she could change her attitudes she could be happy. But against this Larsen placed an alternative reading of Helga's progress, that her alienation was not just in her head but was produced by existing forms of social relations and therefore subject to elimination only by a change in those social relations. That Larsen incorporated this alternative definition of alienation in her text has political significance, for the representation of alienation as a state of mind reduces history to an act of thought and leads to a political conservatism. If people cannot change their conditions, only how they feel about them, they can only legitimize and approve the status quo, and social criticism becomes irrelevant.

Larsen in *Quicksand*, however, represented the full complexity of the modern alienated individual. *Quicksand* is the first text by a black woman to be a conscious narrative of a woman embedded within capitalist social relations. In the opening pages, Helga was represented as an isolated figure but a consumer, a character initially defined through the objects that surround her. Though Helga was a teacher and Larsen described a school, she utilized the language of the factory and the ideology of Taylorism in her creation of Naxos. Alienated from her work, she experienced no emotional or intellectual sustenance from her teaching. Like a small, insignificant part in a big machine, Helga made no difference and felt that an essential part of her and the students' humanity was denied in favor of the production of uniformity:

> [Naxos] had grown into a machine. It was now a show place in the black belt, exemplification of the white man's magnanimity, refutation of the black man's inefficiency. Life had died out of it. It was . . . only a big knife . . . cutting all to a pattern, the white man's pattern. Teachers as well as students were subjected to the paring process, for it tolerated no innovations, no individualisms. (9)

Students were described as products, automatons who goosestepped in massed phalanxes (28). Consciously created as subject to an industrial time and discipline, the dullness of the outward appearance of everyone at Naxos was represented as being symbolic of the acceptance of their oppressed social condition. Within this order, Helga was an expression of powerlessness, the alienated individual who could not change her social condition and felt only a sense of individual failure.

The critique of Naxos as a black college was a critique of the policy of racial uplift and of black intellectual leadership. As a product of Fisk herself, Larsen was directing a bitter attack toward black educators as race representatives. She detached her protagonist from their narrow-minded adherence to the dictates of white Southern expectations of Negro passivity and separated her from their class perspective. Helga had neither a community nor a network of black kinship. She had no black family and thus lacked the connections which Larsen condemned for being so important to black middle-class society, a society that Larsen represented as being as exclusive as its white counterpart. This critique of the black middle class was continued in the section of the novel set in Harlem. In direct contrast to Fauset, Larsen did not feel that the middle class were the guardians of civilized behavior and moral values. Harlem intellectuals were criticized for two major acts of hypocrisy: their announced hatred of white people and deprecation of any contact with white society while imitating their clothes, manners, and ways of life, and the proclamation of the undiluted good of all things Negro which disguised a disdain, contempt, and amusement for the actual culture and behavior of the majority of black people. Larsen used Helga, who was both black intellectual and member of the middle class but stood outside both, as a figure who could question the limits of middle-class intellectual pretension.

Larsen augmented this questioning of the representative nature of a black elite and accentuated Helga's social displacement by her particular use of the figure of the mulatto. The mulatto, as I have already described, is most usefully regarded as a convention of Afro-American literature which enabled the exploration in fiction of relations which were socially proscribed.[16] The mulatto figure is a narrative device of mediation; it allows for a fictional exploration of the relationship between the races while being at the same time an imaginary expression of the relationship between the races. One mode of representing this social tension is the "passing" novel, in which the protagonist pretends to be white, exemplified by Fauset's *Plum Bun* and Larsen's second novel, *Passing*.[17] But in *Quicksand* this option was refused. Larsen's particular use of the mulatto figure allowed her protagonist to be both inside and outside contemporary race issues. Helga was simultaneously critical of what she regarded as an all-pervasive concern with race problems and subject to racism. The section of the novel set in Copenhagen confronted directly the question of the representation of blacks by whites. Helga's portrait was painted by a leading Danish artist, who created an animalistic, sensuous creature on his canvas. Larsen displaced to Europe an issue of central concern to the intellectuals of the Harlem renaissance: white fascination with the "exotic" and the "primitive." Outside the black community, Helga became a mere object for white consumption.

Social relations which objectified the body permeate the text. Helga herself was represented as a consumer, a woman who defined a self through the acquisition of commercial products, consumer goods, and commodities. As a woman, she is at the center of a complex process of exchange. Money was crucial to Larsen's narrative, structuring power relations, controlling social movement, and defining the boundaries of Helga's environment. Money replaces kinship as the prime mediator of social relations: Helga's white uncle sent her money as he could not afford to acknowledge her relationship to him. This money allowed her social movement; she bought her way out of a Jim Crow car and eventually out of Harlem. In Chicago, Helga spent money, buying and consuming rather than facing her desperate conditions. While the possession of money disguised her real social predicament, the lack of money forced degradation and the recognition that in the job market her social position as a black woman was narrowly defined as domestic worker.

Although money permitted Helga's movement within the text, the direction of her journey reproduces the tensions of migration into a structure of oppositions between country and city. Helga's first movement in the text is from South to North, from the rural outskirts of Atlanta to industrial Chicago. Immediately upon arrival in Chicago, Helga became one of a crowd. Her initial identification was with the anonymity of the city, where she had the appearance of freedom but no actual home or friends. This anonymity brought brief satisfaction and contentment, while Helga could maintain her position as consumer, but she discovered her vulnerability as an object of exchange when her money ran out. Larsen represented the city as a conglomeration of strangers, where social relations were structured through the consumption of both objects and people. The imagery of commerce and this process of exchange dominated the text as it moved to New York and Copenhagen. This polarity between rural and urban experience frames the text; in the closing pages, all cities are finally abandoned and Helga is metaphorically and, the reader is led to assume, literally buried in the rural South.

Helga was a consumer, but as a woman she was also potentially a consumable object. Larsen's representation of sexual politics delineated the dilemma of the woman's body as a commercialized object. Helga's sexuality was not only objectified in relation to art, but when she failed to get a job as a maid in Chicago she had offers of money for sexual services. Helga, as an unmarried woman, was brought to a recognition of her exchange value which denied her humanity while cementing her fragile dependence on money. Larsen represented the ideologies of consumerism, of capitalism, and of sexuality as being intimately connected, and in the process of this critique she revealed the inability of the structure of the romance to adequately express the experience of women while she also posed a challenge to the readers' expectations of the form of the novel.

Larsen stressed the contradictory nature of the search for a female self by refusing the romance and structuring the relation of the individual to the social formation through the interconnection of sexual, racial, and class identity. The conclusion of the text offered no imaginary resolutions to the contradictions Larsen raised. As readers, we are left meditating on the problematic nature of alternative possibilities of a social self. Consider the metaphor of quicksand; it is a condition where individual struggle and isolated effort are doomed to failure. Helga's search led to the burial, not the discovery, of the self. The only way out of quicksand is with external help; isolated individual struggle ensured only that she would sink deeper into the quagmire. The question that remains is, to what social group does Helga attach herself in order to be saved? Unlike Fauset, whom I have described as an ideologue for an emergent middle class, Larsen found it impossible to portray the experience of the black middle class as representative of the race. The black bourgeoisie was attacked on many levels: for its hypocrisy, for its articulation of the race "problem," and for its moral and aesthetic code.

But Larsen did not consider the crisis of representation facing Harlem intellectuals only in terms of class. Her particular use of the figure of the mulatto allowed Larsen to negotiate issues of race as they were articulated by both white and black. However, Larsen's representation of both race and class are structured through a prism of black female sexuality. Larsen recognized that the repression of the sensual in Afro-American fiction in response to the long history of the exploitation of black sexuality led to the repression of passion and the repression or denial of female sexuality and desire. But, of course, the representation of black female sexuality meant risking its definition as primitive and exotic within a racist society. Larsen attempted to embody but could not hope to resolve these contradictions in her representation of Helga as a sexual being, making Helga the first truly sexual black female protagonist in Afro-American fiction. Racist sexual ideologies proclaimed the black woman to be a rampant sexual being, and in response black women writers either focused on defending their morality or displaced sexuality onto another terrain. Larsen confronted this denial directly in her fiction. Helga consistently attempted to deny her sensuality and repress her sexual desires, and the result is tragedy. Each of the crises of the text centered on sexual desire until the conclusion of the novel, where control over her body was denied Helga and her sexuality was reduced to its biological capacity to bear children. Helga's four children represented her entrapment as she was unable to desert them; her fifth child represented her certain death.

Larsen offered her readers few avenues of resolution. Liberation through money that allowed Helga to explore Europe—the "Old World," white "civilization"—as an alternative to the United States was rejected as a viable alternative. The figure of the mulatto allowed Larsen's protagonist to ask why her future should be yoked to a despised social group, but living in a white world was no alternative. Readers are left with the unresolvable. Harlem was simultaneously represented as a black city which appeared to allow for the unfettered possibilities of black cultural expression and as a cage or ghetto. The novel closes with a representation of "the folk," but they were not represented as a positive alternative to the black urban elite. The rural community was bound together through its allegiance to the black preacher, Helga's husband, who appeared as an Old Testament patriarch. Unlike Hurston's folk, who were represented as embodying in their culture and language the unique "truth" of the Afro-American experience, Larsen's representation of the folk was as the deluded. Their religion, the core of their existence, was the great illusion which robbed them of the crudest truths. In a passage of bitter denunciation, Helga concluded that religion

> ailed the whole Negro race in America, this fatuous belief in the white man's God, this childlike trust in full compensation for all woes and privations in "kingdom come." . . . [It] bound them to slavery, then to poverty and insult, and made them bear it unresistingly, uncomplainingly almost, by sweet promises of mansions in the sky by and by. (297)

In the country, among the folk, Helga felt only suffocation and a great loathing. It was the moment of her greatest oppression and degradation. Chained to her children, she was engulfed by the quicksand while she dreamed of "freedom and cities."

It is important that Larsen returned her readership to the urban landscape and refused a romantic evocation of the folk, for in this movement she stands as a precursor not only to Richard Wright and Ralph Ellison but to a neglected strand of Afro-American women's fiction. In the search for a tradition of black women writers of fiction, a pattern has been established from Alice Walker back through Zora Neale Hurston which represents the rural folk as bearers of Afro-American history and preservers of Afro-American culture. This construction of a tradition of black women writing has effectively marginalized the fictional urban confrontation of race, class, and sexuality that was to follow *Quicksand*: Ann Petry's *The Street* (1946); Dorothy West's *The Living Is Easy* (1948); Gwendolyn Brooks's *Maud Martha* (1951); and the work of Toni Morrison.[18] Afro-American cultural and literary history should not create and glorify a limited vision, a vision which in its romantic evocation of the rural and the folk avoids some of the most crucial and urgent issues of cultural struggle—a struggle that Larsen, Petry, West, Brooks, and Morrison recognized would have to be faced in the cities, the home of the black working class.

Notes

Chapter 1

1. Frances Harper, "Woman's Political Future," in May Wright Sewell, ed., *World's Congress of Representative Women* (Chicago: Rand McNally, 1894), pp. 433–37.

2. Fannie Barrier Williams, "The Intellectual Progress of the Colored Women of the United States since the Emancipation Proclamation," in Sewell, *World's Congress*, pp. 696–711.

3. Anna Julia Cooper, "The Intellectual Progress of the Colored Women of the United States since the Emancipation Proclamation," in Sewell, *World's Congress*, pp. 711–15.

4. Fannie Jackson Coppin, and Sarah J. Early and Hallie Quinn Brown, "The Organized Efforts of the Colored Women of the South to Improve Their Condition," in Sewell, *World's Congress*, pp. 715–17, 718–29.

5. Ida B. Wells, ed., *The Reason Why: The Colored American Is Not in the World's Columbian Exposition* (Chicago: by the author, 1893).

6. Report of Mrs. Potter Palmer, President, to the Board of Lady Managers, September 2, 1891 (Chicago), cited in Ann Massa, "Black Women in the 'White City,'" *Journal of American Studies* 8 (December 1974): 320.

7. Ibid., p. 329.

8. Robert W. Rydell, "The World's Columbian Exposition of 1893: Racist Underpinnings of a Utopian Artifact," *Journal of American Culture* 1 (Summer 1978): 253–75.

9. David F. Burg, *Chicago's White City of 1893* (Lexington: University of Kentucky Press, 1976), p. 75.

10. Alan Trachtenberg, *The Incorporation of America: Culture and Society in the Gilded Age* (New York: Hill and Wang, 1982), p. 209.

11. F. L. Barnett, "The Reason Why," in Wells, *The Reason Why*, p. 79; Elliot M. Rudwick and August Meier, "Black Man in the 'White

City': Negroes and the Columbian Exposition, 1893," *Phylon* 26 (Winter 1965): 361.

12. Rudwick and Meier, "Black Man in the 'White City,'" p. 354; Frederick Douglass, "Introduction," in Wells, *The Reason Why*, p. 4.

13. W. E. B. Du Bois, *The Souls of Black Folk* (1903; reprint New York: Fawcett World Library, 1961), p. 23.

14. Hazel V. Carby, "White Woman Listen: Black Feminism and the Boundaries of Sisterhood," in Centre for Contemporary Cultural Studies, *The Empire Strikes Back: Race and Racism in Seventies Britain* (London: Hutchinson, 1982), pp. 212–35.

15. Barbara Smith, "Toward a Black Feminist Criticism," *Conditions: Two* 1 (October 1977), reprinted in Elaine Showalter, ed., *The New Feminist Criticism: Essays on Women, Literature, and Theory* (New York: Pantheon, 1985), pp. 168–85. References are to this edition; page numbers will be given parenthetically in the text.

16. Mary Helen Washington, ed., *Black-Eyed Susans* (New York: Anchor Press, 1975). The first contemporary anthology of black women's writings, fiction and nonfiction, was Toni Cade, ed., *The Black Woman* (New York: New American Library, 1970).

17. See also Mary Helen Washington, "Teaching Black-Eyed Susans: An Approach to the Study of Black Women Writers," in Gloria T. Hull, Patricia Bell Scott, and Barbara Smith, eds., *All the Women Are White, All the Blacks Are Men, But Some of Us Are Brave* (Old Westbury, N.Y.: Feminist Press, 1982), pp. 208–17.

18. Alice Walker, "One Child of One's Own: A Meaningful Digression within the Work(s)," *In Search of Our Mothers' Gardens* (New York: Harcourt Brace Jovanovitch, 1983), pp. 361–83.

19. Ibid., p. 372.

20. See also the introduction to Barbara Smith, ed., *Home Girls: A Black Feminist Anthology* (New York: Kitchen Table, Women of Color Press, 1983).

21. Hull et al., "The Politics of Black Women's Studies," in *But Some of Us Are Brave*, p. xvii.

22. Ibid.

23. Mary Berry, "Foreword," Hull et al., *But Some of Us Are Brave*, p. xv.

24. My position is that cultural studies is not disciplinary, nor does it seek to be a discipline even in the sense that American studies, Afro-American studies, or women's studies are interdisciplinary; rather it is a critical position which interrogates the assumptions of and principles of critical practice of all three modes of inquiry. As a practitioner of cultural studies notes: "The relation of cultural studies to the other disciplines is rather one of critique: of their historical construction, of their claims, of

their omissions, and particularly of the forms of their separation. At the same time, a critical relationship to the disciplines is also a critical stance to their forms of knowledge production—to the prevalent social relations of research, the labor process of higher education." Michael Green, "The Centre for Contemporary Cultural Studies," in Peter Widdowson, ed., *Re-Reading English* (London: Methuen, 1982), p. 84.

25. Hull et al., "Politics of Black Women's Studies," *But Some of Us Are Brave*, pp. xxi–xxii.

26. Deborah McDowell, "New Directions for Black Feminist Criticism," *Black American Literature Forum* 14 (1980), reprinted in Showalter, *The New Feminist Criticism*, pp. 186–99. References are to this edition; page numbers will be given parenthetically in the text. Barbara Christian, *Black Feminist Criticism: Perspectives on Black Women Writers* (New York: Pergamon Press, 1985).

27. See also Barbara Christian, *Black Women Novelists: The Development of a Tradition, 1892–1976* (Westport, Conn.: Greenwood Press, 1980).

28. Christian, *Black Feminist Criticism*, pp. 1–30.

29. Ibid., pp. x–xi.

30. Hortense Spillers, "Black/Female/Critic," *Women's Review of Books* 2 (September 1985): 9–10.

31. Cornel West, "The Dilemma of the Black Intellectual," *Cultural Critique* 1 (Fall 1985): 116–17.

32. Showalter, "The Feminist Critical Revolution," in *The New Feminist Criticism*, pp. 3–17.

33. This argument is drawn from V. N. Volosinov, *Marxism and the Philosophy of Language* (New York: Seminar Press, 1973). Volosinov was a Soviet theorist associated with the circle of Mikhail Bakhtin.

34. I am particularly drawing on that aspect of cultural studies which has analyzed issues of race and the study of black culture. A key figure is Stuart Hall. For many years the director of the Centre for Contemporary Cultural Studies, he has written a number of major theoretical essays on culture and ideology, including: "Cultural Studies: Two Paradigms," *Media, Culture, and Society* 2 (1980): 57–72; "The Rediscovery of 'Ideology': Return of the Repressed in Media Studies," in Michael Gurevitch, Tony Bennett, James Curran, and Janet Woolacott, eds., *Culture, Society, and the Media* (New York: Methuen, 1982), pp. 56–90; "Culture, the Media, and the 'Ideological' Effect," in James Curran, Michael Gurevitch, and Janet Woolacott, eds., *Mass Communications and Society* (London: Edward Arnold, 1977), pp. 315–48; "Notes on Deconstructing 'The Popular,'" in Ralph Samuel, ed., *People's History and Socialist Theory*, History Workshop Series (London: Routledge and Kegan Paul, 1981); "A 'Reading' of Marx's *1857* Introduction to the Grundrisse," *CCCS Stencilled Papers* 1 (1973); "Rethinking the Base/Superstructure Metaphor," in John Bloom-

field, ed., *Class, Party, and Hegemony* (London: Lawrence and Wishart, 1977), pp. 43–72. Hall's work on race that has been particularly influential includes: *Policing the Crisis: Mugging, the State, and Law and Order* (London: Macmillan, 1978); "Pluralism, Race, and Class in Caribbean Society," in *Race and Class in Post-Colonial Society* (Paris: UNESCO, 1977), pp. 150–82; "Racism and Reaction," in *Five Views of Multi-Racial Britain* (London: Commission for Racial Equality, 1978), pp. 23–35; "Race, Articulation and Societies Structured in Dominance," in *Sociological Theories: Race and Colonialism* (Paris: UNESCO, 1980), pp. 305–45; "The Whites of Their Eyes: Racist Ideologies and the Media," in George Bridges and Rosalind Brunt, eds., *Silver Linings: Some Strategies for the Eighties* (London: Lawrence and Wishart, 1981) pp. 28–52. Younger scholars influenced by Hall and the work of C. L. R. James include the authors of *The Empire Strikes Back* (see note 14 above) and Paul Gilroy, "Managing the 'Underclass': A Further Note on the Sociology of Race Relations in Britain," *Race and Class* 22 (Summer 1980): 47–62; Paul Gilroy, "You Can't Fool the Youths . . . Race and Class Formation in the 1980s," *Race and Class* 23 (Autumn 1981/Winter 1982): 207–22; and Paul Gilroy, *There Ain't No Black In The Union Jack* (London: Hutchinson, 1987). For collections of essays by C. L. R. James, see *The Future in the Present* (London: Allison and Busby, 1977); *Spheres of Existence* (London: Allison and Busby, 1980); *At the Rendezvous of Victory* (London: Allison and Busby, 1984); and his cultural history of cricket in the West Indies, *Beyond a Boundary* (1963; reprint London: Stanley Paul, 1980). In the United States there is the related work of Cedric J. Robinson, *Black Marxism: The Making of the Black Radical Tradition* (London: Zed Press, 1983); Cornel West, *Prophesy Deliverance! An Afro-American Revolutionary Christianity* (Philadelphia: Westminister Press, 1982); and Cornel West, "The Dilemma of the Black Intellectual" see note 31; John Brown Childs, "Afro-American Intellectuals and the People's Culture," *Theory and Society* 13 (1984): 69–90; John Brown Childs, "Concepts of Culture in Afro-American Political Thought, 1890–1920," *Social Text* 4 (Fall 1981): 28–43; and Ronald Takaki, *Iron Cages: Race and Culture in 19th-Century America* (Seattle: University of Washington Press, 1979), which fuses black intellectual tradition, cultural studies, and western Marxism.

35. The phrase is taken from Hall, "Race, Articulation, and Societies Structured in Dominance."

Chapter 2

1. This observation was first made by Angela Davis in her seminal essay "Reflections on the Black Woman's Role in the Community of Slaves," *Black Scholar* 3 (December 1971): 3–15.

2. Catherine Clinton, *The Plantation Mistress: Woman's World in the Old South* (New York: Pantheon, 1982), p. xiv.

3. John Blassingame, *The Slave Community* (New York: Oxford University Press, 1979), p. 224.

4. Ibid., pp. 173, & 154.

5. The exception to this comment is Jacqueline Jones's splendid history, *Labor of Love, Labor of Sorrow: Black Women, Work, and the Family from Slavery to the Present* (New York: Basic Books, 1985). Future feminist and Afro-American historiography will be transformed by this account of black female workers. See also Deborah Gray White, *Ar'n't I a Woman? Female Slaves in the Plantation South* (New York: W. W. Norton, 1985).

6. See Minrose C. Gwin, *Black and White Women of the Old South: The Peculiar Sisterhood in American Literature* (Knoxville: University of Tennessee Press, 1985), pp. 45–109.

7. Barbara Welter, "The Cult of True Womanhood, 1820–1860," *Dimity Convictions: The American Woman in the Nineteenth Century* (Columbus: University of Ohio Press, 1976), pp. 21–41.

8. Ibid., p. 21.

9. Julia Cherry Spruill, *Women's Life and Work in the Southern Colonies* (1938; reprint New York: W. W. Norton, 1972).

10. Ann Scott, *The Southern Lady: From Pedestal to Politics, 1830–1930* (Chicago: University of Chicago Press, 1970), p. x.

11. Clinton, *The Plantation Mistress*, p. 6.

12. Ibid., p. 8.

13. Ibid., p. 37.

14. Ibid., p. 15.

15. Spruill, *Women's Life and Work*, p. 220.

16. Welter, "The Cult of True Womanhood," p. 23.

17. Clinton, *The Plantation Mistress*, p. 94.

18. Caroline Lee Hentz, *Eoline, or Magnolia Vale* (Philadelphia: T. B. Peterson, 1852), p. 53.

19. Metta Victoria Victor, *Maum Guinea and Her Plantation Children* (New York: Beadle and Co., 1861), p. 120.

20. Spruill, *Women's Life and Work*, p. 232.

21. Barbara Berg, *The Remembered Gate: Origins of American Feminism, The Woman and the City, 1800–1860* (Oxford: Oxford University Press, 1978), p. 84.

22. For further discussion of the influence of the literary figure of the Southern belle, see: Irving H. Bartlett and C. Glenn Cambor, "The History and Psychodynamics of Southern Womanhood," *Women's Studies* 2 (1974): 9–24; John C. Ruoff, "Frivolity to Consumption: Or, Southern Womanhood in Antebellum Literature," *Civil War History* 18 (1972): 213–

29; Mary Elizabeth Massey, "The Making of a Feminist," *Journal of Southern History* 39 (1973): 3–22; Kathryn L. Seidel, "The Southern Belle as an Antebellum Ideal," *Southern Quarterly* 15 (1977): 387–401.

23. John Pendleton Kennedy, *Swallow Barn, or A Sojourn in the Old Dominion* (Philadelphia: Carey and Lee, 1832).

24. Thomas R. Drew, "Dissertation on the Characteristic Differences between the Sexes, and on the Position and Influence of Woman in Society," *Southern Literary Messenger* 1 (May 1835): 493–512, quoted in Aileen S. Kraditor, ed., *Up from the Pedestal* (New York: New York Times Book Co., 1968), pp. 45–47.

25. Clinton, *The Plantation Mistress*, p. 93.

26. Frederick Douglass, *Narrative of the Life of Frederick Douglass an American Slave* (1845; reprinted New York: New American Library, 1968), p. 48.

27. Ibid., p. 52.

28. Quoted in Sudie Duncan Sides, "Southern Women and Slavery," *History Today* 20 (January 1970): 57.

29. See Kate Drumgoold, *A Slave Girl's Story: The Autobiography of Kate Drumgoold* (New York: n.p., 1895), for an effective juxtaposition of the relationship she had with two mothers, her own and her white mother/mistress. See also Phillis Wheatley, *Letters of Phillis Wheatley, the Negro Slave Poet of Boston* (Boston: John Wilson and Son, 1864), for an account of being treated more like a child than a servant.

30. Douglass, *Narrative*, p. 48.

31. Mary Boykin Chesnut, *A Diary from Dixie*, Ben Ames Williams, ed. (Boston: Houghton Mifflin, 1949), p. 199.

32. Ibid., p. 200.

33. Scott, *The Southern Lady*, p. 36.

34. Clinton, *The Plantation Mistress*, p. 13.

35. Josiah Quincy, "Journal of Josiah Quincy Junior, 1773," *Massachusetts Historical Society, Proceedings* 49 (June 1916): 424–81; cited in Spruill, *Women's Life and Work*, p. 177.

36. Welter, "The Cult of True Womanhood," p. 27.

37. Chesnut, *Diary from Dixie*, pp. 21–22.

38. Ibid., p. 162.

39. Francis Smith Foster, *Witnessing Slavery: The Development of the Ante-bellum Slave Narratives* (Westport, Conn.: Greenwood Press, 1979), p. 131.

40. David Levy, "Racial Stereotypes in Antislavery Fiction," *Phylon* 31 (1970): 265–79.

41. E. D. E. N. Southworth, *Retribution: A Tale of Passion* (Philadelphia: T. B. Peterson, 1856); Sara Josepha Hale, *Liberia, or, Mr. Peyton's Experiment* (New York: H. Long and Brother, 1852); Mary Hayden Pike,

Ida May: Story of Things Actual and Possible (New York: Phillips, Sampson and Co., 1854); and Victor, *Maum Guinea.*

42. Hentz, *Eoline*, pp. 26–27.

43. Victor, *Maum Guinea*, p. 146.

44. Ibid., p. 157.

45. Ibid., p. 171.

46. Harriet Elizabeth Beecher Stowe, *Uncle Tom's Cabin; or, Life among the Lowly* (Boston: John P. Jewett and Co., 1852).

47. William Lloyd Garrison, *The Liberator* (February 21, 1835), quoted in Marion Starling, *The Slave Narrative: Its Place in Literary History* (1946; reprinted Boston: G. K. Hall, 1982).

48. William Craft, *Running a Thousand Miles for Freedom, or the Escape of William and Ellen Craft from Slavery* (London: W. Tweedie, 1860), reprinted in Arna Bontemps, ed., *Great Slave Narratives* (Boston: Beacon Press, 1969), pp. 269–331.

49. Ibid., p. 271.

50. Lucy Delany, *From the Darkness Cometh the Light, or Struggles for Freedom* (St. Louis: J. T. Smith, n. d.).

51. Ibid., p. 50.

52. Drumgoold, *A Slave Girl's Story*, p. 33.

53. Mary Prince, *A West Indian Slave, Related by Herself with a Supplement by the Editor, to Which Is Added the Narrative of Asa-Asa, a Captured African* (London: F. Westley and A. H. Davis, 1831), p. 4.

54. Caroline Gilman, *Recollections of a Southern Matron*, quoted in Welter, "The Cult of True Womanhood," p. 29.

55. Foster, *Witnessing Slavery*, p. 135.

56. Davis, "Reflections on the Black Woman's Role."

Chapter 3

1. Nancy Prince, *A Narrative of the Life and Travels of Mrs. Nancy Prince. Written by Herself* (Boston: by the author, 1850), preface. Page numbers will be given parenthetically in the text.

2. See the recent edition of *The Life and Religious Experience of Jarena Lee; Memoirs of the Life, Religious Experience, Ministerial Travels and Labors of Mrs. Zilpha Elaw*; and *A Brand Plucked from the Fire: An Autobiographical Sketch by Mrs. Julia A. J. Foote*, in William L. Andrews, ed., *Sisters of the Spirit: Three Black Women's Autobiographies of the Nineteenth Century* (Bloomington: Indiana University Press, 1986).

3. Harriet E. Wilson, *Our Nig; or, Sketches from the Life of a Free Black, in a Two-Story White House, North. Showing That Slavery's Shadows Fall Even There*, introduction by Henry Louis Gates, Jr. (Boston: by

the author, 1859; reprint New York: Random House, 1983). References are to the 1983 edition; page numbers will be given parenthetically in the text.

4. Harriet Jacobs, [Linda Brent], *Incidents in the Life of a Slave Girl, Written by Herself,* L. Maria Child, ed. (Boston: for the author, 1861). A paperback edition with an introduction by Walter Teller was published in New York by Harcourt Brace Jovanovich in 1973; the pages cited in parentheses are in this edition.

5. John Blassingame, "Critical Essay on Sources," *The Slave Community: Plantation Life in the Antebellum South,* 2nd ed. (New York: Oxford University Press, 1979), pp. 367–82.

6. Ibid., p. 373.

7. Ibid., p. 367 (emphasis added).

8. This evidence has focused on the discovery of a collection of Jacobs's letters to Amy Post held in the Post family papers at the University of Rochester library. See Dorothy Sterling, ed., *We Are Your Sisters: Black Women in the Nineteenth Century* (New York: W. W. Norton, 1984); and Jean Yellin, "Written by Herself: Harriet Jacobs' Slave Narrative," *American Literature* 53 (November 1981): 479–86; "Texts and Contexts of Harriet Jacobs' Incidents in the Life of a Slave Girl: Written by Herself," in Charles T. Davis and Henry Louis Gates, Jr., eds., *The Slave's Narrative* (New York: Oxford University Press, 1985), pp. 262–82; and her introduction to a new annotated edition of *Incidents in the Life of a Slave Girl* (Cambridge: Harvard University Press, 1987). Yellin has also verified details of Jacobs's life in Edenton, North Carolina, and is preparing to write her biography.

9. Harriet Jacobs, [Linda Brent], *The Deeper Wrong: Or, Incidents in the Life of a Slave Girl, Written by Herself,* L. Maria Child, ed. (London: W. Tweedie, 1862).

10. For Jacobs on Willis, see Yellin, "Texts and Contexts," pp. 265, 279n.

11. Jacobs to Post, May 18 and June 18 (1857?), cited in Yellin, "Written by Herself," pp. 485–86.

12. Jacobs to Post, October 8 (1860?), in ibid., p. 483.

13. Jacobs to Post, June 21 (1857?), cited in Yellin, "Texts and Contexts," p. 269.

14. I am grateful to Jean Yellin for reading an earlier draft of this chapter and helping me clarify my ideas. Yellin argues that "Jacobs' narrator dramatizes the failure of her efforts to adhere to the sexual patterns she had been taught to endorse . . . and tentatively reaches toward an alternative moral code" ("Texts and Contexts," pp. 270–71). I am arguing that this alternative is the development of a discourse of black womanhood and that, far from being tentative, this movement away from the ideology of true womanhood is assertive.

15. Yellin, "Written by Herself," p. 482.

16. Yellin, "Texts and Contexts," p. 276.

17. See the discussion of incidents in relation to plot in Nina Baym, *Novels, Readers and Reviewers: Responses to Fiction in Antebellum America* (Ithaca: Cornell University Press, 1984), pp. 75–79.

18. Nina Baym's observations on morality in novels and reviews of novels are enlightening in any consideration of the extent to which writers could challenge convention. See *Novels, Readers and Reviewers*, pp. 173–89, where she makes the argument that female sexuality was consistently policed by reviewers: "Two basic Victorian assumptions about female character—that women do not experience sexual desire and that they are naturally suited to monogamous marriage where they are the servants of their husbands, their children, and society at large—are here exposed as cultural constrictions whose maintenance requires constant surveillance, even to the supervision of novel reading" (183).

19. Barbara Welter, *Dimity Convictions: The American Woman in the Nineteenth Century* (Colombus: Ohio University Press, 1976), p. 23.

20. Jacobs intended that this note of rebellion be repeated in her final chapter which was about John Brown, but at the suggestion of Lydia Maria Child the chapter was dropped. Had it been retained, it would have strengthened this interpretation of the importance of the linking of freedom and death.

Chapter 4

1. Frances E. W. Harper, *Iola Leroy; or, Shadows Uplifted,* 2nd ed. (Philadelphia: Garrigues Brothers, 1893), pp. 262–63. Page numbers will be cited parenthetically in the text.

2. Benjamin Brawley, *Early Negro American Writers* (Chapel Hill: University of North Carolina Press, 1935), pp. 290–92; Hugh M. Gloster, *Negro Voices in American Fiction* (Chapel Hill: University of North Carolina Press, 1948; New York: Russell and Russell, 1965), pp. 30–32; Vernon Loggins, *The Negro Author, His Development in America* (New York: Columbia University Press, 1931), p. 325. Loggins maintains that *Iola Leroy* was published in 1893, not 1892.

3. Gerda Lerner, *Black Women in White America* (New York: Random House, 1973), p. 244.

4. Sandra M. Gilbert and Susan Gubar, *The Madwoman in the Attic: The Woman Writer and the Nineteenth-Century Literary Imagination* (New Haven: Yale University Press, 1979), p. 64.

5. Ibid., p. 83.

6. William Still, introduction to Harper, *Iola Leroy,* p. 1.

7. For biographical information on Harper, see the entries by Louis Filler in Edward T. James, Janet Wilson James, and Paul S. Boyer, eds., *Notable American Women: A Biographical Dictionary, 1607–1950* (Cambridge: Harvard University Press, 1971); and Daniel Walden in Rayford W. Logan and Michael R. Winston, eds., *Dictionary of American Negro Biography* (New York: W. W. Norton, 1982). See also William Still, *The Underground Railroad* (Philadelphia: Porter & Coates, 1872), pp. 755–80.

8. Quoted in Philip S. Foner, ed., *The Voice of Black America: Major Speeches by Negroes in the United States, 1797–1971* (New York: Simon and Schuster, 1972), p. 6.

9. Quoted in Brawley, *Early Negro American Writers,* pp. 290–91.

10. Phebe Hanaford, *Daughters of America; or Women of the Century* (Augusta, Maine: True & Co., 1882), p. 326.

11. Still, *The Underground Railroad,* pp. 767–68.

12. Quoted in "Annual Meeting of the American Equal Rights Association," *The Revolution,* May 20, 1869, pp. 305–7.

13. Quoted in "Annual Meeting of the American Equal Rights Association: Second Day's Proceedings," *The Revolution,* May 27, 1869, pp. 321–22.

14. Still, *The Underground Railroad,* p. 772.

15. Frances E. W. Harper, "Colored Women of America," *Englishwoman's Review,* January 15, 1878.

16. Frances E. W. Harper, "Woman's Political Future," in May Wright Sewell, ed., *World's Congress of Representative Women* (Chicago: Rand McNally, 1894), pp. 433–37.

17. Ibid., p. 435.

18. Gloster, *Negro Voices,* p. 30; William Wells Brown, *Clotelle* (Boston: James Redpath, 1864).

19. Sterling A. Brown, Arthur P. Davis, and Ulysses Lee, eds., *The Negro Caravan: Writings by American Negroes* (New York: Dryden Press, 1941; New York: Arno Press, 1969), p. 139.

20. Nina Baym, *Woman's Fiction: A Guide to Novels by and about Women in America 1820–1870* (Ithaca: Cornell University Press, 1978), pp. 11–12. Page numbers will be cited parenthetically in the text.

21. Frances E. W. Harper, *Poems on Miscellaneous Subjects* (Boston: J. B. Yerrington & Son, 1854); "The Two Offers," *Anglo-African Magazine* 1 (September 1859): 288–91 and (October 1859): 311–13; "The Triumph of Freedom—A Dream," *Anglo-African Magazine* 2 (January 1860): 21–22; *Moses: A Story of the Nile* (n.p., 1869); *Poems* (Philadelphia: n.p., 1871); *Sketches of Southern Life* (1872; Philadelphia: Ferguson Brothers, 1893); *Idylls of the Bible* (Philadelphia: George S. Ferguson, 1901); *The Sparrow's Fall and Other Poems* (n.p., n.d.).

22. See Alfred Habegger, *Gender Fantasy and Realism in American Literature* (New York: Columbia University Press, 1982).

23. What follows is an analysis of the structure of *Iola Leroy* in its relation to Baym's models of women's fiction in the United States. I am grateful to Richard Slotkin for pointing out to me that many boy/man heroes follow formulaic conventions that are the same as for heroines: "heroes from Washington to Leatherstocking, to Tom Sawyer and Huckleberry Finn and Horatio Alger are all orphans and so 'self-made'" (personal communication). While concentrating on women's fiction, I recognize the necessity for analyses of the relationship between the fiction formulas of heroes and of heroines.

24. See in particular Judith R. Berzon, *Neither White nor Black: The Mulatto Character in American Fiction* (New York: New York University Press, 1978); and Barbara Christian, *Black Women Novelists: The Development of a Tradition, 1892-1976* (Westport, Conn.: Greenwood Press, 1980).

25. For a very interesting discussion of the representation of black English, see Sylvia Wallace Holton, *Down Home and Uptown: The Representation of Black Speech in American Fiction* (Rutherford, N.J.: Fairleigh Dickinson University Press, 1984), especially "Black English in Fiction, 1790-1900: The Identification of an American Dialect," pp. 55-94.

26. Brown, *Clotelle,* p. 22.

27. Ibid.

28. August Meier, *Negro Thought in America, 1880-1915* (Ann Arbor: University of Michigan Press, 1963).

29. Harper, "Women's Political Future," pp. 433-37.

30. W. E. B. Du Bois, "The Talented Tenth," in Booker T. Washington, ed., *The Negro Problem: A Series of Articles by Representative Negroes of Today* (New York: James Pott & Co., 1903), pp. 33-75; reprinted in Julius Lester, ed., *The Seventh Son: The Thought and Writings of W. E. B. Du Bois,* Vol. 1 (New York: Random House, 1971), pp. 385-403. See also W. E. B. Du Bois, "Harvard and the South"; "The Afro-American"; "The True Meaning of a University," MS, 1894, cited in Meier, *Negro Thought,* p. 304.

31. Frances E. W. Harper, "Duty to Dependent Races," *National Council of Women of the United States, Transactions* (Philadelphia: National Council of Women of the United States, 1891), pp. 86-91.

32. Quoted in ibid., pp. 89-90.

33. Ibid., p. 90.

34. See Christian, *Black Women Novelists,* p. 4.

35. See also Harper, "Women's Political Future," p. 436, for exactly the same story told to the World's Congress of Representative Women.

36. Harper, "Colored Women of America," pp. 10-15.

37. Christian, *Black Women Novelists,* p. 29.

38. Ibid., p. 26.

39. It is illuminating to contrast this relationship with the use of history in Jessie Fauset's *The Chinaberry Tree* (Philadelphia: Frederick A. Stokes & Co., 1931), where Colonel Halloway's love for Aunt Sal was dominated by conventions of romantic love. Systemic considerations in this text were displaced to the level of scandal.

40. Du Bois, "The Talented Tenth," pp. 385–86.

41. Frances E. W. Harper, "The Great Problem," in Alice Moore Dunbar, ed., *Masterpieces of Negro Eloquence* (New York: Bookery Publishing Company, 1914), pp. 101–6. The address was delivered at the Centennial Anniversary of the Pennsylvania Society for Promoting the Abolition of Slavery, held in Philadelphia, April 14, 1875. "The Women's Christian Temperance Union and the Colored Woman," *AME Church Review* 4 (1888): 313–16 was followed by an article called "National Women's Christian Temperance Union," *AME Church Review* 5 (1889): 242–45.

42. Harper, "Women's Political Future," pp. 433–34.

43. Though I cannot go into Harper's temperance work at length, she felt that the potential of Frances Willard's Women's Crusade was unlimited. By 1888, Harper had progressed from the position of superintendent of "work among colored people" for the city of Philadelphia to state and eventually national superintendent of "work among colored people of the North." Although it was a segregated organization in the majority of its unions, Harper was convinced that black women should be persuaded to join. At one time the only black woman on the executive committee, Harper became one of three who constantly had to battle against women who "fail to make in their minds the discrimination between social equality and Christian affiliation" and supported continued segregation. Nevertheless, this commitment to temperance provided the moral and spiritual imperative to her vision of "a nation wearing sobriety as a crown and righteousness as the girdle of her loins" (219). Harper felt that the WCTU had the organizational and mobilizing ability of the abolitionist movement, and she would often compare them. As a movement, the WCTU provided the structure within which Harper, as intellectual, could agitate, and temperance novels must have provided models of didacticism for *Iola Leroy.* Above all, Harper held that "the Women's Christian Temperance Union has in its hands one of the grandest opportunities that God ever pressed into the hands of womanhood of any country. Its conflict is not the contest of a social club, but a moral warfare for an imperiled civilization." See Harper, "Women's Christian Temperance Union," pp. 315, 316.

44. Harper, "Women's Political Future," p. 434.

Chapter 5

1. A similar argument, though in a different context, is made by Terry Eagleton in *The Rape of Clarissa* (Minneapolis: University of Minnesota Press, 1984), p. 4. As he states clearly, "I am interested less in what fiction 'mirrors' than in what it *does*. For Richardson's novels are not mere images of conflicts fought out on another terrain, representations of a history which happens elsewhere; they are themselves a material part of those struggles, pitched standards around which battle is joined, instruments which help to constitute social interests rather than lenses which reflect them."

2. *The Woman's Era* was a journal started in 1894, published in association with "The Woman's Era Club" in Boston. It was edited by its president, Josephine St. Pierre Ruffin.

3. "Forget-me-not" (Emma Dunham Kelley), *Megda* (Boston: James H. Earle, 1891); Anna Julia Cooper, *A Voice from the South: By a Black Woman of the South* (Xenia, Ohio: Aldine Publishing House, 1892); Ida B. Wells, *Southern Horrors: Lynch Law in All Its Phases* (New York: The New York Age Print, 1892), reprinted in Ida Wells-Barnett, *On Lynchings* (New York: Arno Press, 1969).

4. Victoria Earle, *Aunt Lindy. A Story Founded on Real Life* (New York: J. J. Little, 1893); N. F. Mossell, *The Work of the Afro-American Woman* (Philadelphia: George S. Ferguson Co., 1894).

5. This is obviously only a very partial account of the activity of Afro-American women during the decade. For useful collections of nineteenth-century sources and for references, see the bibliography.

6. Sources for all quotations will be cited parenthetically in the text. A detailed biography of Cooper has recently been published in conjunction with an exhibition of her life and work, so I will concentrate on her theoretical exposition of race and gender. See Louise Daniel Hutchinson, *Anna Julia Cooper: A Voice from the South* (Washington, D.C.: Smithsonian Institution Press, 1981). See also Sharon Harley, "Anna Julia Cooper: A Voice for Black Women," in Sharon Harley and Rosalyn Terborg-Penn, eds., *The Afro-American Woman: Struggles and Images* (Port Washington, N.Y.: Kennikat Press, 1978), pp. 87–96.

7. May Wright Sewall, ed., *World's Congress of Representative Women* (Chicago: Rand McNally, 1894), pp. 711–15.

8. Ida B. Wells, ed., *The Reason Why: The Colored American Is Not in the World's Columbian Exposition* (Chicago: by the author, 1893). This pamphlet was published with the help of Frederick Douglass, who attended the World's Fair as the representative of Haiti.

9. Thomas C. Holt, "The Lonely Warrior: Ida B. Wells and the Strug-

gle for Black Leadership," in John Hope Franklin, ed., *Black Leaders of the Twentieth Century* (Urbana: University of Illinois Press, 1982), pp. 39–61.

10. The exception is Bettina Aptheker, who published a paper comparing the political activism of Wells and Jane Addams. Bettina Aptheker, ed., *Lynching and Rape: An Exchange of Views*, Occasional Paper 25 (San Jose, Calif.: American Institute for Marxist Studies, 1977).

11. Alfreda M. Duster, ed., *Crusade for Justice: The Autobiography of Ida B. Wells* (Chicago: University of Chicago Press, 1970), p. 47.

12. Ibid., p. 64.

13. Ibid., pp. 65–66; and Wells, *Southern Horrors*, p. 4.

14. *A Red Record* (1895) and *Mob Rule in New Orleans* (1900) are reprinted in *On Lynchings*. All quotations will be from this edition and will be cited parenthetically in the text, using the abbreviations SH or RR. *Southern Horrors* was published as *U. S. Atrocities* in London in 1892, on Wells's first tour.

15. The term *moral panic* has been developed as an analytic concept to explain the phenomenon of the emergence of a perceived threat to the values and interests of a society in its mass media. My use is directly influenced by the work of Stuart Hall, Chas Critcher, Tony Jefferson, John Clarke, and Brian Roberts in *Policing the Crisis: Mugging, the State, and Law and Order* (London: Macmillan, 1978), pp. 16–28. The term was originally used by Stan Cohen in *Folk Devils and Moral Panics: The Creation of the Mods and Rockers* (London: MacGibbon and Kee, 1972), p. 28.

16. Aptheker, *Lynching and Rape*, p. 29.

17. Duster, *Crusade for Justice*, p. 81. But the gathering of black women from Philadelphia, Boston, New York, and other cities would indicate that organization was already embryonic.

18. Mary Church Terrell, *A Colored Woman in a White World* (Washington, D.C.: Ransdell Publishing Co., 1940), p. 148.

19. Elizabeth Lindsay Davis, *Lifting As They Climb: The National Association of Colored Women* (Washington, D.C.: National Association of Colored Women, 1933), p. 14.

20. Ibid., pp. 14–15. See also Duster, *Crusade for Justice*, p. 242, for Wells's claim that the slurs were directed at her and through her to all black women.

21. Davis, *Lifting As They Climb*, p. 18.

22. Ibid., p. 19.

23. Ibid., p. 30.

24. Victoria Earle Matthews, *The Awakening of the Afro-American Woman*, address delivered at the Annual Convention of the Society of

Christian Endeavor, San Francisco, July 11, 1897 (New York: by the author, 1897), pp. 6–7.

25. Ibid., pp. 9–10.

26. Davis, *Lifting As They Climb*, p. 22.

27. Adele Logan Alexander, "How I Discovered My Grandmother . . .," *Ms.*, November 1983, pp. 29–33. I am grateful to Adele Logan Alexander for sharing with me the materials she has found while working on the biography of her grandmother.

28. Victoria Earle Matthews, *The Value of Race Literature*, address delivered at the First Congress of Colored Women of the United States, Boston, July 30, 1895 (n. p.).

29. Ibid., p. 18.

30. Ibid., p. 19.

31. Ibid., pp. 22–23.

Chapter 6

1. Pauline E. Hopkins, *Contending Forces* (Boston: Colored Co-operative Publishing Co., 1900; reprinted Carbondale: Southern Illinois University Press, 1978). All references will be to the 1978 edition; page numbers will be given in parentheses in the text.

2. "Prospectus . . . of the New Romance of Colored Life, *Contending Forces*," *Colored American Magazine* 1 (September 1900): 195–96.

3. Dorothy B. Porter, "Hopkins, Pauline Elizabeth," in Rayford W. Logan and Michael R. Winston, eds., *Dictionary of American Negro Biography* (New York: W. W. Norton, 1982), pp. 325–26.

4. Ann Allen Shockley, "Pauline Elizabeth Hopkins: A Biographical Excursion into Obscurity," *Phylon* 33 (Spring 1972): 22–26. The essay, undated, is in the Pauline E. Hopkins papers at Fisk University Library, Nashville.

5. In the short biographical sketch of Hopkins in *Colored American Magazine* 2 (January 1901): 218, it was reported that a Mr. Fred Williams, the stage manager of the Boston Museum, advised her to become a writer of fiction in story form rather than a dramatist.

6. "Prospectus . . .," p. 196.

7. See August Meier, "Booker T. Washington and the Negro Press: With Special Reference to the Colored American Magazine," *Journal of Negro History* 38 (January 1953): 67–90. Meier hardly mentions the early years of the journal, and when he does he fails to mention Hopkins at all. It is clear, however, that Washington's period of ascendancy in the journal coincides with Hopkins's decision to leave. See also A. A. Johnson and

R. M. Johnson, "Away from Accommodation: Radical Editors and Protest Journalism, 1900–1910," *Journal of Negro History* 62 (October 1977): 325–38, for a description of Hopkins's tenure as editor. See also William Stanley Braithwaite, "Negro America's First Magazine," *Negro Digest* (December 1947): 21–26, reprinted in Philip Butcher, ed., *The William Stanley Braithwaite Reader* (Ann Arbor: University of Michigan Press, 1972), pp. 114–21. Braithwaite acknowledged the editorial influence of Hopkins but obviously did not like her. His description of her as "temperamental" and as a novelist who "regarded herself as a national figure . . . and as such felt free to impose her views and opinions upon her associates in the conduct of both the book and the magazine publications" would indicate that Braithwaite resented her power and perhaps as a contributor had smarted under her critical eye. Indeed, Braithwaite has praise only for the men on the journal and seemed to think that Hopkins should have remained in grateful and silent submission for having had the opportunity to publish in the *Colored American Magazine*. See also Brian Joseph Benson, "Colored American," in Walter C. Daniels, ed., *Black Journals of the United States* (Westport, Conn.: Greenwood Press, 1982), pp. 123–30, who mistakenly refers to Hopkins as the editor throughout the period during which the journal was published from Boston.

8. "Editorial and Publishers' Announcements," *Colored American Magazine* 1 (May 1900): 60–64.

9. The series "Famous Men of the Negro Race" appeared as follows: "Frederick Douglass," 2 (December 1900): 121–32; "William Wells Brown," 2 (January 1901): 232–36; "Robert Browne Elliot," 2 (February 1901): 294–301; "Edwin Garrison Walker," 2 (March 1901): 358–66; "Lewis Hayden," 2 (April 1901): 473–77; "Charles Lenox Remond," 3 (May 1901): 35–39; "Sergeant William H. Carney," 3 (June 1901): 84–89; "Hon. Mercer Langston," 3 (July 1901): 177–84; "Senator Blanche K. Bruce," 3 (August 1901): 257–61; "Robert Morris," 3 (September 1901): 337–42; "Booker T. Washington," 3 (October 1901): 436–41. The series "Famous Women of the Negro Race" appeared as follows: "Phenomenal Vocalists," 4 (November 1901): 45–53; "Sojourner Truth," 4 (December 1901): 124–32; "Harriet Tubman," 4 (January/February 1902): 210–23; "Some Literary Workers," 4 (March 1902): 274–80; "Literary Workers," 4 (April 1902): 366–71; "Educators," 5 (May 1902): 41–46; "Educators," 5 (June 1902): 125–30; "Educators," 5 (July 1902): 206–13; "Club Life among Colored Women," 5 (August 1902): 273–77; "Artists," 5 (September 1902): 362–67; "Higher Education of Colored Women in White Schools and Colleges," 5 (October 1902): 445–50; "Heroes and Heroines in Black," 6 (January 1903): 206–21.

10. "Munroe Rogers," 6 (November 1902): 20–26; [Sarah Allen], "The Latest Phases of the Race Problem in America," 6 (February 1903): 244–51; "Reminiscences of the Life and Times of Lydia Maria Child," 6 (Febru-

ary 1903–May/June 1903); "Echoes from the Annual Convention of Northeastern Federation of Colored Women's Clubs," 6 (October 1903): 709–13.

11. Richard Ohmann has defined this relationship between a low price and a dependence on advertising as "the principle behind the mass magazines of our century." "Where Did Mass Culture Come From? The Case of Magazines," *Berkshire Review* 16 (1981): 89.

12. R. S. Elliot, "The Story of Our Magazine," *Colored American Magazine* 3 (May 1901): 43. Elliot, who was white, was employed by the company for his expertise in marketing and layout. This readership figure is obviously exaggerated to generate confidence and to encourage advertisers. Brian Joseph Benson, in "Colored American," p. 130, states that the highest circulation figure for the journal was 15,000; however, the Ayers directory for 1904 cites a circulation of 17,840. See N. W. Ayers & Son, *American Newspaper Annual* (Philadelphia: N. W. Ayers & Son, 1904). But Elliot's exaggeration does not negate the success of the *Colored American Magazine* as comparison with the weekly *New York Age* indicates. In 1892, the year before the magazine "revolution," when Ida B. Wells published for the first time in the *New York Age*, it had a circulation of 4,500. Ayers, *American Newspaper Annual*, 1892.

13. "Editorial and Publishers' Announcements," *Colored American Magazine* 6 (May/June 1903): 466.

14. "Editorial and Publishers' Announcements," *Colored American Magazine* 1 (May 1900): 60.

15. Ohmann, "Where Did Mass Culture Come From?" pp. 91–92.

16. "Announcement," *Colored American Magazine* 1 (May 1900): 3.

17. "Editorial and Publishers' Announcements," 1, p. 60.

18. "Editorial and Publishers' Announcements," 6, p. 467.

19. U. S. Department of Commerce, Bureau of the Census, *Negro Population in the United States 1790–1915* (New York: Arno Press, 1968), p. 409.

20. Ibid., p. 411. I have not included the figures for the West.

21. Ibid., pp. 416–17.

22. Ibid., p. 508.

23. In 1910, the total number of blacks in professional service was recorded as being 67,245. Ibid., p. 510.

24. W. E. B. Du Bois, *Atlanta University Publications* (New York: Octagon Books, 1968), Vol. 2. See also U.S. Dept. of Commerce, *Negro Population*, p. 510.

25. Du Bois, *University Atlanta*, p. 93.

26. See Mamie Fields, *Lemon Swamp and Other Places* (New York: Free Press, 1983), for a vivid representation of the black community in Charleston, North Carolina, from the 1890s through the 1920s. The structure of the community is revealed through an exploration of the social

relations among servants, artisans, professionals, and owners of small businesses. Though the *Colored American Magazine* is not referred to, and there wasn't an agent in Charleston, it is the type of community that would have been the journal's ideal target audience.

27. Elliot, "The Story of Our Magazine," p. 47.

28. Pauline E. Hopkins [Sarah Allen], *Hagar's Daughter. A Story of Southern Caste Prejudice, Colored American Magazine* 2–4 (March 1901–March 1902); *Winona. A Tale of Negro Life in the South and Southwest,* 5 (May–October 1902); *Of One Blood. Or, the Hidden Self,* 6 (November 1902–November 1903).

29. Hopkins, "The Mystery Within Us," *Colored American Magazine* 1 (May 1900): 14–18; "Talma Gordon," 1 (October 1900): 271–90; "General Washington. A Christmas Story," 2 (December 1900): 95–104; "A Dash for Liberty," 3 (August 1901): 243–47; "Bro'r Abr'm Jimson's Wedding. A Christmas Story," 4 (December 1901): 103–12; "The Test of Manhood," 6 (December 1902): 113–19; "As the Lord Lives He Is One of Our Mother's Children," 6 (November 1903): 795–801.

30. Hopkins, "Famous Women of the Negro Race, Educators." p. 130.

31. Robert L. Allen, *Reluctant Reformers* (Garden City, N.Y.: Anchor Press, 1975), p. 88.

32. Christopher Lasch, *The World of Nations: Reflections on American History, Politics and Culture* (New York: Alfred A. Knopf, 1973), p. 74. The structure of the following argument draws on Lasch's analysis and observations in his essay, "The Anti-Imperialists, the Philippines, and the Inequality of Man," in *The World of Nations,* pp. 70–79.

33. Lasch, *The World of Nations,* p. 71.

34. Quoted in Lasch, *The World of Nations,* p. 74.

35. Lasch, *The World of Nations,* p. 79.

36. Hopkins, "Munroe Rogers," p. 22.

37. Allen, *Reluctant Reformers,* p. 91.

38. See the afterword to the 1978 edition of Hopkins, *Contending Forces,* by Gwendolyn Brooks, pp. 403–9.

39. Sappho, "Fragment 132," quoted in Sarah B. Pomeroy, *Goddesses, Whores, Wives, and Slaves: Women in Classical Antiquity* (New York: Shocken, 1975), p. 54.

Chapter 7

1. See Sally Mitchell, *The Fallen Angel: Chastity, Class and Women's Reading 1835–1880* (Bowling Green, Ohio: Bowling Green University Popular Press, 1981), p. 151, for her analysis of the shift toward the physical nature of action in the penny weekly magazines of the 1870s. On dime

novel conventions, see Michael Denning, *Mechanic Accents: Dime Novels and Working-Class Culture in 19th-Century America* (London: Verso, 1987).

2. See John G. Cawelti, *Adventure, Mystery, and Romance: Formula Stories as Art and Popular Culture* (Chicago: University of Chicago Press, 1976), pp. 264–65, for his argument about the importance of spectacle in social melodrama.

3. Pauline Hopkins, *Hagar's Daughter, Colored American Magazine* 2–4 (March 1901–March 1902). All quotations will be from this first publication, and volume and page numbers will be given parenthetically in the text.

4. Compare Hopkins, *Hagar's Daughter*, 3: 33–34, with William Wells Brown, *Clotelle* (Boston: James Redpath, 1864), pp. 51–52.

5. A good example of the use of this particular device to explore and represent the black community in a racist fashion was Old Cap. Collier, *Black Tom the Negro Detective, or, Solving a Thompson Street Mystery*, Old Cap. Collier Library, 486 (April 22, 1893).

6. Alfred Habegger, *Gender, Fantasy, and Realism in American Literature* (New York: Columbia University Press, 1982), pp. 172–73; and Mitchell, *The Fallen Angel*, p. 75.

7. Mitchell, *The Fallen Angel*, pp. 75–76.

8. J. Randolph Cox, "The Detective Hero in the American Dime Novel," *Dime Novel Roundup* 50 (February 1981): 5.

9. Ibid., pp. 7–8.

10. Genesis 16 and 21.

11. Numbers 12.

12. Pauline Hopkins, *Winona: A Tale of Negro Life in the South and Southwest, Colored American Magazine* 5, nos. 1–6 (May–October 1902). References will be to this publication, and volume and page numbers will be cited parenthetically in the text.

13. Pauline Hopkins, *Of One Blood. Or, The Hidden Self, Colored American Magazine* 6 (November 1902–November 1903). References will be to this publication, and volume and page numbers will be cited parenthetically in the text.

14. Pauline Hopkins, "Famous Women of the Negro Race 7. Educators," *Colored American Magazine* 5 (June 1902): 130.

15. Basil Davidson, *The Lost Cities of Africa* (Boston: Little, Brown, 1959), p. 47.

16. Ibid., pp. 47–48.

17. Pauline Hopkins [Sarah A. Allen], "The Test of Manhood," *Colored American Magazine* 6 (December 1902): 113–19.

18. "Venus and Apollo Modelled from Ethiopians," *Colored American Magazine* 6 (May/June 1903): 465. See also *A Primer of Facts pertaining*

to the Early Greatness of the African Race and the Possibility of Restoration by Its Descendents, with Epilogue (Cambridge, Mass: P. E. Hopkins & Co., 1905).

19. There is confusion about Hopkins's editorial role on the *Colored American Magazine*. William Braithwaite, in "Negro America's First Magazine," *Negro Digest* (December 1947): 21–26, refers to Hopkins's editorial influence; see note 7, Chapter Six herein. Dorothy Porter also refers to her "editorship" though is unclear about dates, in "Pauline Elizabeth Hopkins," in Rayford W. Logan and Michael Winston, eds., *Dictionary of American Negro Biography* (New York: W. W. Norton, 1982), pp. 325–26. See also Walter C. Daniel, *Black Journals of the United States* (Westport, Conn.: Greenwood Press, 1982), pp. 123–30, who acknowledges the confusion but lists Hopkins as editor from November 1903 to September 1904 in his history of publication. Perhaps the strongest evidence of her editorial influence lies not in verifiable dates but in the text of the *Colored American Magazine*.

20. Pauline Hopkins, "Toussaint L'Overture," *Colored American Magazine* 2 (November 1900): 10, 24.

21. Ibid., p. 10.

22. Pauline Hopkins, "Heroes and Heroines in Black," *Colored American Magazine* 6 (January 1903): 211.

23. Ibid., p. 206.

Chapter 8

1. The three major contemporary texts are Jervis Anderson, *This Was Harlem: A Cultural Portrait, 1900–1950* (New York: Farrar Straus Giroux, 1982); Nathan Irvin Huggins, *Harlem Renaissance* (New York: Oxford University Press, 1971); David Levering Lewis, *When Harlem Was in Vogue* (New York: Vintage, 1982). The term has recently been used to describe contemporary black cultural production, particularly black women novelists who are linked to this first renaissance by the figure of Zora Neale Hurston; "a second black literary Renaissance, in which women are taking a significant part, seems well under way," according to Mary V. Dearborn, *Pocahontas's Daughters: Gender and Ethnicity in American Culture* (New York: Oxford University Press, 1986), p. 61.

2. Alain Locke, ed., *The New Negro* (New York: Albert & Charles Boni, 1925; New York: Atheneum, 1970).

3. "Announcement," *Colored American Magazine* 1 (May 1900): 2.

4. For the best account of the relationship among the various intellectual attitudes toward black culture during this period, see John Brown

Childs, "Afro-American Intellectuals and the People's Culture," *Theory and Society* 13 (1984): 69–90, an informative and stimulating analysis of the vanguardism inherent in concepts of intellectuals as the "Talented Tenth," in Alain Locke's and Charles Johnson's approach to folk culture, and in Chandler Owen's and A. Philip Randolph's socialist "New" Negro. See notes 2 and 5, this chapter.

5. *Messenger* (August 1920): 73, quoted in Sterling D. Spero and Abram L. Harris, *The Black Worker* (New York: Antheneum, 1969), p. 389. See also Jervis Anderson, *A. Philip Randolph: A Biographical Portrait* (New York: Harcourt Brace Jovanovich, 1972), p. 98; William H. Harris, *Keeping the Faith: A. Philip Randolph, Milton P. Webster, and the Brotherhood of Sleeping Car Porters, 1925–37* (Urbana: University of Illinois Press, 1977), pp. 21, 98; and Theodore G. Vincent, ed., *Voices of a Black Nation: Political Journalism in the Harlem Renaissance* (San Francisco: Ramparts Press, 1973).

6. *Messenger*, p. 73, quoted in Spero and Harris, *The Black Worker*, pp. 389–90.

7. See, for examples of the conflicts over patronage, the second edition of Zora Neale Hurston's *Dust Tracks on a Road: An Autobiography*, Robert E. Hemenway, ed. (Urbana: University of Illinois Press, 1984); Claude McKay, *A Long Way from Home: An Autobiography* (1937; New York: Harcourt, Brace & World, 1970); and Langston Hughes, *The Big Sea: An Autobiography* (1940; New York: Hill and Wang, 1963). Hughes's second autobiography, *I Wonder As I Wander: An Autobiographical Journey* (1956; New York: Hill and Wang, 1964), opens with the acknowledgment of the loss of his patron.

8. R. S. Elliot, "The Story of Our Magazine," *Colored American Magazine* 3 (May 1901): 44. The journal did eventually have a black patron, Colonel William H. Dupress, to whom it was sold for debt. See Walter C. Daniel, ed., *Black Journals of the United States* (Westport, Conn.: Greenwood Press, 1982), p. 125.

9. Elliot, "The Story of Our Magazine," p. 44.

10. Nella Larsen, *Quicksand* (New York: Alfred A. Knopf, 1928; Westport, Conn.: Negro Universities Press, 1969). Page references to the latter edition will be given parenthetically in the text.

11. Compare the responses of Robert Bone, *The Negro Novel in America* (New Haven: Yale University Press, 1958); Arthur P. Davis, *From the Dark Tower: Afro-American Writers 1900–1960* (1974; Washington, D.C.: Howard University Press, 1981); and Addison Gayle, Jr., *The Way of the New World: The Black Novel in America* (Garden City, N.Y.: Anchor Press, 1976), with the black feminist critique of Barbara Christian, *Black Women Novelists: The Development of a Tradition, 1892–1976* (Westport,

Conn.: Greenwood Press, 1980), and the recent reconsideration of Nella Larsen and Jessie Fauset as ethnic writers in Dearborn, *Pocahontas's Daughters*.

12. And as the "founder of the tradition of contemporary black women writers." She is considered by all the critics cited in note 11, but the two people most responsible for the critical acclaim accorded Hurston's work are Robert Hemenway, *Zora Neale Hurston: A Literary Biography* (Urbana: University of Illinois Press, 1977), and Alice Walker, who wrote the foreword to Hemenway's text and edited *I Love Myself When I Am Laughing . . . : A Zora Neale Hurston Reader* (Old Westbury, N.Y.: Feminist Press, 1979). Zora Neale Hurston, *Jonah's Gourd Vine* (Philadelphia: J. B. Lippincott, 1934); *Mules and Men* (Philadelphia: J. B. Lippincott, 1935); *Their Eyes Were Watching God* (Philadelphia: J. B. Lippincott, 1937); *Tell My Horse* (Philadelphia: J. B. Lippincott, 1938); *Moses, Man of the Mountain* (Philadelphia: J. B. Lippincott, 1939); *Dust Tracks on a Road: An Autobiography* (Philadelphia: J. B. Lippincott, 1942); *Polk County, a Comedy of Negro Life on a Sawmill Camp* (unpublished, 1944); *Seraph on the Suwanee* (New York: C. Scribner's Sons, 1948).

13. Jessie Redmond Fauset, *There Is Confusion* (New York: Boni & Liveright, 1924); *Plum Bun* (New York: Frederick A. Stokes, 1928); *The Chinaberry Tree* (New York: Frederick A. Stokes, 1931); *Comedy American Style* (New York: Frederick A. Stokes, 1933).

14. Fauset's middle-class code, however, was not merely imitative of white middle-class behavior, of which she could be extremely critical; rather, she tried to describe a particularly black middle-class ideology which was more moral and more civilized than the white racist society in which it existed.

15. Deborah E. McDowell, "Introduction: A Question of Power or the Rear Guard Faces Front," in Fauset, *Plum Bun* (1929; reprint London: Routledge Kegan Paul, 1985), pp. ix–xxiv.

16. See Chapter Four, pp. 88–90.

17. Nella Larsen, *Passing* (New York: Alfred A. Knopf, 1929).

18. Ann Petry, *The Street* (Boston: Houghton Mifflin, 1946); Dorothy West, *The Living Is Easy* (1948; Old Westbury, N.Y.: Feminist Press, 1982); Gwendolyn Brooks, *Maud Martha* (1951; New York: Harper & Brothers, 1953); Toni Morrison, *The Bluest Eye* (New York: Simon and Schuster, 1972); *Sula* (New York: Alfred A. Knopf, 1973); *Song of Solomon* (New York: New American Library, 1977).

Bibliography of Texts
by Black Women Authors

Allen, Sarah A. *See* Hopkins, Pauline Elizabeth.

Andrews, William A. *Sisters of the Spirit: Three Black Women's Autobiographies of the Nineteenth Century*. Bloomington: Indiana University Press, 1986.

Anonymous [probably Pauline Hopkins]. "Venus and Apollo Modelled from Ethiopians." *Colored American Magazine* 6 (June 1903): 465.

Aunt Sally. *Aunt Sally, or the Cross the Way of Freedom. Narrative of the Slave-Life and Purchase of the Mother of Rev. Isaac Williams of Detroit, Michigan*. Cincinnati: American Reform Tract and Book Society, 1858.

Belinda. "The Cruelty of Men, Whose Faces Were Like the Moon." Petition of an African Slave to the Legislature of Massachusetts. *The American Museum or Repository of Ancient and Modern Fugitive Pieces, &c. Prose and Poetical* 1 (June 1787).

Blake, Margaret Jane. *Memoirs of Margaret Jane Blake of Baltimore, Md. and Selections in Prose and Verse by Sarah R. Leavering*. Philadelphia: Press of Innes and Son, 1897.

Brown, Jane. *Narrative of the Life of Jane Brown and Her Two Children*. Hartford: n.p., 1860.

Burton, Annie Louise. *Memoirs of Childhood's Slavery Days*. Boston: n.p., 1909.

Cooper, Anna Julia. *A Voice from the South: By a Black Woman of the South*. Xenia, Ohio: Aldine Publishing House, 1892.

Delany, Lucy. *From the Darkness Cometh the Light, or Struggles for Freedom*. St. Louis: Publishing House of J. T. Smith, n.d.

Drumgoold, Kate. *A Slave Girl's Story: the Autobiography of Kate Drumgoold*. New York: n.p., 1898.

Du Bois, Silvia. [C. Wilson Larison.] *A Biography of the Slave Who Whipt*

Her Mistres and Gand Her Fredom. Ringos, N.J.: by the author, 1883.

Earle, Victoria. See Matthews, Victoria Earle.

Early, Sarah J., and Hallie Quinn Brown. "The Organized Efforts of the Colored Women of the South to Improve Their Condition." In May Wright Sewell, ed., *World's Congress of Representative Women.* Chicago: Rand McNally, 1894.

Eldridge, Elleanor. *Elleanor's Second Book.* Providence: B. T. Albro, 1842.

———. [Francis Harriet Greene McDougall.] *Memoirs of Elleanor Eldridge.* Providence: B. T. Albro, 1838.

Fauset, Jessie. *The Chinaberry Tree.* Philadelphia: Frederick A. Stokes, 1931.

———. *Comedy American Style.* New York: Frederick A. Stokes, 1933.

———. *Plum Bun.* New York: Frederick A. Stokes, 1928.

———. *There Is Confusion.* New York: Boni & Liveright, 1924.

Fields, Mamie. *Lemon Swamp and Other Places.* New York: Free Press, 1983.

Harper, Frances Ellen Watkins. "Colored Women of America." *Englishwoman's Review*, January 1878, pp. 10–15.

———. "Duty to Dependent Races." *National Council of Women of the United States, Transactions.* Philadelphia: National Council of Women of the United States, 1891, pp. 86–91.

———. *Idylls of the Bible.* Philadelphia: George S. Ferguson, 1901.

———. *Iola Leroy, or Shadows Uplifted.* Philadelphia: Garrigues Brothers, 1892.

———. *Moses: A Story of the Nile.* n.p., 1869.

———. "National Woman's Christian Temperance Union." *AME Church Review* 5 (1889): 242–45.

———. *Poems on Miscellaneous Subjects.* Boston: J. B. Yerrington and Son, 1854.

———. *Sketches of Southern Life.* Philadelphia: Ferguson Brothers, 1872.

———. *The Sparrow's Fall and Other Poems.* n.p., n.d.

———. "The Triumph of Freedom—A Dream." *Anglo-African Magazine*, January 1860, pp. 21–22.

———. "The Two Offers." *Anglo-African Magazine*, September 1859, pp. 288–91; October 1859, pp. 311–13.

———. "The Woman's Christian Temperance Union and the Colored Woman." *AME Church Review* 4 (1888): 313–16.

———. "Woman's Political Future." In May Wright Sewell, ed., *World's Congress of Representative Women.* Chicago: Rand McNally, 1894.

Hopkins, Pauline Elizabeth. "As the Lord Lives, He Is One of Our Mother's Children." *Colored American Magazine* 6 (November 1903): 795–801.

——. "Bro'r Abr'm Jimson's Wedding. A Christmas Story." *Colored American Magazine* 4 (December 1901): 103–12.

——. *Contending Forces: A Romance Illustrative of Negro Life North and South.* Boston: Colored Co-operative Publishing Co., 1900.

——. "A Dash for Liberty." *Colored American Magazine* 3 (August 1901): 243–47.

——. "Echoes from the Annual Convention of Northeastern Federation of Colored Women's Clubs." *Colored American Magazine* 6 (October 1903): 709–13.

——. "Elijah William Smith." *Colored American Magazine* 6 (December 1902): 96–100.

——. "Escape from Slavery. A Musical Drama." n.p., 1880.

——. "Famous Men of the Negro Race." *Colored American Magazine* 2–3 (December 1900–October 1901).

——. "Famous Women of the Negro Race." *Colored American Magazine* 4–5 (November 1901–October 1902).

——. "General Washington. A Christmas Story." *Colored American Magazine* 2 (December 1900): 95–104.

——. [Sarah A. Allen.] *Hagar's Daughter. A Story of Southern Caste Prejudice. Colored American Magazine* 2–4 (March 1901–March 1902).

——. "Heroes and Heroines in Black." *Colored American Magazine* 3 (January 1903): 206–11.

——. [Sarah A. Allen.] "Latest Phases of the Race Problem in America." *Colored American Magazine* 6 (February 1903): 244–51.

——. "Munroe Rogers." *Colored American Magazine* 6 (November 1902): 20–26.

——. "The Mystery Within Us." *Colored American Magazine* 1 (May 1900): 14–18.

——. [Sarah A. Allen.] "A New Profession." *Colored American Magazine* 6 (September 1903): 661–63.

——. *Of One Blood. or, the Hidden Self. Colored American Magazine* 6 (November 1902–November 1903).

——. *A Primer of Facts pertaining to the Early Greatness of the African Race and the Possibility of Restoration by Its Descendents.* Cambridge, Mass.: P. E. Hopkins & Co., 1905.

——. "Reminiscences of the Life and Times of Lydia Maria Child." *Colored American Magazine* 6 (February–June 1903).

——. "Talma Gordon." *Colored American Magazine* 1 (October 1900): 271–90.

———. [Sarah A. Allen.] "The Test of Manhood." *Colored American Magazine* 6 (December 1902): 113–19.

———. "Toussaint L'Overture." *Colored American Magazine* 2 (November 1900): 9–24.

———. "Whittier, the Friend of the Negro." *Colored American Magazine* 3 (September 1901): 324–30.

———. *Winona: A Tale of Negro Life in the South and Southwest. Colored American Magazine* 4–5 (May–October 1902).

Hurston, Zora Neale. *Dust Tracks on a Road: An Autobiography.* Philadelphia: J. B. Lippincott, 1942. Reprint, Robert B. Hemenway, ed. Urbana: University of Illinois Press, 1984.

———. *Jonah's Gourd Vine.* Philadelphia: J. B. Lippincott, 1934.

———. *Moses, Man of the Mountain.* Philadelphia: J. B. Lippincott, 1939.

———. *Mules and Men.* Philadelphia: J. B. Lippincott, 1935.

———. *Polk County, a Comedy of Negro Life on a Sawmill Camp.* Unpublished, 1944.

———. *Seraph on the Suwanee.* New York: C. Scribner's & Sons, 1948.

———. *Tell My Horse.* Philadelphia: J. B. Lippincott, 1938.

———. *Their Eyes Were Watching God.* Philadelphia: J. B. Lippincott, 1937.

Jacobs, Harriet. [Linda Brent.] *Incidents in the Life of a Slave Girl.* Boston: by the author, 1861.

Keckley, Elizabeth. *Behind the Scenes by Elizabeth Keckley, Formerly a Slave, but More Recently Modiste and Friend to Mrs. Abraham Lincoln, or Thirty Years a Slave and Four Years in the White House.* New York: n.p., 1868.

Kelley, Emma Dunham. *Megda.* Boston: James H. Earle, 1891.

Larsen, Nella. *Passing.* New York: Alfred A. Knopf, 1929.

———. *Quicksand.* New York: Alfred A. Knopf, 1928.

Lee, Jarena. *Religious Experience and Journal of Mrs. Jarena Lee, Giving an Account of Her Call to Preach the Gospel,* 2nd ed. Philadelphia: n.p., 1849.

Matthews, Victoria Earle. [Victoria Earle.] *Aunt Lindy. A Story Founded on Real Life.* New York: J. J. Little, 1893.

———. *The Awakening of the Afro-American Woman.* An address delivered at the Annual Convention of the Society of Christian Endeavor, San Francisco, July 11, 1897. New York: by the author, 1897.

———. "Value of Race Literature." An address to the National Conference of Colored Women, Boston, July 30, 1895.

Morrison, Toni. *The Bluest Eye.* New York: Simon and Schuster, 1972.

———. *Song of Solomon.* New York: New American Library, 1977.

———. *Sula.* New York: Alfred A. Knopf, 1973.

Mossell, N. F. [Gertrude Bustill Mossell.] *The Work of the Afro-American Woman*. Philadelphia: George S. Ferguson Co., 1894.

Petry, Ann. *The Street*. Boston: Houghton Mifflin, 1946.

Plato, Ann. *Essays, Including Biographies and Miscellaneous Pieces in Prose and Poetry*. Hartford: n.p., 1841.

Prince, Mary. *The History of Mary Prince, a West Indian Slave, Related by Herself*. London: F. Westley & A. H. Davis, 1831.

Prince, Nancy. *A Narrative of the Life and Travels of Mrs. Nancy Prince. Written by Herself*. Boston: by the author, 1850.

Smith, Amanda Berry. *An Autobiography of Mrs. Amanda Smith: The Colored Evangelist*. Chicago: Meyer & Brother, 1893.

Stewart, Maria W. *Meditations from the Pen of Mrs. Maria Stewart*. Washington, D.C.: Enterprise Publishing Co., 1879.

Taylor, Susie King. *Reminiscences of My Life in Camp with the 33rd. United States Colored Troops*. Boston: by the author, 1902.

Terrell, Mary Church. *A Colored Woman in a White World*. Washington, D.C.: Ransdell Publishing Co., 1940.

———. "Lynching from a Negro's Point of View." *North American Review* 177 (June 1904): 853–68.

Truth, Sojourner. *Narrative of Sojourner Truth*. Boston: by the author, 1875.

Veney, Bethany. *The Narrative of Bethany Veney, or Aunt Betty's Story*. Worcester, Mass.: by the author, 1889.

Wells, Ida B. [Ida B. Wells Barnett.] "Lynch Law in America." *Arena* 23 (January 1900): 15–24.

———. "Lynching and the Excuse for It." *Independent* 53 (May 1901): 1133–36.

———. *On Lynchings: Southern Horrors; A Red Record; Mob Rule in New Orleans*. New York: Arno Press, 1969.

———. *The Reason Why: The Colored American is not in the World's Columbian Exposition*. Chicago: by the author, 1893.

———. "The White Man's Problem." *Arena* 23 (January 1900): 1–30.

Williams, Fanny Barrier. "Club Movement among Colored Women of America." In J. E. MacBrady, ed., *A Negro for a New Century*. Chicago: American Publishing House, 1900.

———. "The Intellectual Progress of the Colored Women of the United States since the Emancipation Proclamation." In May Wright Sewell, ed., *World's Congress of Representative Women*. Chicago: Rand McNally, pp. 696–711.

———. "A Northern Negro's Autobiography." *Independent* 57 (July 1904): 96.

Wilson, Harriet E. *Our Nig; or, Sketches from the Life of a Free Black*. Boston: by the author, 1859.

General Bibliography

Alexander, Adele Logan. "How I Discovered My Grandmother." *Ms. Magazine*, November 1983, pp. 29–33.

Allen, Robert L. *Reluctant Reformers*. Garden City, N.Y.: Anchor Press, 1975.

Anderson, Jervis. *This Was Harlem: A Cultural Portrait, 1900–1950*. New York: Farrar Straus Giroux, 1982.

"Annual Meeting of the American Equal Rights Association." *The Revolution* 3 (May 20, 1869): 305–8.

"Annual Meeting of the American Equal Rights Association: Second Day's Proceedings." *The Revolution* 3 (May 27, 1869): 321–22.

Aptheker, Bettina, ed. *Lynching and Rape: An Exchange of Views*. Occasional paper no. 25. San Jose, Calif.: American Institute for Marxist Studies, 1977.

———. *Women's Legacy: Essays on Race, Sex, and Class in American History*. Amherst: University of Massachusetts Press, 1982.

Ayer, N. W., & Son. *American Newspaper Annual*. Philadelphia: N. W. Ayer & Son, 1904.

Bancroft, Frederick. *Slave Trading in the Old South*. New York: Frederick Ungar Publishing Co., 1959.

Bartlett, Irving H., and C. Glenn Cambor. "The History and Psychodynamics of Southern Womanhood." *Women's Studies* 2 (1974): 9–24.

Bauer, Raymond, and Alice Bauer. "Day to Day Resistance to Slavery." *Journal of Negro History* 27 (October 1942): 415–17.

Baym, Nina. *Novels, Readers, and Reviewers: Responses to Fiction in Antebellum America*. Ithaca: Cornell University Press, 1984.

———. *Woman's Fiction: A Guide to Novels By and About Women in America 1820–1870*. Ithaca: Cornell University Press, 1978.

Benson, Brian Joseph. "Colored American." In Walter C. Daniels, ed., *Black Journals of the United States*. Westport, Conn.: Greenwood Press, 1982.

Berg, Barbara. *The Remembered Gate: Origins of American Feminism. The Woman and the City, 1800–1860.* Oxford: Oxford University Press, 1978.

Berzon, Judith R. *Neither White nor Black: The Mulatto Character in American Fiction.* New York: New York University Press, 1978.

Blassingame, John W. *The Slave Community: Plantation Life in the Antebellum South,* 2nd ed. Oxford: Oxford University Press, 1979.

———, ed. *Slave Testimony.* Baton Rouge: Louisiana State University Press, 1977.

Bradford, Sarah H. *Harriet, the Moses of Her People.* New York: J. Little & Co., 1901.

Bragg, George. "Frances Harper." *Men of Maryland.* Baltimore: Church Advocate Press, 1925.

Braithwaite, William S. "Negro America's First Magazine." *Negro Digest* (December 1947): 21–26. In Philip Butcher, ed., *The William Stanley Braithwaite Reader.* Ann Arbor: University of Michigan Press, 1972, pp. 114–21.

Brawley, Benjamin Griffith. *Early Negro American Writers.* Chapel Hill: University of North Carolina Press, 1935.

———. *The Negro Genius.* New York: Dodd, Mead, 1937.

———. *The Negro in Literature and Art.* New York, Duffield & Co., 1929.

Brown, Hallie Quinn. *Homespun Heroines and Other Women of Distinction.* Xenia, Ohio: Aldine Publishing Co., 1926.

Brown, Sterling A., Arthur P. Davis, and Ulysses Lee. *The Negro Caravan: Writings by American Negroes.* New York: Dryden Press, 1941.

Brown, William Wells. *Clotelle.* Redpath's Books for the Campfires. Boston: James Redpath, 1864.

Browne, Martha. [Mattie Griffith.] *Autobiography of a Female Slave.* New York: J. S. Redfield, 1857.

Burg, David F. *Chicago's White City of 1893.* Lexington: University of Kentucky Press, 1976.

Butterfield, Stephen. *Black Autobiography in America.* Amherst: University of Massachusetts Press, 1974.

Cade, Toni, ed. *The Black Woman.* New York: New American Library, 1970.

Campbell, Horace. "Rastafari: Culture of Resistance." *Race and Class* 22 (Summer 1980): 1–22.

Carby, Hazel V. "White Woman Listen: Black Feminism and the Boundaries of Sisterhood." In Centre for Contemporary Cultural Studies, *The Empire Strikes Back: Race and Racism in Seventies Britain.* London: Hutchinson, 1982.

Carroll, Berenice A., ed. *Liberating Women's History.* Urbana: University of Illinois Press, 1976.

Cash, Wilbur. *The Mind of the South*. New York: Alfred Knopf, 1941.

Cawelti, John G. *Adventure, Mystery, and Romance: Formula Stories as Art and Popular Culture*. Chicago: University of Chicago Press, 1976.

Centre for Contemporary Cultural Studies. *The Empire Strikes Back: Race and Racism in Seventies Britain*. London: Hutchinson, 1982.

Chesnut, Mary Boykin. *A Diary from Dixie*. Ben Ames Williams, ed. Boston: Houghton Mifflin, 1949.

———. *Mary Chesnut's Civil War*. C. Vann Woodward, ed. New Haven: Yale University Press, 1981.

Child, Lydia Maria. *The American Frugal Housewife*, 30th ed. New York: Samuel S. and William Wood, 1844.

Childs, John Brown. "Afro-American Intellectuals and the People's Culture." *Theory and Society* 13 (1984): 69–90.

———. "Concepts of Culture in Afro-American Political Thought, 1890–1920." *Social Text* 4 (Fall 1981): 28–43.

Christian, Barbara. *Black Feminist Criticism: Perspectives on Black Women Writers*. New York: Pergamon Press, 1985.

———. *Black Women Novelists: The Development of a Tradition 1892–1976*. Westport, Conn.: Greenwood Press, 1980.

Clark, Alice. "Frances Ellen Watkins Harper." *Negro History Bulletin* 5 (January 1942): 83.

Clinton, Catherine. *The Other Civil War: American Women in the Nineteenth Century*. New York: Hill and Wang, 1984.

———. *The Plantation Mistress: Woman's World in the Old South*. New York: Pantheon, 1982.

Conrad, Earl. *Harriet Tubman*. New York: Paul S. Eriksson, 1943.

Cott, Nancy F. "Passionlessness: An Interpretation of Victorian Sexual Ideology, 1790–1850." *Signs* 4 (Winter 1978): 219–33.

Cox, J. Randolph. "The Detective Hero in the American Dime Novel." *Dime Novel Roundup* 50 (February 1981): 2–18.

Craft, William. *Running a Thousand Miles for Freedom, or, the Escape of William and Ellen Craft from Slavery*. London: W. Tweedie, 1860; reprint, Arna Bontemps, ed. *Great Slave Narratives*. Boston: Beacon Press, 1969.

Dannett, Sylvia G. L. *Profiles of Negro Womanhood 1619–1900*, Vol. 1. Chicago: Educational Heritage, 1964.

Davidson, Basil. *The Lost Cities of Africa*. Boston: Little Brown, 1959.

Davis, Angela. "Racism and Contemporary Literature on Rape." *Freedomways* 16 (1976): 25–33.

———. "Reflections on the Black Woman's Role in the Community of Slaves." *Black Scholar* 3 (December 1971): 3–15.

———. *Women, Race and Class*. New York: Random House, 1981.

Davis, Arthur P. *From the Dark Tower: Afro-American Writers 1900–1960*. Washington, D.C.: Howard University Press, 1981.

Davis, Elizabeth Lindsay. *Lifting As They Climb: The National Association of Colored Women*. Washington, D.C.: National Association of Colored Women, 1933.

Davis, Lenwood G. *The Black Woman in American Society. A Selected Annotated Bibliography*. Boston: G. K. Hall, 1975.

Dearborn, Mary V. *Pocahontas's Daughters: Gender and Ethnicity in American Culture*. New York: Oxford University Press, 1986.

Denning, Michael. *Mechanic Accents: Dime Novels and Working-Class Culture in 19th-Century America*. London: Verso, 1987.

Dill, Bonnie Thornton. "Race, Class, and Gender: Prospects for an All-inclusive Sisterhood." *Feminist Studies* 9 (Spring 1983): 131–50.

Doenecke, Justus D. "Myths, Machines and Markets: The Columbian Exposition of 1893." *Journal of Popular Culture* (Winter 1972): 535–49.

Douglass, Frederick. *Narrative of the Life of Frederick Douglass an American Slave*. Boston: Boston Anti-Slavery Society, 1845.

Drew, Thomas R. "Dissertation on the Characteristic Differences between the Sexes, and on the Position and Influence of Woman in Society." *Southern Literary Messenger* 1 (May 1835): 493–512.

Du Bois, W. E. B. *Black Reconstruction in America, 1860–1880*. New York: Harcourt Brace & Co., 1935.

———. *The Souls of Black Folk*. New York: Fawcett World Library, 1961.

———. "The Talented Tenth." In Booker T. Washington, ed., *The Negro Problem: A Series of Articles by Representative Negroes of Today*. New York: James Pott & Co., 1903.

———, ed. *Atlanta University Publications*, Vols. 1 and 2. New York: Octagon Books, 1968.

Eagleton, Terry. *The Rape of Clarissa*. Minneapolis: University of Minnesota Press, 1982.

Elliot, R. S. "The Story of Our Magazine." *Colored American Magazine* 3 (May 1901): 43.

Epstein, Barbara Leslie. *The Politics of Domesticity, Women Evangelism and Temperance in Nineteenth Century America*. Middletown, Conn.: Wesleyan University Press, 1981.

Ferguson, Alfred R. "The Abolition of Blacks in Abolitionist Fiction, 1830–1860." *Journal of Black Studies* 5 (1974): 134–56.

Fishburn, Katherine. *Women in Popular Culture: A Reference Guide*. Westport, Conn.: Greenwood Press, 1982.

Flexner, Eleanor. *Century of Struggle: The Woman's Rights Movement in the United States*, 2nd ed. Cambridge: Harvard University Press, 1975.

Foner, Philip S. *The Voice of Black America: Major Speeches by Negroes in the United States, 1797–1971*. New York: Simon and Schuster, 1972.

Forrest, Mary. [Mrs. Julia Deane Freeman.] *Women of the South Distinguished in Literature*. New York: Derby & Jackson, 1861.

Foster, Frances Smith. "Changing Concepts of the Black Woman." *Journal of Black Studies* 3 (June 1973): 433–54.

———. *Witnessing Slavery: The Development of the Ante-Bellum Slave Narratives*. Westport, Conn.: Greenwood Press, 1979.

Fredrickson, George M. *The Black Image in the White Mind: The Debate on Afro-American Character and Destiny, 1817–1914*. New York: Harper and Row, 1971.

Gayle, Addison. *The Way of the New World: The Black Novel in America*. Garden City, N.Y.: Anchor Press, 1976.

Genovese, Eugene D. "Life in the Big House." In Nancy Cott, ed., *A Heritage of Her Own*. New York: Touchstone, 1979, pp. 290–97.

———. *Roll, Jordan, Roll: The World the Slaves Made*. New York: Random House, 1976.

Gibson, J. W., and W. H. Crogman, eds. *Progress of the Race*. Atlanta: J. L. Nichols Co., 1903.

Giddings, Paula. *When and Where I Enter: The Impact of Black Women on Race and Sex in America*. New York: William Morrow, 1984.

Gilbert, Sandra M., and Susan Gubar. *The Madwoman in the Attic: The Woman Writer and the Nineteenth-Century Literary Imagination*. New Haven: Yale University Press, 1979.

Gilroy, Paul. '*There Ain't No Black in the Union Jack': The Cultural Politics of Race and Nation*. London: Hutchinson, 1987.

———. "You Can't Fool the Youths . . . Race and Class Formation in the 1980s." *Race and Class* 23 (Summer 1981): 207–22.

Gloster, Hugh M. *Negro Voices in American Fiction*. Chapel Hill: University of North Carolina Press, 1948.

Goodson, Martia Graham. "The Slave Narrative Collection: A Tool for Reconstructing Afro-American Women's History." *Western Journal of Black Studies* 3 (Summer 1979): 116–22.

Green, Michael. "The Centre for Contemporary Cultural Studies." In Peter Widdowson, ed., *Re-Reading English*. London: Methuen, 1982, pp. 77–90.

Griffith, Mattie. *Autobiography of a Female Slave*. New York: Redfield, 1857.

Grimke, Sarah M. *Letters on the Equality of the Sexes and the Condition of Women*. Boston: Issac Knapp, 1838.

Gurko, Miriam. *The Ladies of Seneca Falls*. New York: Macmillan, 1974.

Gutman, Herbert G. *The Black Family in Slavery and Freedom.* New York: Random House, 1977.

———. "Marital and Sexual Norms among Slave Women." In Nancy Cott, ed., *A Heritage of Her Own.* New York: Touchstone, 1979, pp. 298–311.

Gwin, Minrose C. *Black and White Women of the Old South: The Peculiar Sisterhood in American Literature.* Knoxville: University of Tennessee Press, 1985.

Habegger, Alfred. *Gender Fantasy and Realism in American Literature.* New York: Columbia University Press, 1982.

Hale, Sarah Josepha. *Northwood: A Tale of New England.* Boston: Bowles and Dearborn, 1827.

Hall, Jacqueline Dowd. *The Revolt against Chivalry: Jessie Daniel Ames and the Women's Campaign against Lynching.* New York: Columbia University Press, 1979.

Hall, Stuart. "Cultural Studies: Two Paradigms." *Media, Culture and Society* 2 (1980): 57–72.

———. "Culture, the Media and the 'Ideological' Effect." In James Curran, Michael Gurevitch, and Janet Woolacott, eds., *Mass Communications and Society.* London: Edward Arnold, 1977, pp. 315–48.

———. "Notes on Deconstructing 'the popular.'" In Ralph Samuel, ed. *People's History and Socialist Theory.* History Workshop Series. London: Routledge & Kegan Paul, 1981.

———. "Pluralism, Race and Class in Caribbean Society." In *Race and Class in Post Colonial Society.* Paris: UNESCO, 1977, pp. 150–82.

———. *Policing the Crisis: Mugging, the State, and Law and Order.* London: Macmillan, 1978.

———. "Race, Articulation and Societies Structured in Dominance." In *Sociological Theories: Race and Colonialism.* Paris: UNESCO, 1980, pp. 305–45.

———. "Racism and Reaction." In *Five Views of Multi-Racial Britain.* London: Commission for Racial Equality, 1978, pp. 23–35.

———. "A 'Reading' of Marx's 1857 Introduction to the Grundrisse." *CCCS Stencilled Papers* 1 (1973).

———. "The Rediscovery of 'Ideology': Return of the Repressed in Media Studies." In Michael Gurevitch, Tony Bennett, James Curran, and Janet Woolacott, eds., *Culture, Society and the Media.* New York: Methuen, 1982, pp. 56–90.

———. "Rethinking the Base/Superstructure Metaphor." In John Bloomfield, ed., *Class, Party and Hegemony.* London: Lawrence and Wishart, 1977, pp. 43–72.

————. "The Whites of Their Eyes: Racist Ideologies and the Media." In George Bridges and Rosalind Brunt, eds., *Silver Linings: Some Strategies for the Eighties.* London: Lawrence and Wishart, 1981.

Hanaford, Phebe A. *Daughters of America; or Women of the Century.* Augusta, Maine: True & Co., 1882.

Harding, Vincent. *The Other American Revolution.* Afro-American Culture and Society, no. 4. Los Angeles: University of California, Los Angeles, and Institute of the Black World, 1980.

————. *There Is a River: The Black Struggle for Freedom in America.* New York: Harcourt Brace Jovanovich, 1981.

Harley, Sharon and Rosalyn Terborg-Penn. *The Afro-American Woman: Struggles and Images.* Port Washington, N.Y.: Kennikat Press, 1978.

Harris, Trudier. *From Mammies to Militants: Domestics in Black American Literature.* Philadelphia: Temple University Press, 1982.

Harris, William H. *Keeping the Faith: A. Philip Randolph, Milton P. Webster, and the Brotherhood of Sleeping Car Porters, 1925–37.* Urbana: University of Illinois Press, 1977.

Hemenway, Robert. *Zora Neale Hurston: A Literary Biography.* Urbana: University of Illinois Press, 1977.

Hentz, Caroline Lee. *Eoline, or Magnolia Vale.* Philadelphia: T. B. Peterson, 1852.

————. *Linda: The Young Pilot of the Belle Creole, a Tale of Southern Life.* Philadelphia: A. Hart, 1850.

Hine, Darlene C. "Female Slave Resistance: The Economics of Sex." *Western Journal of Black Studies* 3 (Summer 1979): 123–27.

Holt, Thomas C. "The Lonely Warrior: Ida B. Wells and the Struggle for Black Leadership." In John Hope Franklin, ed., *Black Leaders of the Twentieth Century.* Urbana: University of Illinois Press, 1982.

Holton, Sylvia Wallace. *Down Home and Uptown: The Representation of Black Speech in American Fiction.* Rutherford, N.J.: Fairleigh Dickinson University Press, 1984.

Hughes, Langston. *The Big Sea: An Autobiography.* 1940. Reprint New York: Hill and Wang, 1963.

————. *I Wonder as I Wander: An Autobiographical Journey.* 1956. Reprint New York: Hill and Wang, 1964.

Huggins, Nathan Irvin. *Harlem Renaissance.* New York: Oxford University Press, 1971.

Hull, Gloria T., Patricia Bell Scott, and Barbara Smith, eds. *All the Women Are White, All the Blacks Are Men, but Some of Us Are Brave.* Old Westbury, N.Y.: Feminist Press, 1982.

Hutchinson, Louise Daniel. *Anna Julia Cooper: A Voice from the South.* Washington, D.C.: Smithsonian Institution Press, 1981.

James, C. L. R. *At the Rendezvous of Victory.* London: Allison and Busby, 1984.

———. *Beyond a Boundary.* 1963. Reprint London: Stanley Paul, 1980.

———. *The Future in the Present.* London: Allison and Busby, 1977.

———. *Spheres of Existence.* London: Allison and Busby, 1980.

James, Edward T., Janet Wilson James, and Paul S. Boyer, eds. *Notable American Women: A Biographical Dictionary, 1607–1950.* Cambridge: Harvard University Press, 1971.

Johnson, A. A., and R. M. Johnson. "Away from Accommodation: Radical Editors and Protest Journalism, 1900–1910." *Journal of Negro History* 62 (October 1977): 325–38.

Jones, Anne Goodwyn. *Tomorrow Is Another Day: The Woman Writer in the South, 1859–1936.* Baton Rouge: Louisiana State University Press, 1981.

Jones, Jacqueline. *Labor of Love, Labor of Sorrow: Black Women, Work, and the Family from Slavery to the Present.* New York: Basic Books, 1985.

Kelley, Mary. *Private Woman, Public Stage: Literary Domesticity in Nineteenth Century America.* New York: Oxford University Press, 1983.

Kendricks, Ralph, and Claude Levitt, eds. *Afro-American Voices 1770's–1970's.* Los Angeles: Oxford Book Co., 1970.

Kennedy, John Pendleton. *Swallow Barn, or a Sojourn in the Old Dominion.* Philadelphia: Carey & Lee, 1832.

Kraditor, Aileen S., ed. *Up from the Pedestal: Selected Writings in the History of American Feminism.* New York: New York Times Book Co., 1968.

Lasch, Christopher. *The World of Nations: Reflections on American History, Politics and Culture.* New York: Alfred A. Knopf, 1973.

Lerner, Gerda. *Black Women in White America.* New York: Random House, 1973.

Lester, Julius, ed. *The Seventh Son: The Thought and Writings of W. E. B. Du Bois*, Vol. 1. New York: Random House, 1971.

Levy, David. "Racial Stereotypes in Antislavery Fiction." *Phylon* 31 (1970): 265–79.

Lewis, David Levering. *When Harlem Was in Vogue.* New York: Vintage, 1982.

Locke, Alain, ed. *The New Negro.* New York: Albert and Charles Boni, 1925.

Loewenberg, Bert James, and Ruth Bogin. *Black Women in Nineteenth Century American Life.* Philadelphia: Pennsylvania State University Press, 1976.

Logan, Rayford, and Michael R. Winston. *Dictionary of American Negro Biography*. New York: W. W. Norton, 1982.

Loggins, Vernon. *The Negro Author, His Development in America*. New York: Columbia University Press, 1931.

Majors, Monroe A. *Noted Negro Women*. 1893. Reprint Freeport, N.Y.: Books for Libraries Press, 1971.

Massa, Ann. "Black Women in the 'White City.'" *Journal of American Studies* 8 (December 1974): 319–37.

Massey, Mary Elizabeth. "The Making of a Feminist." *Journal of Southern History* 39 (1973): 3–22.

McDowell, Deborah. "New Directions for Black Feminist Criticism." *Black American Literature Forum* 14. In Elaine Showalter, ed., *The New Feminist Criticism: Essays on Women, Literature and Theory*. New York: Pantheon, 1985, pp. 186–99.

McKay, Claude. *A Long Way from Home: An Autobiography*. 1940. New York: Harcourt Brace & World, 1970.

Meier, August. "Booker T. Washington and the Negro Press: With Special Reference to the Colored American Magazine." *Journal of Negro History* 38 (January 1953): 67–90.

———. *Negro Thought in America, 1880–1915*. Ann Arbor: University of Michigan Press, 1963.

Melder, Keith. *Beginnings of Sisterhood: The American Women's Rights Movement, 1800–1850*. New York: Shocken, 1977.

Mitchell, Sally. *The Fallen Angel: Chastity, Class and Women's Reading 1835–1880*. Bowling Green, Ohio: Bowling Green University Popular Press, 1981.

Nichols, Charles. *Many Thousands Gone: The Ex-slaves' Account of Their Bondage and Freedom*. Bloomington: Indiana University Press, 1969.

Nichols, J. L., and William Crogman, eds. *Progress of a Race*, 2nd. ed. Naperville, Ill.: J. L. Nichols Co., 1929.

Ohmann, Richard. "Where Did Mass Culture Come From? The Case of Magazines." *Berkshire Review* 16 (1981): 85–101.

Omolade, Barbara. "Black Women and Feminism." In Hester Feisenstein and Alice Jardine, eds., *The Future of Difference*. Boston: G. K. Hall, 1980, pp. 247–57.

Palmer, Phyllis Marynick. "White Women/Black Women: The Dualism of Female Identity and Experience in the United States." *Feminist Studies* 9 (Spring 1983): 151–70.

Penn, Irvine Garland. *The Afro-American Press and Its Editors*. Springfield, Mass.: Willey & Co., 1891.

Pierson, Emily Catherine. *Jamie Parker, the Fugitive*. Hartford: n.p., 1851.

Pike, Mary Hayden. *Ida May: Story of Things Actual and Possible*. New York: Phillips, Sampson & Co., 1854.

Pomeroy, Sarah B. *Goddesses, Whores, Wives, and Slaves: Women in Classical Antiquity*. New York: Shocken, 1975.

Quarles, Benjamin. "Frederick Douglass and the Woman's Rights Movement." *Journal of Negro History* 25 (January 1940): 35–44.

Quincy, Josiah. "Journal of Josiah Quincy Junior." *Massachusetts Historical Society Proceedings* 49 (June 1916): 424–81.

Reynolds, Thomas J. *Dinah, a Black Mamma*. Magnolia, Ark.: by the author, 1906.

Robinson, Cedric J. *Black Marxism: The Making of the Black Radical Tradition*. London: Zed Press, 1983.

Robinson, Wilhelmina S. *Historical Negro Biographies*. International Library of Negro Life and History. New York: Publishers Co., 1967.

Rosenberg, Charles E. "Sexuality, Class and Role in Nineteenth Century America." *American Quarterly* 25 (May 1973): 131–53.

Rudwick, Elliot M., and August Meier. "Black Man in the 'White City': Negroes and the Columbian Exposition, 1893." *Phylon* 26 (Winter 1965): 354–61.

Ruoff, John C. "Frivolity to Consumption: Or, Southern Womanhood in Antebellum Literature." *Civil War History* 18 (1972): 213–29.

Rydell, Robert W. "The World's Columbian Exposition of 1893: Racist Underpinnings of a Utopian Artifact." *Journal of American Culture* 1 (Summer 1978): 253–75.

Scott, Ann. *The Southern Lady: From Pedestal to Politics, 1830–1930*. Chicago: University of Chicago Press, 1970.

Scruggs, L. C. *Women of Distinction*. Raleigh, N.C.: by the author, 1893.

Seidel, Kathryn L. "The Southern Belle as an Antebellum Ideal." *Southern Quarterly* 15 (1977): 387–401.

Sewell, May Wright, ed. *World's Congress of Representative Women: A Historical Resume*. Chicago: Rand McNally, 1894.

Shockley, Ann Allen. "Pauline Elizabeth Hopkins: A Biographical Excursion into Obscurity." *Phylon* 33 (Spring 1972): 22–26.

Showalter, Elaine, ed. *The New Feminist Criticism: Essays on Women, Literature and Theory*. New York: Pantheon, 1985.

Sicherman, Barbara, and Carol Hurd Green, eds. *Notable American Women: A Biographical Dictionary, the Modern Period*. Cambridge: Harvard University Press, 1980.

Sides, Sudie Duncan. "Southern Women and Slavery." *History Today* 20 (January 1970): 54–60; (February 1970): 124–30.

Sims, Janet L. *The Progress of Afro-American Women, a Selected Bibliog-*

raphy and Resource Guide. Westport, Conn.: Greenwood Press, 1980.

Smith, Barbara. "Toward a Black Feminist Criticism." *Conditions Two* 1 (October 1977). In Elaine Showalter, ed., *The New Feminist Criticism: Essays on Women, Literature and Theory*. New York: Pantheon, 1985, pp. 168–85.

———, ed. *Home Girls: A Black Feminist Anthology*. New York: Kitchen Table, Women of Color Press, 1983.

Southworth, E. D. E. N. *Retribution: A Tale of Passion*. Philadelphia: T. B. Peterson, 1856.

Spero, Sterling D., and Abram L. Harris. *The Black Worker*. New York: Atheneum, 1969.

Spillers, Hortense. "Black/Female/Critic." *Women's Review of Books* 2 (September 1985): 9–10.

Spruill, Julia Cherry. *Women's Life and Work in the Southern Colonies*. Chapel Hill: University of North Carolina Press, 1938. Reprint New York: W. W. Norton, 1972.

Stage, Sarah J. "Out of the Attic: Studies of Victorian Sexuality." *American Quarterly* 27 (October 1975): 480–86.

Stanton, Elizabeth Cady. *History of Woman Suffrage*. New York: Fowler & Wells, 1881.

Starling, Marion. *The Slave Narrative: Its Place in Literary History*. Boston: G. K. Hall, 1982.

Sterling, Dorothy, ed. *We Are Your Sisters: Black Women in the Nineteenth Century*. New York: W. W. Norton, 1984.

Still, William. *The Underground Railroad*. Philadelphia: Porter & Coates, 1872.

Stowe, Harriet Beecher. *Uncle Tom's Cabin; or, Life among the Lowly*. Boston: John P. Jewett & Co., 1852.

Strasser, Susan. *Never Done*. New York: Pantheon, 1982.

Taylor, William R. *Cavalier and Yankee*. New York: Anchor, 1963.

Terborg-Penn, Rosalyn. "Discontented Black Feminists: Prelude and Postscripts to the Nineteenth Amendment." In Lois Scharf and Joan M. Jensen, eds., *Decades of Discontent: The Women's Movement, 1920–1940*. Westport, Conn.: Greenwood Press, 1983.

Trachtenberg, Alan. *The Incorporation of America: Culture and Society in the Gilded Age*. New York: Hill and Wang, 1982.

Truman, Ben C. *History of the World's Fair Being a Complete and Authentic Description of the Columbian Exposition from Its Inception*. Philadelphia: Standard Publishing Co., 1893.

U.S. Department of Commerce. Bureau of the Census. *Negro Population in the United States 1790–1915*. New York: Arno Press, 1968.

Victor, Metta Victoria. *Maum Guinea and Her Plantation Children.* New York: Beadle & Co., 1861.

Vincent, Theodore G., ed. *Voices of a Black Nation: Political Journalism in the Harlem Renaissance.* San Francisco: Ramparts Press, 1973.

Voloshinov, V. N. *Marxism and the Philosophy of Language.* New York: Seminar Press, 1973.

Walker, Alice. "One Child of One's Own: A Meaningful Digression within the Work(s)." *In Search of Our Mothers' Gardens.* New York: Harcourt Brace Jovanovich, 1983, pp. 361–83.

———, ed. *I Love Myself When I Am Laughing . . . : A Zora Neale Hurston Reader.* Old Westbury, N.Y.: Feminist Press, 1979.

Washington, Mary Helen. "Teaching Black-Eyed Susans: An Approach to the Study of Black Women Writers." In Gloria Hull, Patricia Bell Scott, and Barbara Smith, eds., *All the Women Are White, All the Blacks Are Men, but Some of Us Are Brave.* Old Westbury, N.Y.: Feminist Press, 1982, pp. 208–17.

———, ed. *Black-Eyed Susans.* New York: Anchor Press, 1975.

Welter, Barbara. *Dimity Convictions: The American Woman in the Nineteenth Century.* Columbus: University of Ohio Press, 1976.

West, Cornel. "The Dilemma of the Black Intellectual." *Cultural Critique* 1 (Fall 1985): 109–24.

———. *Prophesy Deliverance! An Afro-American Revolutionary Christianity.* Philadelphia: Westminster Press, 1982.

White, Deborah Gray. *Ar'n't I a Woman? Female Slaves in the Plantation South.* New York: W. W. Norton, 1985.

Williams, Ora. *American Black Women in the Arts and Social Sciences: A Bibliographic Survey.* Metuchen, N.J.: Scarecrow Press, 1966.

Woodward, C. Vann. *The Strange Career of Jim Crow,* 2nd ed. New York: Oxford University Press, 1966.

———, ed. *Mary Chesnut's Civil War.* New Haven: Yale University Press, 1981.

Yellin, Jean. "Incidents in the Life of Our National Letters." Paper presented at the Seminar on Women and Society, Columbia University, April 12, 1982.

———. "Texts and Contexts of Harriet Jacobs' Incidents in the Life of a Slave Girl: Written by Herself." *The Slave's Narrative.* Charles T. Davis and Henry Louis Gates, Jr., eds. New York: Oxford University Press, 1985.

———. "Written by Herself: Harriet Jacobs' Slave Narrative." *American Literature* 53 (November 1981): 479–86.

Index

Abolitionism, 34–35, 44, 61, 63, 65, 121, 129–31, 151–52
British, 130–31
African Methodist Episcopal Church, 65, 109
Alexander, Adele Logan, 119
Alienation, 169–70
Allen, Sarah A., 145
Allen, Sarah A., [pseudonym]. *See* Hopkins, Pauline Elizabeth
Amalgamation. *See* Miscegenation
AME Church. *See* African Methodist Episcopal Church
American Equal Rights Association, 67–68
Anthony, Susan B., 67–68
Antislavery Society of Maine, 65
Atlanta Constitution, 85

Baym, Nina, 72–77
Beauty, ideologies of, 159–60
Berg, Barbara, 26
The Remembered Gate, 26
Berry, Mary, 10–11
Black feminism, 11, 95–120
Black feminist critics, 10–15
Black feminist literary criticism. *See* Black feminist theory
Black feminist theory, 3, 7–19, 95–120

black feminist literary criticism, 7–16, 53
Black manhood, 35–36, 46, 113, 143–44
Black readership, 125–27
Black womanhood, discourse of, 6, 32, 39, 59–61, 144
Black women's organizations, 4, 39, 96–97, 116–20, 122
Colored Women's League (Washington), 116
Congress of Colored Women of the United States, 96
Ida B. Wells Club (Chicago), 116
National Association of Colored Women, 39, 96–97, 117, 118
National Federation of Afro-American Women, 96
National League of Colored Women, 96
Tuskegee Woman's Club, 119
Woman's Columbian Association, 4
Women's Columbian Auxiliary Association, 4
Women's Era Club (Boston), 116, 120, 122
Women's Loyal Union (New York), 116
Black women's studies, 10–11

Blassingame, John, 21–22, 45–46,
        48
    The Slave Community, 21, 45–
        46
Board of Lady Managers. *See*
        World's Congress of
        Representative Women
Brooks, Gwendolyn, 175
    Maud Martha, 175
Brown, Hallie Quinn, 3–4, 96
Brown, John, 154–55
Brown, Sterling, 71
Brown, William Wells, 71–72, 80–
        81, 121–22, 146–47
    Clotelle, 71–72, 80–81, 146–47

Chesnut, Mary Boykin, 28–29,
        31–32
Chicago Tribune, 111
Child, Lydia Maria, 47
Christian, Barbara, 11, 13–15
    *Black Feminist Criticism:
        Perspectives on Black Women
        Writers*, 11, 13–15
Christian Recorder, 66
Class, 17–18, 73, 166–69, 171, 173,
        175
Clinton, Catherine, 20, 24–25, 27,
        30
    The Plantation Mistress, 20
Colonization, internal, 133–36,
        137–40, 142, 143–44. *See also*
        Imperialism
    of women's bodies, 143–44
Colored American Magazine, 120,
        121–27, 145, 155, 158, 159–60,
        162, 163, 164, 165–66
Colored Co-operative Publishing
        Company, 120, 121, 124,
        166

Columbian Exposition. *See*
        World's Columbian
        Exposition
Congress of Representative
        Women. *See* World's Congress
        of Representative Women
Consumer, figure of, 170, 172–73
Cooper, Anna Julia, 3, 6, 7, 96–
        108, 114–17, 118, 120
    A Voice From the South, 96,
        97–108, 114–15
Coppin, Fannie Jackson, 3–4, 96
Craft, William and Ellen, 35–36
    *Running a Thousand Miles for
        Freedom*, 35–36
Cult of true womanhood, 21, 23–
        34, 39, 42, 47, 49–50, 53, 55–
        57, 61, 74, 100, 131, 148
    dissection of, 47, 49–50, 55–57
    and fiction, 33–34
    as ideology, 23–25, 30–32, 39, 55
    and sexuality, 27, 30
    tenets of, 23, 25
Cultural studies, 178–79 *n*, 179–
        80 *n*

Davis, Angela, 39
Davis, Arthur P., 71
Davis, Elizabeth Lindsay, 118
Delany, Lucy, 36–37
    *From the Darkness Cometh the
        Light, or Struggles for
        Freedom*, 36–37
Desire, 174, 185 *n*
Diaspora, as narrative convention,
        136, 157
Dime novels and story papers,
        144, 145–46, 149–50, 194–95 *n*
Disguise, 145, 147–49, 156
    and passing, 147–48
Domestic novels, 33–34, 72–77

Douglass, Frederick, 5, 27–29, 68, 110
  Narrative of the Life of Frederick Douglass an American Slave, 27–29
Drew, Thomas R., 27
Drumgoold, Kate, 37–51
  A Slave Girl's Story, 37, 51
Du Bois, W. E. B., 84–85, 91–94, 96, 97, 108, 126–27
  and the "Talented Tenth," 84–85, 91–92

Earle, Victoria. *See* Matthews, Victoria Earle
Early, Sarah J., 3–4, 96
Education, 97, 99–101
Ellison, Ralph, 175
Emerson, Ralph Waldo, 134
Ethiopianism, 156–58, 159–60

Father, as narrative figure, 143–44
Fauset, Jessie, 166–68, 171
  Plum Bun, 167, 171
  The Chinaberry Tree, 167–68
Folk, 77–78, 164–65, 166, 169
Formulaic conventions, 147–53, 187 *n. See also* Disguise
  detective, 149–50
  magical resolutions, 150–51
  masculinized female, 148–49
  narrative limits of, 152–53
Fortune, Thomas T., 110
Foster, Frances Smith, 32, 38–39
  Witnessing Slavery: The Development of the Antebellum Slave Narratives, 32, 38–39
Free Soil Movement, 155
Free Speech, 109–10

Garrison, William Lloyd, 34–35
Garvey, Marcus, 166
Gates, Henry Louis, 43
Gilbert Sandra, 63–65
Gilman, Caroline, 38, 39
  Recollections of a Southern Matron, 38, 39
Gloster, Hugh, 71
  Negro Voices in American Fiction, 71
Grady, Henry W., 85–86
Greenwood, Grace, 66–67
Gubar, Susan, 63–65

Hale, Sara Josepha, 33
Hanaford, Phebe, 67
  Daughters of America; or Women of the Century, 67
Harper, Fenton, 65
Harper, Frances, 3, 7, 62–94, 95, 96, 97, 99, 101, 108, 109, 114, 115, 118, 120, 143
  Iola Leroy; or, Shadows Uplifted, 62–64, 71–94, 96, 143
Hentz, Caroline Lee, 26, 33
  Eoline, or Magnolia Vale, 26, 33
Hopkins, Pauline Elizabeth, 7, 95, 97, 101, 105, 106, 108, 113, 120, 121–62, 164, 166, 167
  Contending Forces, 120, 121–22, 128–44, 145, 146, 158, 162
  Hagar's Daughter, 127, 145–53
  Of One Blood, 127, 155–61
  Winona, 127, 146, 153–55
Hull, Gloria T., 10
  All the Women Are White, All the Blacks Are Men, But Some of Us Are Brave, 10–11
Hurston, Zora Neale, 164, 166, 175

Imperialism, 96, 97, 101–2, 114, 133–36, 140, 141–42, 162

Independent, 66–67

Inheritance, 76, 128, 132–33, 135–37, 146, 167

Intellectual leadership, 6, 7, 19, 15, 17, 67, 77–80, 82–88, 90–94, 96–97, 99, 115–20, 130, 162, 164–67, 170–72

and black women, 6, 7, 17, 19, 77–80, 84, 96–97, 99, 114–20, 162, 166–67

by an elite, 84–85, 87–88, 90–94, 115–20, 164–67

and the folk, 77–78, 80, 82–83, 164–65

and the people, 166

Jacobs, Harriet, 6, 39, 40, 45–61, 71

Incidents in the Life of a Slave Girl, 40, 45–61

Jim Crow, 64, 89–90, 93, 104, 111, 128, 172

Jordan, June, 108

Kelley, Emma Dunham, 96

Megda, 96

Language, 8, 9, 16–17, 78, 83, 170

existence of black female, 8, 9, 16

Larsen, Nella, 166, 168–75

Passing, 171

Quicksand, 166, 168–75

Lee, Ulysses, 71

Lesbian aesthetic, 9, 12

Levy, David, 33

Liberator, 35

Literacy, 83, 126

Literary stereotypes, 14, 22

Logan, Adella Hunt, 119

Lynching, 93, 96, 109–14, 115–16, 128, 129, 136–38, 141

McDowell, Deborah, 11–13, 167

Magazine fiction, 145–62

Magazines, 122–26. See also *Colored American Magazine*

Matthews, Victoria Earle, 96, 117–18

Aunt Lindy, 96

The Awakening of the Afro-American Women, 117–18

Meier, August, 83–84

Messenger, 165

Migration, 164, 166–67, 172

Miscegenation, 35–36, 45, 46, 91, 109–11, 113, 128, 134–35, 137, 140–41, 142–43, 160–61

as incest, 160–61

as rape, 141

Missouri Press Association, 116

Moral panic, 112, 190 *n*

Morrison, Toni, 7, 175

Mossell, Gertrude, 96

The Work of the Afro-American Woman, 96

Motherhood, ideologies of, 20, 25, 49–50, 56–57, 59–61, 142–43, 144. *See also* Cult of true womanhood; Sexual ideologies; Womanhood, ideologies of

Mulatta. *See* Mulatto characters

Mulatto characters, 34, 63, 73, 88–91, 135, 137, 140–41, 171, 173, 174

NACW. *See* Black women's organizations
Narratives of free women, 40–45, 95
National American Woman Suffrage Association, 119
National Association of Colored Women. *See* Black women's organizations
NAWSA. *See* National American Woman Suffrage Association
"New Negro," 165
New York Age, 110
New York Voice, 113

Occupations of black people, 126–27
Octoroon characters. *See* Mulatto characters
Ohmann, Richard, 125
Owen, Chandler, 165

Pan-Africanism, 158–61
Passing, 90, 119, 147–48, 158–59, 171
Patronage, 165–66
Petry, Ann, 175
    The Street, 175
Pike, Mary Hayden, 33
Popular fiction, 33–34, 72, 83, 144, 145–53, 194–95 *n. See also* Dime novels and story papers; Formulaic conventions
    and disguise, 147–48
Post, Amy, 48–49
Prince, Mary, 37–38
    A West Indian Slave, 37–38
Prince, Nancy, 40–43, 52, 61
    A Narrative of the Life and Travels of Mrs. Nancy Prince, 40–43, 52

Quadroon. *See* Mulatto characters
Quincy, Josiah, 30

Race literature, 120, 122–23, 125
Randolph, Asa Philip, 165
Rape, 22, 39, 105, 109, 110–14, 128, 131–32, 133, 136, 138–39, 140–41, 142–44
Reconstruction, 5, 63, 64, 68–69, 83, 89–90, 113
Renaissance, 7, 163, 196 *n*
    black women's, 7
    Boston, 163
    Harlem, 163–62, 172
Representation, 164–67, 169–70, 171–72, 173–75
    of blacks by whites, 171–72
    of class, 166–69, 171, 173, 175
    of the folk, 164–65, 174–75
    of sexuality, 174
Reproduction, 24–25, 54–55, 98
Revolution, 67–68
Ruffin, Josephine St. Pierre, 116–17

Sappho, of Lesbos, 142
Scott, Ann, 23, 29–30
    The Southern Lady, 23, 29–30
Scott, Patricia Bell, 10
    All the Women Are White, All the Blacks Are Men, But Some of Us Are Brave, 10–11
Separation of the races. *See* Jim Crow
Sexual ideologies, 6, 17–18, 20–29, 59–61, 96, 99, 111–13, 114–15, 116, 141, 173–75, 185 *n. See also* Cult of true womanhood; Motherhood, ideologies of; Womanhood, ideologies of

Sexual ideologies (*continued*)
　of black women, 20, 22, 27, 30–
　　39, 116
　and desire, 174–75, 185 *n*
　and objectification, 171–72, 173
　under slavery, 20–39
Showalter, Elaine, 16
Sisterhood, 6, 17, 50–55, 102–3,
　117
Slave narratives, 7, 22, 32, 35–39,
　　40, 43, 44, 45–61, 95. *See also*
　　Narratives of free women
　by men, 27–29, 35–36, 59–60
　by women, 36–39, 40, 45–61
Slave rebels, 60
Slotkin, Richard, 187 *n*
Smith, Barbara, 7–11
　All the Women Are White, All
　　the Blacks Are Men, But
　　Some of Us Are Brave, 10–11
Social Darwinism, 128, 140
Societies structured in dominance,
　concept of, 17
Southern belle, 26–27
Southern Literary Messenger, 27
Southworth, E. D. E. N., 33
Spacks, Patricia Meyer, 9–10
　The Female Imagination, 9–10
Spillers, Hortense, 15
Spruill, Julia Cherry, 23
　Women's Life and Work in the
　　Southern Colonies, 23
Stanton, Elizabeth Cady, 67–68
Starling, Marion, 38–39
Still, William, 64–66
Stowe, Harriet Beecher, 29, 34, 48,
　　49–50, 76
　The Key to Uncle Tom's Cabin,
　　49–50
　Uncle Tom's Cabin, 29, 34, 76
Suffrage movement, 4, 6, 18, 67–
　　68, 70, 102–3, 106–7, 114–15,
　　116, 119, 123, 142

racism in, 6, 18, 67–68, 102–3,
　106–7, 116, 119

Taylorism, ideology of, 170
Temperance movement, 4, 6, 18,
　　121–22. *See also* Women's
　　Christian Temperance Union
　racism in, 6, 18
Terrel, Mary Church, 116
The Women's Era, 119
Tillman, Benjamin R., 134
Tradition, 13, 14, 123
Tragic mulatto. *See* Mulatto
　characters
True womanhood. *See* Cult of true
　womanhood

Underground Railroad, 65
Universal Negro Improvement
　Association, 166
Uplifting, 63, 70, 92–94, 168

Victor, Metta Victoria, 26, 33–34
　Maum Guinea and Her
　　Plantation Children, 26, 33

Walker, Alice, 7, 9–10, 108
Washington, Booker T., 84, 93, 95,
　　108, 122
Washington, Mary Helen, 9
　Black-Eyed Susans, 9
Watkins, Frances Ellen. *See*
　　Harper, Frances
Watkins, William (Rev.), 65
WCTU. *See* Women's Christian
　　Temperance Union
Wells, Ida B., 4, 7, 96, 108–16,
　　118, 120, 141
　A Red Record, 110–11, 112–14

Crusade for Justice, 109
Mob Rule in New Orleans, 110
Southern Horrors: Lynch Law in All its Phases, 110–12
The Reason Why: The Colored American Is Not in the World's Columbian Exposition, 4, 107
Welter, Barbara, 25, 59
West, Cornel, 15
West, Dorothy, 175
The Living is Easy, 175
White supremacy, doctrine of, 140–41
Willard, Frances, 113–14
Williams, Fannie Barrier, 3, 96
Willis, Nathaniel P., 47
Wilson, Harriet, 43–45, 61, 71
Our Nig; or, Sketches from the Life of a Free Black, 43–45
Windheyer, Margaret, 70
Womanhood, ideologies of, 6, 17, 20–39, 49–50, 54–57, 59–61, 98, 104–7, 111–17, 141. *See also* Cult of true womanhood; Motherhood, ideologies of; Sexual ideologies
black, 20, 22, 32–39, 98, 104–5, 115–16

Southern white, 20, 29–30, 98, 106, 111
under slavery, 20–39
Womanhood Suffrage League of New South Wales, Australia, 70
Woman's Columbian Association. *See* Black women's organizations
Women's Christian Temperance Union, 68, 94, 113–14, 188 *n*
Women's fiction, conventions of, 72–77
Women's movement, 18–19
World's Columbian Exposition, 3–6. *See also* World's Congress of Representative Women
racist attitudes in, 5
White city, 5
World's Congress of Representative Women, 3–6, 69–70, 96, 107–8
Board of Lady Managers, 4–5
Wright, Richard, 175

Yellin, Jean Fagan, 46